A Packet of Letters

copy

July 25. 1864

Dear Monsignor Talbot

I have received your letter, inviting me to preach next Lent in your Church at Rome, to "an audience of Protestants more educated than could ever be the case in England."

However, Birmingham people have souls; and I have neither taste nor talent for the sort of work, which you cut out for me — and I beg to decline your offer   I am &c   JHN

A copy, in Newman's hand, of a famous letter to George Talbot

A PACKET OF LETTERS

A Selection from the Correspondence
of
John Henry Newman

Edited with an introduction by
JOYCE SUGG

'Your father told me he had put my letters to him in packets. I should be greatly obliged...if your Mother would
lend them me. I would take care they went back to her—
but I make the request with the proviso that it does not
give any great trouble.'
(Letter to Wilfred Wilberforce, 11 March 1875)

CLARENDON PRESS · OXFORD
1983

Oxford University Press, Walton Street, Oxford OX2 6DP
London Glasgow New York Toronto
Delhi Bombay Calcutta Madras Karachi
Kuala Lumpur Singapore Hong Kong Tokyo
Nairobi Dar es Salaam Cape Town
Melbourne Auckland
and associates in
Beirut Berlin Ibadan Mexico City Nicosia

Published in the United
States by Oxford University
Press, New York

British Library Cataloguing in Publication Data
Newman, John Henry
A packet of letters: a selection from the
correspondence of John Henry Newman.
1. Newman, John Henry   2. Catholic Church—
Clergy—Correspondence
I. Title   II. Sugg, Joyce
262'.135'0924   BX4705.N5
ISBN 0-19-826442-9
0-19-826448 8 pbk

Library of Congress Cataloging in Publication Data
Newman, John Henry, 1801–1890.
A packet of letters.
Includes bibliographical references and
index.
I. Newman John Henry, 1801–1890.
2. Cardinals—England—Correspondence.
I. Sugg, Joyce.   II. Title.
BX4705.N5A4 1983   282'.092'4 [B]   82–4444
ISBN 0-19-826442-9   AACR2
0-19-826448 8 pbk

Set by Syarikat Seng Teik Sdn. Bhd., Kuala Lumpur, Malaysia
Printed in Great Britain at
The University Press, Oxford
by Eric Buckley
Printer to the University

Contents

Introduction

Newman had a great opinion of letters as the best kind of
biography, allowing a man to speak for himself. He wrote to
his sister Jemima in 1863 (letter 92), 'It has ever been a hobby
of mine (unless it be a truism, not a hobby) that a man's life
lies in his letters. This is why Hurrell Froude published St
Thomas à Beckett's letters with nothing of his own except
what was necessary for illustration or connection of parts. . . .
Biographers varnish; they assign motives; they conjecture feelings; they interpret Lord Burleigh's nods; they palliate or defend.' Not surprisingly, then, Newman took pains to collect
his own letters, copies or autographs. When he was writing the
Apologia he wrote to friends asking for the loan of his letters to
them and he made copies before he returned them. The process
had begun much earlier, however, for as early as 1828 he was
keeping selections from family letters, and it continued, for,
almost to the end of his long life, he was busy with his letters,
sorting, transcribing, correcting, and elucidating by an added
word here or there. There are several references in later letters
to borrowings, and packets of his letters travelled between his
friends' houses and the Birmingham Oratory where he had
pigeon-holes for them which can be seen there still.

After Newman's death, William Neville, his literary executor, asked for the loan of letters and thousands were sent in.
Neville copied and sorted and he was succeeded in this work
by other Oratorians, Richard and Lewis Bellasis and, later,
Henry Tristram.

Many letters, or parts of them, have been used by biographers. The Anglican period of Newman's life has been best
represented with Anne Mozley's *Letters and Correspondence of
John Henry Newman* (1891) and *Correspondence of John Henry
Newman with John Keble and Others 1839–1845* (1917) edited by
Joseph Bacchus at the Birmingham Oratory. The large biography by Wilfrid Ward, *Life of John Henry Cardinal Newman*
(1912) contained passages from the letters, both from the

Anglican and Catholic periods, and Ward intended to bring out an additional volume containing only letters. Newman's Oratorian executors, however, not best pleased with Ward's presentation of his subject, refused permission, though they did allow the publication of some letters in appendices at the end of the two volumes of his biography. Groups of letters were published in other books too (such as *Newman's University Idea and Reality* by Fergal McGrath, published in 1951) but for seventy years after Newman's death only a small part of his letters had reached the public. Charles Stephen Dessain, writing from the Birmingham Oratory in 1961, said that this was surprising 'when we take into account the intrinsic interest and attractiveness of these letters, the attention paid nowadays to the Victorians, the growing appetite for ample collections of correspondence, the veneration long felt for their writer among men of every creed, and latterly, the possibility of his canonisation'.[1]

Father Dessain had taken upon himself the great task of collecting still more of Newman's letters (there are more than twenty thousand extant) and of editing them together with memoranda and diaries. He decided against giving the whole correspondence but to quote letters *to* Newman where this was necessary for the understanding of his own letters. Since it was the letters from the Catholic period that were more numerous and had rested in greater oblivion he decided to publish these first and saw the twenty-one volumes 1845–90 through the press, helped in the work by Thomas Gornall S.J. and by Vincent Ferrer Blehl S.J. Another Jesuit, Edward Kelly, helped with one volume. Sadly, Father Dessain died suddenly in 1976, having accomplished this heavy task of editing with 'scholarship, skill and devotion', as one of the next editors commented. At this time (1981) about half of the Anglican volumes have been published, edited by Ian Ker and by Thomas Gornall S.J. When complete, Newman's letters will fill thirty-one volumes. The availability of the letters, of such value in themselves, has made a great difference to modern writers on Newman. Meriol Trevor's two-volume biography, *Newman: The Pillar of the Cloud* and *Newman: Light in Winter* (1962) came out before the publication of Father Dessain's volumes but she was able to use a great mass of unpublished letters and memoranda, more than previous biographers had had—hence the vividness and detail of her account.

To read all Newman's letters is an extraordinary experience. Obviously, one man's letters, even if that one man was at the centre of great ecclesiastical movements, will not give all the information, background, views that appertain to the rise and progress of the Oxford Movement or to the history of the Catholic Church in England in the nineteenth century. But letters give an immediacy and a personal slant that make events and movements of thought extraordinarily vivid. How fascinating it is to see events unfolding—even when the outcome is known! Everyone knows, who knows anything about Newman, that he was elected a Fellow of Oriel in 1822 and (wise after the event) we know that this election was the beginning of his remarkable career. To read letters written on the very day of his success is to be involved, made responsive to that young Oxford man's delight. Again, though everyone knows that Newman was made a Cardinal in his old age and many know that he nearly lost this honour because of Manning's opposition, there is no substitute, in terms of immediacy, for a reading of the letters that chart surprise, expectation, debate, disappointment, and finally pleasure mingled with some fear that the necessary journey to Rome would be very difficult for an old, feeble man. The day-by-day unfolding of events is so interesting that in smaller matters, unimportant to the historian or philosopher, the reader is spell-bound, as in reading a well-told tale. For here the outcome is not known beforehand. Will this sick Oratorian recover? Will Marianne and Emily Bowden both become nuns? What will happen to Eleanor Bretherton who as a child went to confession to Father Newman and was something of a pet of his and who, when grown-up, married a poor man who could not give her the comfort her delicate health required? There are glimpses of scores of lives enmeshed with Newman's own life.

One views the nineteenth century, in these letters, through the interstices of religious concerns but the details are so clear and interesting from Newman's pen that a little secular comment goes a long way. So we can learn what it was like to witness a cholera epidemic, to travel about on the steam trains, to know the suffering caused by the Crimean War. If there is one overriding impression of Newman's time it is of a century when medical men were powerless against certain diseases that we do not now fear in the Western world—notably cholera and tuberculosis. Moreover, pre-natal care and obstetrics were crude: many women died in childbed and infant mortality was high. Newman's relatives and friends were not poor: they could afford doctors and medicines and even foreign travel to a warmer climate but the letters are full of the expectation and the facing of death, often the death of the young. Newman's youngest sister died at nineteen (probably of peritonitis), his great friends, Hurrell Froude and John Bowden, died when quite young men—and the list of those to be prayed for on the anniversary of their death-day grew very long, even before Newman became an old man and endured what all old men must, the passing of their contemporaries. If the recurring death-beds are the dominant fact, the dominant impression is not of melancholy. Newman had many disappointments and "baulks" (to use his own word) besides the loss of dear friends to make him sad but the overriding impression of the volumes and packs of letters is of serenity and buoyant faith.

Just as events are put under the microscope in a large collection of letters, so is the character of the writer. The detail that emerges, the strong sense of a voice actually speaking, make the reader conscious not only of the broad lines of character but of all sorts of tiny facets of personality, likes and dislikes, characteristic use of words, habits. Newman was strongly attached to his books so that he viewed a house largely as a place to put one's books: bookshelves were important pieces of furniture to him and a lay-brother who did not dust them was a trial. He was a prodigious walker. He loved springtime and noted the details of growing trees and plants, the colours in the changing landscape. He hated underdone meat. Though he sometimes used the term 'John Bull' in a pejorative sense (believing that John Bull, the average Englishman, was increasingly insensitive to revealed religion) he was something of a John Bull himself when travelling abroad: he was usually unlucky with the weather, particularly during his visits to Rome, and he had a marked distrust of foreign climates. He was a courteous man and the courtesy grew with age.

All this and much more is in the full edition of Newman's

letters and, moreover, the publishing of the letters *in toto* fulfils Newman's desire that he should be allowed to speak for himself. By the act of selection an editor "interprets Lord Burleigh's nods".[2] With the full collection before him, a person anxious to follow a particular topic, such as the history of the Oxford Movement, the conflict between the Birmingham and London Oratories, the beginning of the Irish Catholic University, can deduce a great many facts and follow Newman's train of thought on the matter. But in reading a selection it is not possible to have a clear impression of the sequence of events, thoughts, opinions.

Why, then, should a selection of the letters be made? Father Dessain answered the question at the very moment that he was explaining his reasons for editing all the letters. 'He lived so long', he says, speaking of Newman. 'He had so many friends, he was engaged upon such various enterprises, for so much of his life he carried on an intense apostolate by means of letters, that his output became enormous. . . .'[3] These writings deserve a wide public but not everyone has the time and opportunity to read thirty-one large volumes. Geoffrey Tillotson, selecting from Newman's prose and poetry for a book for the Reynard Library in 1955, was anxious to give some letters, only complaining that 'among the sermons and letters there is an unbroken level of excellence, which limits the power of choice as in a sortilegy'.[4] A more extensive collection of letters was published in 1957, selected by Muriel Spark and Derek Stanford. These collections are in addition to those mentioned earlier which were brought out as part of a biography. Now that all the goods are on the table, so to speak, with the letters published *in extenso*, or soon to be published, it seems time to present a new selection.

What should be the criteria for choosing? The first rule must surely be that the letters should be those that depict most clearly Newman's quality as a man and as a letter-writer. The second rule would seem to be a negative one: that a letter should not be included if it is difficult to read, standing by itself, nor should it be chosen if it requires extensive annotation. The general reader will not wish to delve into many explanations in small print and it is the general reader who is being considered here.

It is possible to illustrate, even in a small selection, the kinds of letter that Newman wrote. Some groups of letters are more interesting than others, some groups tend more to obscurity. In any case, the reader will wish to know what valuable minerals lie in those rocks that have been quarried and to know why the quarrying has been more extensive here or there.

1. The first group of letters is to do with money or business. Newman was a good mathematician and he did not reserve this particular talent for the study or the examination room: for much of his life he was responsible for casting accounts. He had much business to transact—with publishers, with church architects, builders, with parents and with teachers who were concerned with the Oratory School. The Catholic University involved him in all kinds of business and so did the sorting out of personnel, the establishment of workable regulations for the Oratories. Like all ecclesiastics, he had to ask for money at times and he knew how to do this gracefully but straightforwardly and to write his thanks with equal grace. These letters are a very important testimony to the fact that Newman was an efficient man of business, one who knew that life must be lived and money must be handled. He was no skulker in an ivory tower. However, letter by letter they make dull reading and are not well represented in this selection.

2. Some letters comment on the happenings of the day. More particularly, letters to friends like Lord Blachford and Lord Emly, themselves men of affairs, contain comment on political events. In his youth, Newman was something of a High Tory. However, to put a political label on him does less than justice to the individuality and flexibility of his mind (see, for example, letters 129 and 114). The reader will notice how, in the letter to William Monsell (114), Newman's recollections go back to the governments of his youth, range over successive legislation, bring him to the current scene in England and America. It is a letter from a man who has read the newspapers thoughtfully for years. However, it would not do to include many letters which comment upon public affairs for, alas for ministries and armies, the details of their successes and failures are soon forgotten and many such topical references would need lengthy annotation.

It seems strange, to modern minds, that a charitable man like

Newman, who laboured for and among the poor in Birmingham, should not concern himself with reforms, the levelling of the unequal society of Victorian England. He believed that sincere religion would work like leaven through society, bringing justice and harmony, but he seems, on the evidence of the letters, detached from movements of social reform.

One would expect regular comment on church affairs from Newman and it comes in a steady stream, from references to the actions of bishops and clergy of the Church of England to comment on the First Vatican Council. See, for example, letters 18 and 123.

3. There is plenty of literary and some artistic criticism in the letters, besides many apt and amusing references from novels, used to illustrate a point, or lines from poems used illustratively, brought from a well-stocked mind. It is interesting to hear Newman's comments on Jane Austen, on Scott, and on Lewis Carroll and also to hear his strictures on Pugin's church architecture or, rather, on those disciples of Pugin who maintained that his was the only style to be called truly religious (55).

4. There are some letters which are devoted to describing places, a traveller's commentary. This little group has representation, even though it forms a small part of the whole, because these letters are so vivid, so acutely observed.

5. A much larger group of letters is concerned with Christian doctrine, stating, elucidating, persuading, arguing. These are not good subjects for an anthology, for they are often very long and form series; there is one batch of letters, for instance, to his brother Charles who moved away from Christianity as a young man and another series, written at a much later date, to his nephew, John Rickards Mozley.

6. Perhaps the largest group of letters and one of the most interesting is concerned with spiritual advice. Newman was much sought after as a counsellor—by his own Oratorians, by people thinking of becoming Catholics, by new converts, by people in trouble, by parents worried about their wayward children, by young people thinking of a vocation to the religious life. There are a good many letters of this kind selected here. Their merit as letters and their interest are great. They are clearly from a wise head and heart and, though it is probably

dangerous to adopt too readily the advice proffered to someone else (as it is not good to take someone else's medicine), much of what Newman says can be taken to heart today.

7. It would be possible to divide Newman's letters in another way than by subject—into formal and informal ones. By this method, however, an editor would still be classifying by subject, for style and matter go together, most markedly in the case of a great prose writer like Newman. There is a group of letters that can only be called formal letters: they were called forth because Newman was reckoned to be a leader and an important voice, because he was the acknowledged spokesman for moderate English Catholics, was a University Rector, became a Cardinal. They were written to newspapers, in formal acknowledgement to various public and church bodies, to Popes, Cardinals, Prime Ministers. For the most part they are stately and gracious but occasionally Newman shows a cutting wit. Such is the very telling letter to jolt people from a dangerous kind of credulity during the No Popery troubles of the fifties (58) and the marvellous brief letter which he sent to the snobbish Monsignor Talbot, the famous one in which he stated that he would stay and work where he was for 'Birmingham people have souls' (102).

8. Now come those letters which are more intimate and personal. One group is concerned with his writings. There are snippets in letters that tell us that he was writing this book or essay or that. He does not, in general, set out his plans for a book or recapitulate arguments he has set down in what he is writing for the press. But he does speak, more than once, of his methods of writing and offers some interesting comment on style in general — see 27 and 118.

9. The informal letters to friends are delightful, and there are many of them. They are full of warmth and show a constant concern for the health and fortunes of those dear to the writer. Some of these letters are tender, some very funny. The ones written to his greatest friend, Ambrose St John, show Newman entirely spontaneous and at ease. They are represented here (letter 120, for example) but not in numbers because they have a curious kind of obscurity. When we write to our nearest friend we feel free to use a kind of chatty shorthand because the reader will be sure to know what we mean,

and Newman's letters to Ambrose St John are allusive and quirky.

It is sad to note how one group of very personal letters—those to his family—occur so markedly in the early volumes and are so scarce later on. The early family letters are open and affectionate. Then the occasional hint of irritation can be noted, particularly in letters to or about Newman's brothers (24). After his conversion to Rome his two sisters and two brothers (mother, father, and youngest sister were dead by then) more or less ceased to communicate; his sister Jemima did revive the correspondence later, however.

When Newman founded the Oratory School he did not take the post of headmaster but he did write the boys' reports, and these reports can be seen as a little sub-group of the personal letters for they are written in a personal way to the parents and are clearly based on a real knowledge of each boy. The pupils of the Oratory School were lucky to have Newman as assessor—he was honest in his statements but always hopeful that lack of success or faults of character would be overcome in time (88).

10. Some letters are directly autobiographical. In this selection at one or two points in Newman's life there are two letters or a cluster of letters which are concerned with the same happening; it is good to see the event from different angles. One particularly interesting group within this group are letters of reminiscence. Newman had a great memory, particularly for past scenes in his own life and for dates and anniversaries that had a special meaning for friends—he was the sort of person who never forgets birthdays. His looking back at past scenes was not a habit born of nostalgia or regret; it was more a deep sense of the wholeness of a life and of the abiding care of God. It is because of Newman's own conviction of the importance of remembering one's own life that it seems best to arrange all the letters chronologically. Topics recur and they could be grouped together but, since the subject is Newman, it seems in accord with his own habit of mind to let them unfold as the years unfold. Moreover, although it is a mistake to speak as though Newman the Anglican and Newman the Catholic were very different, the year 1845, the year of his reception into the Catholic church, does mark a great transition to different scenes

with different friends and an account that was not chronological would obscure the pattern.

11. Lastly, there are the letters that are self-revelatory. Every letter reveals the writer—even the business letter, even a letter on a mundane topic, like the one Newman wrote when he was enquiring about the best kind of kitchen range to buy for the Oratory School's kitchen. With a man of great personality who had a distinct literary style, whatever he was writing, the lines are drawn with a particular clarity. But some letters deliberately draw aside the veil of reserve (and Newman, the articulate man who wrote so many letters, was in fact reserved) and show something of his inner self. These we have besides the small references to habits and external characteristics which also help to make a portrait.

These hints, touches, revelations, the attitudes of mind that are shown in the letters all show a man who was at once very simple and very complex. One plain statement can be made about him that would describe him truly: that, from the time of his conversion to God (at fifteen) he never wavered in his devotion to Jesus Christ and in his desire to find and hold a dogmatic formulation that would satisfy his Christocentric mind and that, finding what he sought in the Roman Catholic Church, he served that church to the end. He was consistent, single-minded, sincere—in one sense, therefore, simple. Yet, even in reading a small selection of his letters, one is conscious of mystery and ambivalence. Like a great tent held erect by strong guy-ropes pulling in different directions, Newman seems to have traits that are, on the surface, contradictions. He made many friends and he could inspire strong dislike. Affectionate, devoted to his friends, he yet suffered at times from a paralysing shyness with them (23). He speaks plainly of another paradox in a letter written to Capes in 1868:

> I have often been puzzled at myself, that I should be both particularly fond of being alone, and particularly fond of being with friends. Yet I know both the one and the other are true, though I can no more reconcile them than you.

The Abbé Brémond wrote a book called Le *Sécret de Newman* which was translated into English as *The Mystery of Newman*. An Oratorian commented that 'The only mystery about Newman was that he did not give a damn for this world'. But, again, there is paradox and the statement is too simple. He did not pursue wealth or power or pleasure. When, as a young man, he saw someone else's elaborate house he declared plainly that he could not live in such a place.[5] True, he did not give a damn for this world. But it is also clear from his letters that he valued the world, was keenly aware of scenery and natural beauty, loved the smallest details of quotidian life, had, as Geoffrey Tillotson puts it, 'a frank love of particulars'.[6] With what gusto he describes the voyage on a packet boat to the Mediterranean (15)! He is interested even in what it is like to be sea-sick, so that Anne Mozley, the first compiler of his letters and more delicately minded, transcribed the details but with an air of surprise. When he left Littlemore in 1846, he kissed the bed and the mantelpiece because he had been happy there and noted, when packing and disposing, all the different objects that had been part of life, 'passing from a metaphysical MS to a lump of resin or an inkglass'.[7] He was at once an ascetic and a sensuous man. Moreover, (paradox within paradox) he was keenly conscious of the mingling of pleasure and pain that human experience offers, noting often that in the midst of travel or of revisiting the scenes of childhood he knew sorrow even as he enjoyed these things.

In 1868 Newman wrote, 'I am now an old man and my work seems almost over.' His health had been poor during the previous months and sixty-seven is a good age. However, his life had still a good span to go and his work was not over. It is more surprising to find him writing in 1846, 'For me, I am οὐτιδανός [useless], getting old, and fit for the workhouse.' The last phrase puts the whole statement into a slightly joking context but, still, he says it. Such cries, that he is old, that he feels 'knocked up', are scattered through the letters. Was he, then, a feeble man, something of a valetudinarian? Evidence is strongly against such an assessment. His vigour was extraordinary: the amount of writing he did was prodigious and he was engaged in many other activities. There is no real contradiction. He was an unusually industrious man, achieving much despite the 'baulks' that were his chief cross but having to admit every so often that what he did exhausted him physically and nervously. Although he said that writing was always hard work (except when he composed verses, which he could do when he was shaving!) he was fluent in the highest degree and therefore fluent when he complained.

The baulks came during his time as a prominent Anglican and during most of his life as a Catholic. Here there is another paradox, one that arises out of the history of both churches in the nineteenth century rather than out of the disposition and convictions of one man. As an Anglican seeking to set the Church of England in the perspective of history as an inheritor of the doctrines of the early Fathers he was castigated as one too near the doctrines of Rome. Yet as a Catholic his orthodoxy was in doubt and it was not until the Cardinalate in his old age that the cloud was lifted.

As has been suggested earlier, the renowned convert was in fact remarkably consistent in his basic religious views before and after the events of 1845. Yet one impression that comes over from a reading of the letters is that he *did* change a great deal over the years. He mellowed. In youth he was fierce, firstly to himself and then to those he thought wrong-headed, impious, of dangerously liberal religious views. In age he lived simply, but did not go in for the strict fasts and vigils of his days at Littlemore and, though he would always chastise any falling away from the devout life, mildness and benignity were his ruling traits.

His humour flourished most when he was in his sixties and when his life was most dreary. There, too, is a most surprising fact—that Newman, known always as a man of lofty and serious mind, should also be a humorist. 'The ease with which he can be brilliantly witty', says Tillotson, 'seals him of the tribe of the Henry Jameses and Oscar Wildes as certainly as the capacity to write on ecclesiastical matters seals him of the tribe of the Puseys and W. G. Wards.'[8] He could be witty, ironical, satirical of set purpose or amusing in a casual way. Here, quite casually, he comments on two men's false teeth:

Professor Robertson has been here, being a most inquisitive fellow. He looks much older, and his false teeth are visible to the naked eye. Not so bad, however, as Wm Wilberforce's, who has been here, and who throws the whole set out of the gums upon his tongue, and chews them, as an infant might a coral. I never saw anything so strange.[9]

Capes' reply to the letter of March 1868, where Newman confessed himself puzzled at the apparent inconsistency of his loving both solitude and friends, was thus:

... so far from remarking on your twofold likings as an 'apparent inconsistency', which I can no more account for than you can, I have spoken of it as indicating a completeness of character which ordinary observers have not attributed to you; or at least did not attribute to you in former days.[10]

So it seems. He is interesting rather than puzzling, complete rather than inconsistent. Not that Newman was perfect, free from making mistakes, a sage who gave a definitive summary of Christian doctrine and moral precepts. Derek Stanford found many of Newman's Anglican letters very abrasive. It is for the reader to decide whether the abrasive quality (which can be found very occasionally in some later letters too) is there because of a just desire for reform and for doctrinal orthodoxy or smacks of intolerance. Newman himself would wish one to turn to the full collection of his letters and memoranda. He wished his actions and motives to stand in the light and be judged, but judged by facts rather than scattered impressions. He did not claim to be perfect. Sometimes he spoke with a disarming modesty as in the letter to Miss Munro where he said that he had nothing of the saint about him (54). That perhaps may be taken with a good pinch of salt.

Note that this letter, with its frank and interesting self-evaluation, was written to a woman. A paradox of Newman's correspondence is that so many letters *were* written to women. He was reserved with woman, determinedly celibate from an early age. Yet he often expressed himself with more lucidity and freedom to Mrs John Bowden, to Emily Bowles, to Maria Giberne than to his male friends. Hence the frequency of these letters in this selection. Perhaps the ladies of his acquaintance, needing to be put in the picture, to have incidents and views explained, stand more easily for the general reader who is being catered for here.

The number of letters to individual correspondents, be it noted, does not correspond to the quantity of letters to that person. The earliest published editions of his Anglican letters demonstrate the preponderance of letters to Edward Pusey and

John Keble, letters which cannot be adequately represented here. There are many letters extant written to Ambrose St John but not many are reprinted here, for the reason already given. There are also many letters to Frederick Faber but many are on business matters connected with the setting up of the two English Oratories and many are rather dull. Newman was cautious and reserved with Faber because he did not trust him. However, there is a fair spread of correspondents. Newman wrote to so many kinds of people, to popes, dukes, and bishops, to eminent politicians, to Anglican clergymen, fellow Oratorians, to ordinary men and women, to children.

These last mentioned letters are a particularly attractive group. Occasionally in old age Newman missed his mark somewhat and wrote to teenagers as though they were small children—they probably seemed mere infants to him. But in general he could write letters to children that were delightful and within their range, without being avuncular or condescending. Eleanor Bretherton and Chat Bowden must have been very pleased with their letters (79 and 94).

Although it has been a temptation to chop the letters into sections and publish the most interesting extracts (as the first editor, Anne Mozley did), the letters are given whole, for the most part. Occasionally a particularly dull or obscure paragraph or postscript has been omitted but the reader may see the letters as real letters, the informal ones ranging (as our own do) over several topics, unequal in literary merit, varying sometimes in mood from one part to another. They are sometimes like Newman's possessions, mentioned when he was packing at Littlemore, lumps of resin and ink glasses next to metaphysical manuscripts, and are the more human and interesting for that very reason.

It remains to thank the Fathers of the Birmingham Oratory particularly Father Gregory Winterton, for their help in making the letters accessible, and also the patient and knowledgeable archivist of the same Oratory, Mr Gerard Tracey. It will be evident to anyone who has looked at the complete letters how much this selection owes to the scholarship of their editors. The notes on the correspondents have been particularly useful.

The text of the letters is generally that of the complete *Letters and Diaries of John Henry Newman*. Letters 24 to 45, however, have not yet been published in this full edition and some of these have never been published before. Newman's spelling, paragraphs, and punctuation are preserved except that single quotation marks are printed throughout and double ones for quotations within them. Newman customarily used little dashes, to do duty for a comma, a semi-colon or a full stop, when he was writing informally and at speed. Some of the letters were copied later and when a copy provides the text a more formal method of punctuation will be observed. Newman's abbreviations are retained in the address and conclusion of each letter and also the initials that often indicate a name in the text of a letter. If it is not clear from the context who is being referred to, the full name is given in square brackets.

The complete edition adopts a complex system of brackets to distinguish editorial additions (square brackets) from Newman's interlinear explanations (angle brackets), holograph copies (quarter brackets) and Newman's later additions (in double square brackets). A simpler method has been adopted here with Newman's later modifications incorporated into the text.

The address and date are always printed on the same line and at the head of the letter, even where Newman puts them at the end. When he omits or gives an incomplete date the omission is supplied.

A brief outline life of Newman is given, to enable the reader to see the letters in context. There is also a list of his writings, not a complete bibliography because of his enormous output, but a list of his major works and those minor works that are mentioned in these letters.

Summary of Newman's Life

1801   He was born in London on 21 February and

1808–16   was educated at Ealing School, where, in his last year, he came under the Christian influence of Walter Mayers and underwent conversion.

1817–20   He was an undergraduate at Trinity College, Oxford. Although he worked hard and was expected to get a First, he broke down in the final examinations and did badly.

1822   Nevertheless he entered for a Fellowship at Oriel College and was successful.

1824   He was ordained deacon in the Church of England. His father died.

1826   He became a College tutor, a post he held for four years, and then

1828   Vicar of St Mary the Virgin, the University church. This post included the cure of Littlemore, a parish just outside Oxford.

1833   During a tour abroad Newman fell ill in Sicily. The Oxford Movement can be said to date from this year, the movement for the reform of the Church of England and for its return to its Catholic origins. Newman, Keble, and Pusey were its leaders.

1836   Newman's mother died and his sisters married.

1841   Tract 90, which sought to reconcile the Thirty-nine Articles with Catholic doctrine, was condemned by the Heads of Houses of the University and was to be criticized by many of the bishops.

1843   Newman resigned from St Mary's and preached a farewell sermon at Littlemore, where he had been living in retirement.

1845   He resigned from his Oriel Fellowship and was received into the Catholic Church on 9 October.

1846	He left Littlemore for Maryvale, Birmingham, and then set out for Rome with another convert, Ambrose St John.
1847	Having been ordained a priest, he was trained for the Oratory of St Philip Neri, a congregation of secular priests.
1848–9	The English Oratory was founded at Maryvale and, after a year, moved to Alcester Street, Birmingham. Some of Newman's companions went to open the London Oratory, under F. W. Faber.
1850	Papal Aggression agitation. Newman gave *Lectures on Anglican Difficulties* in London.
1851	*Lectures on the Present Position of Catholics* in Birmingham; Achilli, a renegade Dominican friar, brought a libel case which Newman lost two years later after protracted legal delays. He was invited to be Rector of the Catholic University, in Ireland.
1852	The new Oratory building at Edgbaston was opened and the inaugural lectures given for the Catholic University, in Dublin.
1854–8	Newman was Rector of the Catholic University.
1855–6	The London and Birmingham Oratories separated.
1859	The opening of the Oratory School, a public school. Newman tried to save the *Rambler*, a Catholic journal run by laymen, and, because of an article he wrote in it, was delated to Rome for suspected heresy.
1864	A written attack by Charles Kingsley led to the writing of *Apologia Pro Vita Sua*, in weekly instalments.
1867	The Bishops forbade Catholics to attend English Universities. Newman was kept from starting an Oratory in Oxford, a scheme which he had involved himself with over three years.
1870	Vatican Council I. Newman attacked the Ultramontane clique (papal extremists) and his letter was leaked to the press.

1877	Newman was elected the first honorary fellow of Trinity College, Oxford.
1879	He was made a Cardinal by Pope Leo XIII.
1890	He died on 11 August.

Some of Newman's Writings

1826	Article: *Apollonius Tyaneus*
1833–41	*Tracts for the Times* (not all by Newman)
1833	*The Arians of the Fourth Century*
1834–42	*Parochial Sermons*, 6 vols. (many other volumes of sermons published later)
1836–42	Articles in the *British Critic*
1838	*Lectures on Justification*
1845	*An Essay on the Development of Christian Doctrine*
1848	*Loss and Gain*, a novel
1856	*Callista*, a novel
1859	Article: *On Consulting the Faithful in Matters of Doctrine*
1864	*Apologia pro Vita Sua* *P. Terentii Phormio Expurgatus in Usum Puerorum*
1865	*The Dream of Gerontius* *A Letter to the Rev. E. B. Pusey, D.D. on his recent Eirenicon*
1870	*An Essay in Aid of a Grammar of Assent*
1873	*The Idea of a University Defined and Illustrated*. The separate parts of this book had come out in 1852, 1856, and 1859.
1875	*A Letter Addressed to His Grace the Duke of Norfolk*

1

To ELIZABETH NEWMAN

From school, to announce a coming holiday

Ealing December 6th 1811

Dear Aunt,

The joyful 21 again approaches when our books are closed according to delightful custom, and when I hope for the additional pleasure of seeing you all well and happy at home.

Already in imagination I pay my respects to the mince pies, Turkies, and the other good things of Christmas.

In the mean time the Notches on my wooden Calendar diminish apace, but not so the duty and affection with which I am,

Dear Aunt, Your's ever John H Newman

2

To HARRIETT NEWMAN

A rhyme to his sisters, apparently written to put off writing a full letter ·

Ealing April 19. 1815

Tell Jemima,
Once upon a time, a
Letter came from her pen
And I did not answer it then:
Therefore tell her I'm her debtor
Of a long agreeable letter.
Of pleasant school and different places
I'll inform her how the case is:
Pray do send me then a letter, a
Nice epistle: Yours et cetera[1]

John H Newman

3

To MR NEWMAN

The first letter from Trinity College, Oxford

Oxford June 11 1817

The minute I had parted from you, I went straight to the tailor's, who assured me that, if he made twenty gowns, they would fit me no better. . . . If he took it shorter. . . . he would if I pleased, but I might grow etc etc. He tells me it is customary to pay ready money for the cap and gown — he takes 5 per cent off other things, if paid for directly.

I then went HOME, and had hardly seated myself, when I heard a knock at the door, and, opening it, one of the commoners entered, whom Mr Short had sent to me, (having before come himself with this said commoner, when I was out,) to explain to me some of the customs of the College, and accompany me into the Hall at dinner. I have learned from him something I am much rejoiced at. 'Mr Ingram' said he 'was very much liked; he was very good natured; he was presented with a piece of plate the other day from the Collegians. Mr Short on the contrary is not liked; he is strict; all wish Mr Ingram were Tutor still'. Thus I think I have gained by the exchange and that is a lucky thing. Some time after, on my remarking that Mr Short must be very clever, having been second master at Rugby, he replied, 'Do you think so? *I* think him not *too much* so.' Another proof that he is a strict Tutor.

At dinner I was much entertained with the novelty of the thing. Fish, flesh and fowl, beautiful salmon, haunches of mutton, lamb etc and fine, very fine (to my taste) strong beer, served up on old pewter plates, and mis-shapen earthenware jugs. Tell Mama there are gooseberry, raspberry, and apricot pies. And in all this the joint did not go round, but there was such a profusion that scarcely two ate of the same joint. Neither do they sit according to their ranks, but as they happened to come in.

I learned from the same source, whence I learned concerning Mr Short, that there are a *great many* juniors to me. I hear also

2

that there are no more lectures this term, this week being the week for examinations, and next week most of the members go. I shall try to get all the information I am able respecting what books I ought to study, and hope, if my eyes are good-natured to me, to fag. I expect every minute for three or four servants to knock at my door for their fees, which amount altogether to about half a guinea. . . .

Tell Harriett I have seen the fat cook. The wine has this moment come in. 8⅓ per cent is taken off for ready money. Two things I cannot get, milk and beer, so I am obliged to put up with cream for the one and ale for the other.

4

To FRANCIS WILLIAM NEWMAN

Analysing his feelings and aspirations before the final examination

August 17. 1820

Here at Oxford I am most comfortable. The quiet and still-ness of every thing around me tends to calm and lull those emotions, which the near prospect of my grand examination and a heart too solicitous about fame and too fearful of failure are continually striving to excite. I read very much certainly, but I may say (I trust), without deceiving myself or losing sight of my unnumbered transgressions, that God sanctifies my studies by breathing into me all the while thoughts of Him, and enables me to praise Him with joyful lips, when I rise and when I lie down, and when I wake in the night. I know not how in words to describe my state. If I look at the mercies of God, my soul is bright; when I view myself from a different point of view, I wonder how I can dare to assert any growth in grace. I am in dread now, lest I should have written any thing presumptuous. For the calm happiness I now enjoy I cannot feel thankful as I ought. How in my future life, if I do live, shall I look back with a sad smile at these days! however, I am weak, dark, and cold now, and then I trust I shall be strong in the faith, light and fervent.

As to the event of the examination, 'it is in the Lord's hands;

3

let Him do, as it seemeth to Him good'. It is my daily, and (I hope) heartfelt prayer, that I may not get any honours here, if they are to be the least cause of sin to me. As the time approaches, and I have laboured more at my books, the trial is greater. May God give me strength still to say, 'Let me get no honours, if they are to be the slightest cause of sin to me.' And do you, my dear Francis, pray for me in the same way.

5

To WALTER MAYERS

After his failure in the examination

January 1821

Such a host of things has happened since I addressed you last, that I do not know how or where to begin . . . For some time, even when appearances were most favourable, I had a sort of foreboding what would happen. About two months before my trial, the probability of success in my own judgment declined to a first in mathematics and a second in classics; when I went up, to two seconds—after the examination to one second; the Class List came out, and my name was below the line.

. . . My failure was most remarkable. I will grant I was unwell, low-spirited, and very imperfect in my books; yet, when in the Schools, so great a depression came on me, that I could do nothing. I was nervous in the extreme, a thing I never before experienced, and did not expect—my memory was gone, my mind altogether confused. The Examiners behaved with great kindness to me, but nothing would do. I dragged a sickly examination from Saturday to Friday, and after all was obliged to retire from the contest.

I will not attempt to describe the peace of mind I felt when all was over. Before there was darkness and dread—I saw the cataract, to which I was hurrying without the possibility of a rescue. It was as if a surgical operation was day after day being carried on upon me, and tearing away something precious; and all the while 'omnes omnia bona dicebant, et laudabant fortu-

4

nas meas.'[1] They looked at me, and envied me, and laughed at my fears, and could hardly believe them real.

There is a great difference between believing a thing to be good, and feeling it; now I am thankful to say, I am not only enabled to believe failure to be best for me, but God has given me to see and know it. I never could before get my mind to say heartily 'Give me neither poverty nor riches.' I think I can now say it from my soul. I think I see clearly that honour and fame are not desirable. God is leading me through life in the way best adapted for His glory and my own salvation. I trust I may have always the same content and indifference to the world, which is at present the *prevailing* principle in my heart —yet I have great fears of backsliding.

6

To JOHN WILLIAM BOWDEN

This, and the next letter, announce academic success after failure

Friday 12 April 1822

My dear Bowden

I have just been nominated Fellow of Oriel College.—Thank God

I am Yours most truly John Henry Newman

7

To CHARLES ROBERT NEWMAN

Oriel College, Oxford April 13. 1822

Now that the contest and labour is all over, I may be allowed to state, that for the last month or two I have been so far from having a mean opinion of myself, which my Mother some how judged I had conceived, that I have actually considered myself as having a very good chance of succeeding, at the approaching examination. Instead of saying in the letter I wrote about six weeks ago, '*I* think I have no chance,' I merely stated the opinion of every one else.

I am then fellow of Oriel; and, though unable at present to define the advantages that follow, I know enough to say with confidence and thankfulness that I have gained independence, competency, and literary society. Not that I expect any immediate emolument, but I have gained a spell which can conjure me as many pupils as I can desire.

I was not acquainted with a single fellow; my own College was rather undervalued; and the list of Oriel fellows contains the names of many first class men, and they obliged to stand a second year, while of Under-the-line[1] men not one. The examinations commenced this day week (Saturday)—we were locked up for above 8 hours—on Monday above 9. on Tuesday about 4, and then brought up before the fellows for vivâ voce, which trial continued through Wednesday and Thursday. In the course of these days we had to do a Latin Essay, a translation of some Spectator, answers to twelve Mathematical and Philosophical, and to ten Logical Questions; besides construing passages in nine Greek and Latin authors before the Electors. There were ten candidates and two vacancies.

The examination throughout was most kind and considerate, and we were supplied with sandwiches, fruit, cake, jellies, and wine—a blazing fire, and plenty of time.

I think myself honoured inexpressibly by being among such kind, liberal, candid, moderate, learned and pious men, as every act shows the fellows of Oriel as a body to be. There's a eulogium for you!

Yesterday I took my seat in Chapel, and dined with a large party in the Common Room. Today I have breakfasted and dined there, and shall in future, as a constant thing. I sat next Keble yesterday at dinner, and, as I have heard him represented, he is more like an undergraduate than the first man in Oxford—so perfectly unassuming and unaffected in his manner.

The confusion it has made in Oxford is very considerable; and my friends at Trinity were so kindly rejoiced that they could not read a word the rest of the day. Kinsey is in raptures, and Ogle declares that nothing has given him so great gratification since he came to his present situation, it being uncertain whether he means, since he took his first class, since he became M D, since he undertook the Tutorship of Trinity, or since he married Mrs Ogle.

The last Trinity man who got into Oriel was Dr Mant, about 14 years since.

I sent letters yesterday, besides home, to Bowden, Thresher, Dr Nicholas, and Aunt Newman.

Thus, not by the might of my arm, but by circumstances as seemingly unaccountable in themselves as those by which I lost my class, I am fellow of Oriel. I hope I have not been vain in any thing I have said. I am tied up at Oxford by my pupil, or I should like much to run up. I have not yet gone to the Bank about the money, for which thank my Father

Keep this letter as I may wish to refer to it. Now indeed

> 'I groan no more
> Chained to the literary oar'

JHN

8

To MR NEWMAN

Newman's father had said that his newly-ordained son was over-zealous in visiting parishioners

August 9. 1824

.... So far from this invasion of 'an Englishman's castle' being galling to the feelings of the poor, I am convinced by facts that it is very acceptable. In all places I have been received with civility, in most with cheerfulness and a kind of glad surprise, and in many with quite a cordiality and warmth of feeling. One person says, 'Aye, I was sure that one time or other we should have a proper minister—' another that 'she had understood from such a one that a nice young gentleman was come to the parish—' a third 'begged I would do him the favour to call on him, whenever it was convenient to me' (this general invitation has been by no means uncommon) Another, speaking of the parish she came from said, 'the old man preached very good doctrine but he did not come to visit people at their houses as the new one did'. Singularly enough, I had written down as a memorandum a day or two before I received your letter, 'I am more convinced than ever of the necessity of frequently visiting the poorer classes—they seem so gratified at it, and praise it.' Nor do I visit the poor only—I mean to go all through the parish; and have already visited the shopkeepers and principal people. They it is obvious have facilities for educating their children, which the poor have not—and on that ground it is that a clergyman is more concerned with the children of the latter; though our church certainly intended that not only schoolmasters of the poorer children, but all schoolmasters, high and low, should be under her jurisdiction. The plan was not completed, and we must make the best of what we have got.

I have not tried to bring over any regular dissenter—indeed I have told them all, 'I shall make no difference between you and churchgoers—I count you all my flock, and shall be most happy to do you a service out of Church, if I cannot within it.' A good dissenter is of course incomparably better than a bad Churchman—but a good Churchman I think better than a good dissenter. There is too much irreligion in the place for me to be so mad as to drive away so active an ally as Mr Hinton seems to be.

Thank you for your letter, and pardon my freedom of reply

9

To HARRIETT NEWMAN

Life as a College Tutor

March 21. 1826

I am up to my chin in Apollonius, and very cross, as you may suppose. I *must* send him off by the very beginning of next week, and I have three Sermons to write.

I am just transported into rooms in College with my books in disorder all over the room. I am sure a week's visit any where would do me good. I parted from Whately[1] yesterday, and took a most affectionate leave of him.

I feel pleased you like my Sermons—I am sure I need not caution you against taking any thing I say on trust. Do not be run away with by any opinions of mine. I have seen cause to change my mind in some respects, and I may change again. I see I know very little about any thing, though I often think I know a great deal.

I have a great undertaking before me in the Tutorship here. I trust God may give me grace to undertake it in a proper spirit, and to keep steadily in view that I have set myself apart for His service for ever. There is always the danger of the love of literary pursuits assuming too prominent a place in the thoughts of a College Tutor, or his viewing his situation merely as a secular office, a means of a future provision when he leaves College.

10

To HARRIETT NEWMAN

Life as an Oxford don; memories of his sister Mary

November 23. 1828

It is Sunday evening—the duties of the day are over, and I am by myself. Can I raise my mind more entirely upwards than by writing to you? for I hope we are each associated with each by ties not of this world. Home has the memory of too many trying events to inspire a merely earthly pleasure. What confidence can I have, or you, or any of us, that we shall continue blest in each other's love, except as we are members of Him whose life and rule belong to another world?

You will be glad to hear I am quite well. I ascribe it to my morning ride, which has been regular without one exception as yet. At ten I go to the Schools; leave at five or half past; come home and prepare lectures which last from chapel time till near 10, when I go to bed. On my two holidays, I apply myself to Senior or Junior Treasurer's work, reading Candidates' papers, and examining my College pupils. My spirits are very good, or I could not get through so much.

9

My ride of a morning is generally solitary; but I almost prefer being alone. When the spirits are good, every thing is delightful in the view of still nature, which the country gives. I have learned to like dying trees and black meadows—swamps have their grace, and fogs their sweetness. A solemn voice seems to chant from every thing. I know whose voice it is—it is her dear voice. Her form is almost nightly before me, when I have put out the light and lain down. Is not this a blessing? All I lament is, that I do not think she ever knew how much I loved her.

Dear Pusey is gazetted.[1] I hope he will not over work himself. How desirable it seems to be to get out of the stir and bustle of the world, and not to have the responsibility and weariness of success. Now, if I chose to wish a scheme, and in my solitary rides I sometimes do, I should say 'Oh for some small cure of a few hundreds a year, and no preferment as the world calls it!' but you know this is wishing for idleness, and I do not think I shall have this obscurity, because I wish for it. Yet, see, I talk of the comfort of retirement, because I am abroad—how long should I endure it, were I given it? I do not know myself.

11

To MRS NEWMAN

Written when visiting Hurrell Froude's family in Devon

Dartington—July 7. 1831

I despatched a hasty letter yesterday from Torquay which must have disappointed you from its emptiness—but I wished you to know my progress. As we lost sight of the Needles, twilight came on and we saw nothing of the coast. The night was beautiful, and, on my expression [sic] an aversion to the cabin, Froude[1] and I agreed to sleep on deck. I robbed my berth of a blanket, in which I enveloped my blessed person, and, putting over it my cloke, stretched myself on a bench. At one o'clock I woke; we were passing Portland lights—the swell was then considerable, as it always is there.

Now I know I am writing great nonsense—but, since I should say it in words, if I were with you, I will write it down; in this alone unlike Dr Doddridge, that I shall not keep a copy of it. When I woke a little before four, we were passing the Devonshire coast, about 15 miles off it—by six we were entering Torbay, and by seven we were landed at Torquay. We had debated whether to go to Plymouth, or to land at Dartmouth, or at Torquay—our decision would have been furthered on our finding the steamer's flag was a tricolour, but was ultimately made by a desire for breakfast and change of linen.

The limestone and sandstone rocks of Torbay are very brilliant in their colours, and sharp in their forms; strange to say, I believe I believe I never saw real rocks before in my life. This consciousness keeps me very silent, for I feel I am admiring what every one knows, and it is foolish to observe upon. You see a house said to belong to Sir Walter Raleigh; what possessed him, to prefer the court of Greenwich to a spot like this! Really, the abstract vague desire of distinction does seem to me the most morbid unnatural feeling going. I can understand a man tempted by a definite tangible prize, or a dependent man setting out to seek his fortune; but not that gluttonous indefinite craving for honours and reputation.

I have more to say—but stop to tell you what I think of the country, though I know I am writing in a very dull way, and can only say that the extreme deliciousness of the air and the fragrance of every thing makes me languid, indisposed to speak or write, and pensive. My journey did not fatigue me to speak of, and I have no headache, deafness, or whizzing in my ears but really I think I should dissolve into essence of roses, or be attenuated to an echo if I lived here. Certainly, I am not more original in my remarks and disposed to start a conversation than an echo,—as the people here as yet find, though they may not yet have discovered my relationship to an essence.

What strikes me most is the strange richness of every thing. The rocks blush into every variety of colour—the trees and fields are emeralds, and the cottages are rubies. A beetle picked up at Torquay was as green and gold as the stone it lay on and a squirrel which ran up a tree here just now was not a pale reddish brown, to which I am accustomed, but a bright brown red. Nay, my very hands and fingers look rosy, like Homer's

11

Aurora, and I have been gazing on them with astonishment. All this wonder I know is simple, and therefore of course do not you repeat it. The exuberance of the grass and the foliage is oppressive, as if one had not room to breathe, though this is a fancy—the depth of the valleys and the steepness of the slopes increase the illusion—and the Duke of Wellington would be in a fidget to get some commanding point to see the country from. The scents are extremely fine, so very delicate, yet so powerful, and the colours of the flowers as if they were all shot with white. The sweet peas especially have the complexion of a beautiful face—they trail up the wall, mixed with myrtles, as creepers. As to the sunset, the Dartmoor heights look purple, and the sky close upon them a clear orange. When I turn back to think of Southampton water and the Isle of Wight, they seem by contrast to be drawn in india-ink or pencil. Now I cannot make out that this is fancy for why should I fancy? I am not especially in a poetic mood. I have heard of the brilliancy of Cintra, and still more of the East, and suppose that this region would fade beside them; yet I am content to marvel at what I see, and think of Virgil's description of the purple meads of Elysium—Let me enjoy what I feel, even though I may unconsciously exaggerate.

12

To MRS NEWMAN

A visit to Cambridge

July 16. 1832

Having come to this place with no anticipation, I am quite taken by surprise, and overcome with delight. This doubtless you will think premature in me, in as much as I have seen as yet scarcely any thing, and have been writing letters of business to Mr Rose and Rivingtons. But, really, when I saw at the distance of four miles, on an extended plain, wider than the Oxford, amid thicker and greener groves, the Alma Mater Cantabrigiensis lying before me, I thought I should not be able to contain myself, and, in spite of my regret at her present defects and past history, and all that is wrong about her, I seemed about to cry out, 'Floreat aeternum!' Surely there is a genius loci here, as in my own dear home—and the nearer I came to it, the more I felt its power. I do really think the place finer than Oxford, though I suppose it isn't, for every one says so. I like the narrow streets—they have a character—and they make the University buildings look larger by the contrast. I cannot believe that King's College is not far grander than any thing with us—the stone too is richer, and the foliage more thick and encompassing. I found my way from the inn to Trinity College, like old Oedipus, without guide, by instinct; how I know not. I never studied the plan of Cambridge.

Mr Rose is away—he is very ill—which accounts for his silence. Should you see Froude, tell him, alas! he is married. This has quite troubled and grieved me,—still, if he manages to give his whole soul to the Church, it matters not—though it seems impossible.

Let me know about the cholera—I trust we should have no cases; but it would distress me deeply, should a case occur, while I am away.

13

To GEORGE RYDER

Advice to a younger man on marriage

Oriel. July 22/32

My dear Ryder,

I have been very busy, and now write with an effort—or you should not have been so long without an answer to your letter. It is quite absurd to suppose that you are not *at liberty* both to marry and to go into the Church—indeed I think that country parsons ought, as a general rule, to be married—and I am sure the generality of men ought, whether parsons or not. The celibate is a high state of life, to which the multitude of men cannot aspire—I do not say, that they who adopt it are necessarily better than others, though the noblest ηθος[1] is situated in that state. While I allow you full liberty to marry, yet,

13

if you ask my opinion, I certainly think you too young to marry. Since I do not know who it is your heart is set upon, I may say without seeming to cut at individuals that I think most likely you will make a bad choice. What can you know of others at your age? how likely are you to be captivated by outside show, tho' not show in the common vulgar meaning of the word! Depend upon it, many a man would repent of his marriage, if he did not think it right (as it is) to repress the rising sigh. It is a fearful thing to tie yourself to one person for life. Again I am not at all satisfied at your want of self command. You *gave up* the notion of taking a degree, before you had this impulse—if *it* has been the cause of your changing your mind back, then you have been just swayed by two πάθη[2] to and fro, indolence and love,—you yourself, the proper you, having no power or will of your own.—Do you know yourself enough? Have you not talked a good deal on politics even without feeling what you said? Are you sure you will not sink into a Conservative after all?—a character which may be right or wrong, but could not easily be G.D.R. if he had always really understood the words he used. Again, *supposing* a time of trial is to come, (for argument's sake) what a scrape a man has got into, who did not contemplate its possibility, when he married!—is it not worth while to ascertain whether your hoped-for partner is prepared to be a pilgrim? I think I have now said all that strikes me on the subject, and with best wishes for your coming to a right determination in your difficulties.

I am Ever yrs affly John H Newman

14

To HENRY WILBERFORCE

A warning against indolence

Oriel College Oct 24.32

My dear Henry,

You seem not to have received a letter I wrote you in August from Tunbridge Wells—but I believe it contained nothing very important. As to your difficulties detailed in your last letter, you must not think I do not sympathize in them—which I really do—yet I see not how they interfere with your employing yourself. Take care lest you try to make your deficiences, real though they may be, an excuse for indolence—'I am not good enough' is suspicious, when it is made to account for doing nothing, though it may be sufficient reason for not doing this or that. Are you really in a condition for no service towards God?—if so, why does He keep you on earth? And particularly when this reason for delay is offered by an indolent person it is doubly suspicious. I have already said what struck me you might do, however little prepared you were to take the solemn step of taking orders. I will press no one to that. I wish we all viewed it more seriously than we do. But you can serve the Church as a layman. Come up here and employ yourself. You may be useful theologically and parochially in a hundred ways—and take just so much of direct religious employment as your conscience allows you, but do not say you must be idle, unless you undertake the work of angels. Aut Caesar aut nullus[1] is a bad maxim; and be sure of this, that inactivity is the very reason of temptation; fill your mind with manly objects, and all evil spirits will leave it.

Do not think I account light of the temptations to which you allude, either as to their force, or the miserable after-grief which they bring upon the mind. It is the characteristic of the rebellious passions, whether anger, sullenness, or any other, first to sweep us off our footing, and then to leave us with a polluted, perplexed, despairing conscience, which turns from God through very shame. Thus the temptations of the flesh are distinguished from those of the world, which substitute an evil end and principle of action, and gradually 'choke the word' (in Scripture language) instead of openly opposing it. But let the poignancy of remorse be our cure—surely those sins are more hopeful which bring their punishment with them. It is dangerous to experimentalize, but I confess it seems a sensible thing for a conscience-stricken sinner to inflict some penance on himself as a continual humiliation—abstinence from some pleasure or convenience, which it is in his own power to enforce—or other privation, which may keep his sin in remembrance and withdraw him from temptation. But, in the particular misery you seem to hint at, doubtless occupation is the best preventative—and a good deal of hard bodily exercise—and great vigilance to stop the evil in the beginning, for, when once it outruns its first moments, it is incurable, like the dreadful plague which has visited us.

I believe it is settled that Froude and I go abroad—when is uncertain, either November 9 or December 7. We go by the steamboat to Malta—and thence take whatever direction promises most. Archdeacon Froude goes with us—and perhaps G. Ryder—nay, I hear a *report* that Oxnam has a chance. Rivington's are so dilatory that I shall do nothing with my work, Arians, till my return—which will be in the Spring. It has been finished and off my hands since July.—You do not say how your Father is—or indeed where, but I suppose in Bath, since you have been there. I prefer however directing this to East Farleigh.

Rose tells me the life of Henry More, or Norris would be an interesting subject for his magazine, if you like to undertake it. The former was a remarkable man—I know nothing of the latter—or suppose you were to give a sketch of the life of Loyola and the philosophical peculiarities of his rise—or of St Francis. I am much set on understanding the mode in which the Monastic orders rose, in order to see whether one could not in all simplicity and godly sincerity found such a society, if times get bad. I wish I were to be here next term, if there was a chance of your being in Oxford—but you will find several of your friends—Rogers is to occupy my rooms—Manning is at Merton—and you may manage, as the days grow longer, to go over to Rose Hill and see to my Mother's health, which I shall be anxious about when I am away.

Ever Yrs affectionately John H Newman

15

To HARRIETT NEWMAN

The start of a voyage to the Mediterranean

On board the Hermes. Dec. 12 1832

Dear Harriet,

I hardly thought, after writing to my Mother last night, I should be able so soon to sit down to write a second letter— but we are again out of sight of land, having run out in order to double Cape Finisterre, and there is nothing at present to see on deck except a most beautiful sky and smooth water— towards evening we shall near Oporto and perhaps the Portuguese fleet—so I write while I can. We lost the Lizard about 5 o'clock on Saturday, and after that did not see land till yesterday (Tuesday) morning about 10. The interval was occupied in passing 'the bay', which we did in a straight line almost drawn from Falmouth to Ortegan—Seldom at this time of year is a voyage so prosperous as ours was—there were indeed in the bay the slight remains of the swell which followed the winds of the week before last—but they were not worth speaking of. The weather was dry though dull, and the moon at night very bright. My seasickness, if it may so be called, left me in 24 hours. It is an uncomfortable feeling certainly, but in saying that, I have said the worst and the best of it. Never certainly had I ailment more easy to be borne—and so far from having my spirits depressed, I could do nothing but laugh at the oddity of my plight. It began on going down to dinner on Saturday. The motion is felt much more below, and it is closer. A strange feeling came over me—the heaving to and fro of everything seemed to puzzle me from head to foot, but in such a vague, mysterious way that I could not realize it, or say what was the matter with me or where. On I eat, I was determined, for it is one of the best alleviatives—on I drank, but in so absurdly solemn a way, with such a perplexity of mind, not to say of body, that (as I say) I laughed at myself. How I wished dinner over—yet on I sat—heaving, up and down, to and fro, an endless meaningless motion, a trouble without a crisis, the discomfort of an uneasy dream. I went up stairs and got better.

Then I lay down, and was well—got up at eleven at night—walked about and was better again—went to bed and slept soundly. On Sunday morning I was languid and qualmish—lay down on the deck and got well, but was afraid to stir. We had great difficulty to read the Service. Archdeacon Froude was very bad (as he was till yesterday), and in bed. RHF was getting well, but I did not like to let him try by himself. I was afraid to move, lest consequences should follow. However he read and I was able to respond without inconvenience. I was better and worse all day—and by after bedtime had no more trouble up to this time, when I eat and drink, loll about, read, and write as usual. Seasickness then is *to me* a light evil—lying down is an instant specific for it—and eating a certain alleviation and strengthening. But I am but just now getting reconciled to my berth, which yet is very far superior to most if not all accommodations of the kind. I will not speak of its smallness, more like a coffin than a bed—nor its darkness; but first think of the roll of the vessel to and fro. The first night, my side was sore with the rub, rub of the motion. Then fancy the swinging, neverending swinging—the knocking your head, and bruising your arms, you all the while being shelfed in a cupboard five feet from the floor. Then the creaking of the vessel. It is like half a hundred watchman's rattles, only far louder, mixed with the squeaking of several Brobdignag pigs, while the water dashes dash dash against the sides. Then overhead the loud foot of the watch, who goes tramping up and down the whole night more or less. Then (in the morning) the washing of the deck over your head. Rush comes an engine pipe on the floor above—ceases, is renewed, flourishes about, rushes again—then suddenly ½ a dozen brooms, wish, wash, wish wash, scrib, scrub, roaring and scratching alternately. Then the heavy flump, flump, of the huge dabbing cloth, which is meant to dry the deck in a measure instead of a towel or duster. Last and not least the smell. In spite of air, the berth will smell damp and musty—and at best close—there is no window in it—it opens into the cabin, which at night has been lighted with oil. Added to this the want of room for your baggage, and your higgledy piggledy state—and you will allow I have given you enough of discomforts—yet one day like yesterday outweighs them all, and in fact they are going fast.

To be sure a valetudinarian could not possibly bear it. I think it would have quite knocked me up a year or two since—and as for those who in advanced stages of consumption are sent abroad, it must be a martyrdom—for I repeat our vessel is a *peculiarly* convenient one—but I am glad to say, I am getting over these things. First, we have decided on going on with the vessel to Zante, Patras, and so by Ithaca to Cepalenia and Corfu; and take Malta in as the vessel comes back. That ascertains our remaining on board for a month or more to come. So I shall unpack, which will be a comfort. You must know that each berth has two sleeping shelves, one above another—which are both occupied when the vessel is full; (fancy the misery) but we have no cabin passengers on board but ourselves, so we have our berth each to himself. Now the under shelf I shall have emptied of bedding, and arrange my luggage there. There are several little shelves too, on which I shall arrange various little articles and books—I bought a bag at Falmouth which holds my dirty linen and so altogether shall make myself neat and comfortable. I shall change the arrangements of apparel in bag and portmanteau, and learn to know my property, which at present I do not well embrace in my mind—Next I get to understand my berth and the way of lying in it comfortably; and certainly I cannot deny that it is snug, tho' odd. I get not to mind the noises, and I have caused a more careful ventilation to be kept up in the cabin than was usual, taking care that my berth door should always or generally be open. And this is all I have to say at present, except (as I think I told my Mother) my journey to Falmouth cost about five guineas.

16

To SAMUEL FRANCIS WOOD

Descriptions of his travel—of Malta, Pompeii, Ithaca

Rome March 17 1833

My dear Wood

At length after much wandering, we are settled for 5 or 6 weeks in this great city, the repose and quiet of which is favorable to the recruitment which the mind needs after seeing many sights.—And so I have made it an opportunity of writing to various friends, who have not been out of my mind, tho' not written to before. It seems at first sight strange to call Rome my first resting place, when we were a month at Malta; but that month was not a rest in reality. For twelve days of it we were in the Lazaret,[1] which ought indeed to be as quiet a place as you could wish; and so it was in one way, and yet it was not. Such large rooms; 50 feet long and 22 high, built entirely of stone and destitute of furniture, magnified and multiplied every the least sound; and I did not get more satisfactory sleep of a night than when submitted to the creakings of the bulkheads of the steamer. Indeed we had some curious experience, how tales of midnight ghosts etc. easily arise in such places. Froude and I slept in the same room, and we could not turn in bed, we could not breathe, without a chorus of sounds following from all corners of our vast saloon. Now let it be pitch-dark, and the natural dreariness of the place conjure up superstitious feelings; and let the associations of the place pass before the mind, its almost heathen condition, the present abode of Turks, Jews, and infidels of every kind, and once the seat of pestilence and the scene perhaps of atrocious cruelties,—and you will see that we might easily have manufactured a ghost story, had we been educated in a less sceptical place than Oxford.—However, tho' we did not do this, I at least was defrauded of my due sleep by the noises, and was glad to get released; tho' this did not happen till I caught a cough, which confined me to my bedroom, nearly the whole of the remaining time of my stay at Malta.—But after all I am calumniating the Lazaret—it is really a very habitable place—we were only for one day at all cold—and in summer it must be very pleasant for the sort of thing. We were allowed to row about the harbours, and even along the coast, so that we landed no where. Nor had I much to regret in being a prisoner indoors when we got into Town. Valetta is a very fine place, but there is little to see there in detail. You may see every thing in a day or two—and so much I had in spite of my cough. I went to St Paul's bay, and over St John's Church, walked about the streets and fortifications, and saw a review—There is no part of my time, that I could not better afford to be disabled [sic]—and after all I do believe the solitude was a most composing and recruiting thing after my sea life. I am sure I started from Malta in high spirits and good health, which I have had ever since.—I doubt whether the gratification of travelling does not consist chiefly in the retrospect—there is far too great hurry and excitement at the time to leave room for much actual enjoyment— but afterwards, the memory of every moment and of every little incident from without, awakens strange feelings of regret and almost tenderness. One says to oneself again and again, 'Oh that I had known at the time my own happiness—to be in a place so famous etc.—' the truth is we cannot realize such things at the moment; and we cannot recollect all the associations with which the place is really connected in our minds. I knew I should feel this before setting out—and I have actually experienced it when at the time I most fully entered into the scene before me and made the most of my first sight of it. Yet I begin to feel it, even when I have no particular reason for so doing—thus, e.g., take a good example, Pompeii.—The utmost you can say of it, is, that it is a very *curious* place— beyond this, in me at least, it excites no great interest—I did not go to it with expectations. It was neither the theme of Homer, nor the tomb of Virgil—I had seen ruins enough already to bring before me past times—and all the curiosities of this very place, which are brought together in the Museum at Naples—And what past age did it carry one back to? one of the most profligate and abandoned in history, that age which called for a new religion to be the salt of the earth and save the world hardly and only as if by fire from destruction. There is scarce ground for doubting that the fire from Vesuvius was as strictly judicial as that which overwhelmed the cities of the plain. There is a room set apart in the Museum for odious Mosaics etc collected from Pompeii, which they say are atrocious beyond power of words to stigmatize. The power of which it was an offshoot, was the hateful Roman power, the 4th beast of Daniel's Vision, and the persecutor of the infant Church. A Christian can scarce have any feeling but one of a solemn yet (as thinking of himself) remorseful triumph in seeing the dead carcase of human crime. I expected no great *pleasure* from seeing it, certainly. And the day was unfavorable. For a time we paddled about the ruins in drenching rain, and the road thither is a miserable drive through dirty suburbs of Naples for 14 miles and the first thing one hears is that the city was surprised in the midst of revelry, the amphitheatre being crowded—and the bones of a lion were found in the den close to the arena.—Nor *did* I feel any pleasure at the time—I stared about—saw what was pointed out—and came away. Yet now, at the distance of three weeks from the time, queer relentings come across me, and I almost yearn in my mind over this guilty place, with which I would fain persuade myself I have no sympathy. Why this is, I leave to philosophers to say— here I will but suggest as a theory, that the human heart will in spite of itself claim kindred with every thing human—and in the blackest deformity pities its brethren—enters into their feelings and experiences what bad tendencies they have developed—and imagines their present fearful remorse—according to the old saying, 'Homo sum, humani nihil etc'[2]— And, if we feel this in the worst places, what is felt on the other hand in brighter scenes? where the historical deeds are more comfortable, or the scenery itself is fine?—It is to me a very great loss that I had not with me other friends to see these sights with. How I should have liked to have been with you, or others I could name! One loses half the pleasure by being alone—and I believe I am going alone thro' the next month, when the F.s return home. What a sight it was to see Egesta! and again Scylla and Charybdis—Zacynthus (nemorosa)[3]— Corcyra and above all Ithaca, which was the first poetical place I ever heard of, being used to learn Pope's Odyssey by heart as a child. It was like bringing back childhood again. We passed all along Ithaca twice—first on the West, then on the East. It was quite like a dream—we did not land. I stood on deck gazing uninterruptedly—Oh that I could have touched the shore, to satisfy myself it was not a mere vision—this I thought to myself. And now it is all over, the memory of it has a sort of religious reverence in it—from the notion (I suppose) that it was a favor granted me once and no more—it cannot come again; nor indeed could I wish it, lest I should contract an undue familiarity in my thoughts of it.

I am very anxious about the result of the Merton Election— Rogers has promised (or rather I have asked him) to send me a line immediately afterwards, adding of course the event of the

Oriel, in which I am equally interested. I told him to write to Naples—ask him to direct to me thus—'at Mrs Oates's, 70 Vicolo Freddo—' If you will write too, pray direct to me at the Poste Restante Livorno. I have told Ryder to direct to me Genoa, but (if you see him in Oxford) pray tell him it is safer to direct to Leghorn—I suppose I am sure of being there. It is very vexatious to be so far from home, when interesting events take place. I have not heard from England this three months— at length I have learned a miserable kind of submission to an inconvenience which I cannot obviate.

I propose returning to England in the course of June—at times I am very fidgetty about coming back, and feel unwilling and sick at the thought of staying. Yet, while I am out, I am resolved to see all I conveniently can. When once back, I hope never to stir again. The truth is I have no taste for travelling— it is scarcely more than a pure trouble while it lasts. Even when most satisfactory, it causes the same anxiety as I feel when composing (e.g. a sermon or any thing elsc)—something, viz. which I wish to have got thro' which is an irritation while it lasts, and which has its enjoyment and τέλος in the ἐργόν produced, which is subsequent to the ἐνεργεία[4]—I am making some attempt, while here, to inquire into the history of the Gregorian Chants, but fear it will come to nothing. The greater part of the Music can be got in England, and as for dates and changes I suspect the Italians know little or nothing about them. I am to see Angelo Mai (March 18) this morning, and learn from him if any books in the Vatican will throw light on the subject. And I have got acquainted with an abbé, a very agreeable wellinformed man who has great hoards of old music. I feel very much my want to knowledge on the subject— for tho' I am very fond of music, I am very unlearned in it, having had little opportunity to become acquainted with it as a language.

Ever Yours affectionately John H Newman

17

To JOHN FREDERICK CHRISTIE

Newman's thoughts during his first visit to Rome

Rome April 6. 1833

My dear Christie

This is the first day of the Oriel Examination, and, knowing the unpleasantness to each Elector which that process involves, I sympathize with you all and wish you well through it, and feel almost as if I were a runaway. I am sure, when once back, I shall not of my free will leave England again.

You ought to have had a letter from me, but the post here seems not a little uncertain in its operation at least as regards letters imported. One curious case I heard from the Wilberforces. They were here five weeks and to their surprise got no letters from England. At last they got at the cause of it. The Italians have no W; so the unhappy initial, like puss in the corner, shifts as best it can, being sometimes disposed of among the Hs, sometimes in the list of Ms, sometimes among the Vs, according to the taste of the letter-sorter. Again there is a good deal of jealousy about political matters, particularly at Naples. Also, being afraid of the Cholera they wash all letters till they are quite dirty and illegible, as some letters that I have received.

Till I got here, I have had little leisure to write to any of my friends. I shall regret Rome very much; it is a delightful place, so calm and quiet, so dignified and beautiful, that I know nothing like it but Oxford; and, as being the place of martyrdom and burial of some of the most favoured instruments of God, it has an interest and a solemn charm which no other place can possess except Jerusalem. Before the remains of the Saints the grandeur of pagan Rome crumbles as utterly as have its material structures, and in the ruins which lie scattered on all sides we do but see the 'disjecta membra'[1] of the fourth monster of Daniel's Vision. I confess, I cannot enter into, rather I protest against, the state of mind of those who affect a classical enthusiasm at the sight of Rome. How can we lay aside our Christianity? even as men, to whom 'nihil humanum alienum est',[2] we are bound to triumph over the fall of most hardhearted and crafty Empires, but, as Christians, if we do not raise the song of rejoicing over great Babylon, surely we do not follow those who sing the song of Moses and of the Lamb. Nothing can make the queen of the seven hills any thing but evil, and it surprises me to find clergymen so inconsistent as to praise what God has cursed.

As to my view of the Romanist system, it remains, I believe, unchanged. A union with Rome, while it is what it is, is impossible; it is a dream. As to the individual members of the cruel church, who can but love and feel for them? I am sure I have seen persons in Rome, who thus move me, though they cast out our name as evil. There is so much amiableness and gentleness, so much Oxonianism (so to say) such an amusing and interesting demureness, and such simplicity of look and speech, that I feel for those indeed who are bound with an iron chain, which cripples their energies, and (one would think,) makes their devotion languid. What a strange situation it is, to be with those who think one in a stage of perdition, who speak calmly with one, while they have awful thoughts! what a mixture of grief and indignation, what a perplexity between frankness and reserve comes over one!

Next Tuesday, we go our separate ways; the Froudes homeward, I drawn by an irresistible attraction to the fair levels and richly verdured heights of Sicily. What a country it is! a shadow of Eden, so as at once to enrapture and to make one melancholy. It will be a vision for my whole life; and, though I should not choose, I am not sorry to go alone, in order, as Wordsworth would say, to commune with high nature. I hope to be home at all events not later than the beginning of June. I want to set-to again at my book. I trust I shall be conducted back safely, to be made use of. I do not mind saying this, for I do not think I am actuated by ambitious views, though power, when possessed or in prospect, is a snare. At present to me it is neither in possession or prospect; so let me enjoy my freedom from temptation, while I am sheltered from it; and, should it be ordained that I am never to have the temptation, so much the happier for me. At present I can truly say that I would take the lot of retirement, were the choice offered to me, provided I

saw others maintaining instead of me those views which seem
to me of supreme and exclusive importance. But I am talking
great nonsense, and cannot think how I have come to say it,
though I do not know why I should be ashamed of it either,
for in matter of fact we of Oxford have a high place in trying
times of the Church.

Well, my dear Christie, my thoughts are with you all this
week, and I pray you may be guided to make a selection which
may be for the advantage of Mater Ecclesia. How anxious I
am! it will be all over before you get this. I cannot hear it at
soonest for a month to come. It is a secret which the Sicilian
mountains cannot reveal. I hear L. stands and M. as well as
Marriott and W. Of these I would bet on Marriott.

JHN

J.F. Christie Esqr Oriel College

18

To HENRY WILBERFORCE

An account of his illness in Sicily

Oriel College July 16/33

My dear Henry

I have been so tired and languid since my return, that I have
written no letter which I was not driven to write—else you
were in my thoughts—and I hoped you would hear of my return some how or other. I was tired from my journey, having
been up 6 nights out of the last 7;—which shows my strength.
Indeed I must not call it strength, meaning by that any inherent thing, for my strength is as if the mercy of God externally
holding me up day by day. All sorts of evils came upon me in
Sicily—the fever, of which many were dying on all sides of
me, and which in some places was so bad that they in their
fright called it cholera, was but one though the greatest
(*perhaps*) of the (before strange to me) complaints which suddenly fell upon me (in connexion with it). For a week and
more my nurses etc thought I could not recover—no medicine
was given me which could grapple with the disorder—they

26

know nothing of calomel—they bled me indeed, but took away so little blood that both Mr Babington and Dr Ogle say, it could be of no use to me—In fact the fever ran its course; and when the crisis came, I was spared—and immediately after gained strength in a surprising way. I was so reduced, I could not lift my hand to my mouth to feed myself—much less rise, or (again) sit up, in bed—in four or five days time I could (with help) walk about the room—and in ten days I was able to travel to Palermo – performing one day a journey of 60 miles over a rough country. A determination of blood to my head came on, as I was getting well—but it has gradually gone off, as I get strength. (August 4.—) the only remaining signs of my indisposition now are my hair falling off, and a slight cough, which is very slight.—I was taken ill first in Catania, after spending two nights (unwillingly) in the open air, which I believe is a very dangerous thing in Sicily. However it could not be called more than weakness, and I was able to proceed on my journey. When I got to Leonforte in the very heart of the country, I broke down. For three days I lay without any medical assistance—on the morning of the fourth a notion seized me that my illness was all fancy, so I set out on my mule—After proceeding about 7 miles in great distress from a sort of suffocating feeling, I was forced to betake myself to a hut by the wayside, where I lay the greater part of the day. On a sudden I found fingers at my pulse—a medical man happened by chance to be in a neighbouring cottage and they called him in. His prescription enabled me to get on that evening to Castro Giovanni, the ancient Enna, where I was laid up for 3 weeks. Thence I travelled to Palermo; where the time I had to wait for a vessel was of material service to me in the way of recruiting. After another delay of 3 weeks I set out for Marseilles, and it being the season of calms, was a whole fortnight on the water. Thence I came to England with all speed; and not till I got home, could persuade myself I was not in a dream. So strange has every thing been to me.

I hope it was not presumptuous, but from the beginning of my illness I had so strong a feeling on my mind that I should recover, that, whatever I did in the way of preparation for death (I mean, of giving my servant directions about letters etc) was done as a mere matter of duty. I could not help 'saying, 'I must act as if I were to die, but I think God has work for me yet.'—Thus I cannot answer your questions, never having realized eternity as about to break upon me. Yet I had many serious thoughts. It was a lonely situation, I found myself in, at Leonforte; at a miserable inn. I am not sure my mind was quite clear at all times, so as to be sensible of its desolateness—yet I had once, doubtless when I felt myself lonely, quite a revelation come upon me of God's love to His elect, and felt as if I were one—but of course I mention this, not as laying stress upon it, but as an instance of God's mercy to me;—not that I can describe the feeling in words.—Then again I was much relieved next day, by being able to discover, (as I thought) sins in my conduct, which led God thus to fight against me. This he had been doing ever since I left Rome, and I from time to time had been impatient under the obstacles he put in my way, and had (as it were) asked why He did so. But now I came to think that there was some wilfulness in my coming to Sicily, as I did—and, tho' no one had advised me against it, yet I fancied I ought to have discovered they thought it an over-venturous thing. And then I felt more than I had done the wilfulness of my character generally—and I reflected that I was lying there the very day on which three years before I had sent in my resignation of the Tutorship (or something like it)—and, tho' I could not (and do not) at all repent the doing so, yet I began to understand that the *manner* was hasty and impatient. And then I recollected that the very day before I left Oxford, I had preached a University Sermon against wilfulness, so that I seemed to have been predicting my own condemnation. And I went on to ask myself whether I had not cherished resentment against the Provost—and whether in me was not fulfilled the text I Cor. XI, 29–32, (as I still think it has been).—But after all I was comforted by the thought that, in bringing myself into my present situation, I had not (as I just said) run counter to any advice given me—and I said 'I have not sinned against light—' and repeated this often. And then I thought I would try to obey God's will as far as I could, and, with a dreamy confused notion, which the fever (I suppose) occasioned, thought that in setting off the fourth day from Leonforte, I was walking as long as I could in the way of God's commandments, and putting myself in *the way* of His mercy, as if He would meet me. (Is.xxvi,8) and surely so He did, as I lay in the hut—and though I have no distinct remembrance of the whole matter, yet it certainly seems like some instinct which He put within me and made me follow, to get me to Castro Giovanni, where I had a comfortable room, and was attended most hospitably and kindly.—It is most strange, and shows what is the hardness and inconsistency of my mind, that since I have been in England I have had hardly one feeling of joy and gratitude, tho' the thought of home drew tears into my eyes abroad, as oft as I thought of it—especially in my dreary voyage from Palermo to Marseilles.

Sept. 3. Your letter this morning induces me to send you the above at once. I was afraid I might be teazing you with it, before I heard from you. I suppose you could not come here for this week, previously to your going to Scotland? or on your return?—I should so rejoice to see you. As to the queries of your letter, I would rather talk than write to you. Be assured I shall stick to the State as long as I can—but God forbid I should betray my trust, or diminish the privileges of Christ's Church committed to me. I do not fear a schism. The Clergy will wake—at least great numbers. I will not answer for the Bishop of Winchester, whose vote on the Sacrilege Bill[1] has pained me much. We have set up Societies here—for the defence of the Liturgy and the enforcement of the doctrine of the Apostolical Succession. They are already forming in Oxfordshire, Berkshire, Gloucestershire, Devonshire, Kent and Essex and Suffolk. And we are sure (I believe) of the support of some Bishops. Let us behave like men, and we have nothing to fear. Of course we are lost, if we are cravens.—You will see the writings of many of your friends, if you ever see the British Magazine. We are publishing tracts in our Society, and perhaps may proceed to a Periodical Quarterly. We have already got subscribers for our general plan, The Country clergy *must* rouse, *in order to* save themselves. They will keep possession of their places if they are brave—but woe to them if they knock under—vae victis! My work (the Arians) is passing thro' the Press and appears in October. If you have an opportunity, tell your brother W. I am quite well, with many thanks to him for his kindness

Ever Yrs affly John H Newman . . .

29

19

To R. F. WILSON

There is a system behind the existing system in the church

Oriel College. March 31 1834

Excuse this strange paper. I am writing from the Tower, in the midst of an Audit.

... The Church is certainly in a wretched state, but not a gloomy one to those who regard every symptom of dissolution as a ground of hope. Not that I would do any thing towards the undoing, or will fail both tooth and nail (so be it) to resist every change and degradation to which it is subjected. But, after all, I see a system *behind* the existing one, a system indeed which will take time and suffering to bring us to adopt, but still a firm foundation. Those who live by the breath of state patronage, who think the clergy must be gentlemen, and the Church must rest on the great, not the multitude, of course are desponding. Woe to the profane hands who rob us of privilege or possession, but they can do us no harm. In the mean time, should (by any strange accident) the course of events fall back into its old channel, *I* will not be a disturber of the Church, though it is difficult to see how this return can be.

The state of the Christian Knowledge Society (as you have doubtless heard from Mr Norris) is the most miserable of our miseries. The Evangelicals have taken advantage of the difficulties of the Church to push; but we do not mean to be beaten. There will be probably warm work tomorrow week. I am going up to attend the meeting.

Here we are going on in a humdrum way, only enlivened by Burton and Sewell's pamphlets, which are excellent.[1] Indeed it is most gratifying to see men of ready mind coming forward on the right side. Others are on the move, and doubtless, excepting a few reprobates, in time of trouble we shall all be one way of thinking.

P.S. M.A. fees for degree £24 at outside.

20

To MRS NEWMAN

A visit to Alton where the Newmans had once lived

Sept 20. 1834. Alton

I left Stevens this morning, and got here about two o'clock. As I got near the place, I many times wished I have not come, I found it so very trying. So many strong feelings, distinct from each other, were awakened. The very length of time since I was here was a serious thought, almost half my life; and I so different from what a boy, as I then was, could be;—not indeed in my having any strong stimulus of worldly hope then, which I have not now for, strange though it may seem, never even as a boy had I any vision of success, fortune, or worldly comfort to bound my prospect of the future, but because, after fifteen years, I felt after all that I was hardly the same person as to all external relations, and as regards the particular tempering and colouring of my mind.

And then the number of painful events, and pleasant too, which have gone betwen my past and my present self. And further, the particular season at which we lived here, when I was just entered at Oxford, so that this place is, as it were, the record, as it was the scene, of my Undergraduate studies and opinions. The Oxford reminiscences of that time have been effaced by my constant residence there since, but here I am thrown back upon those years, which never can come again.

There are many little incidents, stored in my memory, which now waken into life. Especially I remember that first evening of my return from Oxford in 1818, after gaining the scholarship at Trinity, and my Father saying, 'What a happy meeting this!' Often and often such sayings of his come into my mind, and almost overpower me, for I consider he did so very much for me at a painful sacrifice to himself—and was so generous and kind; so that whatever I am enabled to do for you and my sisters I feel to be merely and entirely a debt on my part, a debt which he calls me to fulfil.

All these various thoughts so troubled me, as I came along

and the prospect opened clearer and clearer, that I felt quite sick at heart. There was something so mysterious too in seeing old sights, half recollecting them, and doubting. It is like seeing the ghosts of friends. Perhaps it is the impression it makes upon one of God's *upholding* power, which is so awful—but it seemed to me so very strange, that every thing was in its place after so long a time. As we came near, and I saw Monk's Wood, the Church, and the hollow on the other side of the town, it was as fearful as if I was standing on the grave of some one I knew, and saw him gradually recover life and rise again. Quite a lifetime seems to divide me from the time I was here. I wished myself away from the pain of it. And then the excitement caused a re-action, and I got quite insensible and callous—and then again got disgusted with myself, and thought I had made a great fool of myself in coming here at all, and wondered what I should do with myself, now that I was here. Meanwhile the coach went on, and I found myself at the Swan.

I took possession of a bed room and ordered dinner etc etc.

21

To MRS WILLIAM WILBERFORCE

The 'mixture of error' in Romanism

Oriel College. Nov. 17. 1834

(not sent)

My dear Mrs Wilberforce,

Harriet has just had a letter from you, which gives me your direction. Had I written indeed in answer to your very kind letter at once, I should have had no difficulty—but I delayed, and then doubted whether you had not left Sorrento. I delayed writing—yet it was from the great satisfaction, as well as the pleasure, your most acceptable letter gave me—I found my anxiety, as it were, rested—and as being thus at rest, I kept silent, when perhaps I ought to have acknowledged to you how pleased I was. Really, you must not suppose that I do not feel the force and influence of those parts of the Roman Catholic system, which have struck you. To express vividly what I mean, I would say, 'I would be a Romanist, if I could. I wish I could be a Romanist', But I cannot—there is that mixture of error in it, which (though unseen of course by many many pious Christians who have been brought up in it) effectually cuts off the chance of my acquiescing in it. I admire the lofty character, the beauty, the sweetness and tenderness of its services and discipline—I acknowledge them divine in a certain sense, i.e. remnants of that old system which the Apostles founded. On the other hand I grieve to think of our own neglect in realizing the Church system among us, which our Reformers *intended* to be ours, though we have degenerated from their notions; but after all there is that in Romanism which makes it a duty to keep aloof from it, there is a mixture of corruption, which, when seen, it is a duty to protest against—and *we* have been so circumstanced *as to* see it; and instead of shutting our eyes to it, we must feel that we are called upon to protest against it. On the other hand, instead of deserting our own Church, because its members are rebellious, rather let us rally in its defence and try to strengthen its hands. Consider the fallen state of the Jews when our Savior came, how mixed they were with the world, how political, Herod their king a man of Edom, and the Romans their great friends, yet after all did not such as Zechariah, Anna and the rest gain a blessing by quietly going on with *their own* worship as the Saints of old, in spite of the degeneracy around them? and at last they gained by their perseverance the blessing of seeing the Lord's Christ. And so we, though we are thought unfashionable and born centuries too late, may go on in our own Church as our forefathers, secure through Christ's mercy of a blessing from Him, and sure, even though He does not come in our day to make the glory of His second House greater than that of the first, yet that at least we shall be preparing the way for Him, and may be the means of bringing the blessing on our children's children, though it may be delayed.

The more I examine into the R.C. system, the less sound it appears to me to be; and the less safely could I in conscience profess to receive it. I hardly know whether to say any thing on the subject, not knowing whether I shall speak to the point; yet perhaps I ought not to be silent on the nature of my objec-

33

tions to it. E.g. it seems so very irreverent and profane a thing to say that our Savior's own body is carnally present on the Altar. That He is in some mysterious incomprehensible way present I fully believe; but I do not know what way—and since the way is not told us in Scripture or the ancient fathers I dare pronounce nothing. Much less dare I be so irreverent as to determine that His flesh and blood are there as they were on Calvary. Surely He who came into the apartment the doors being shut, has ways of being there innumerable, such as we know not—We believe that now He has a 'spiritual body'—and a spiritual body may be present, the bread and wine still remaining. Therefore it seems safe and according to Scripture to say He is present *in* the bread and wine—but unnecessary and irreverent to insist on our saying that the bread and wine are *changed* into that flesh and blood which were on the Cross.

Again the honor paid to the Saints surely is practically a dishonor to the One God. Is it not practically a polytheism? Are not the Saints the Gods of the multitude in Roman Catholic countries? is there not a natural *tendency* in the human mind to idolatry, and shall the Church, the pillar of the Truth, cherish it instead of repressing it?

Again, after all excuses, is there not something against one's sense of right in praying to images? is there not a still small voice telling us not to do so?

Again, consider what a frightful doctrine purgatory is—not the holiest man who lived but must expect to find himself there on dying, since Christ does not remit all punishment of sin. Now, *if* Christ has promised to wipe away all guilt and all suffering upon death, what a great affront it must be to Him, thus to obscure His mercy, to deprive His people of the full comfort of His work for them!

I feel very much the weakness and poorness of these remarks—but hope you will take them as they are meant in kindness. It requires many words to do justice to them, and conversation rather than writing. I feel the Roman Catholic system to be irreverent towards Christ, degrading Him, robbing Him *practically* of His sole honor, hiding His bounty;— i.e. so far forth as it *is* Roman Catholic—so far as it differs from ours. Its high points are our points too, if it would but keep them, and not give up our jewels. But, while what is good in it is reverent, solemn, and impressive, its corruptions *practically* undo all this excellence. Surely we shall be judged according to our conscience, and if we have a clear sight of what is wrong in Rome, we must not follow our inclinations, because Rome has what is attractive in some part of her devotions. Pray excuse what I feel to be most imperfect. I wish I spoke by mouth, not by letter. Best love to the two Williams.[1] The Revolutionary Ministry is just out—and the Duke of Wellington sent for to the King.

Ever Yrs most sincerely John H. Newman

22

To SIMEON LLOYD POPE

Pope had complained of difficulties and of being alone

Oriel College, December 9 1835

My dear Pope,

I can but express my great regret, as I have often before, that we are at such a great distance from each other—but regret will not mend matters. If I am a bad correspondent, it is really because I am very busy. Day goes after day, each bringing its own work, so that it is with difficulty that I get time to write without a sacrifice.

When did I ever hint you were petulant and unreasonable? not I. Certainly you, have a good deal to harrass you—your being alone is especially against you. But do not suppose that you alone have cares in this world. I suppose every one has in his way. Were you married and at the head of a fine and flourishing family, I may say an increasing family, with nine altogether, four boys and five girls, and a tenth expected, would you not have troubles? or were they all girls, would you not say, 'girls *are* such an expence, and my girls are not particularly showy or well favoured'—or if they were boys, one would be sent away from school for striking a praepositor, another would dabble in wet and dirt till he got the scarlet fever, and the eldest would run off to Gretna Green with some milliner's apprentice. Or Mrs P. would be for ever on the look

35

out for balls and sights, in spite of your grave admonitions that a Parson's wife should keep at home. Or she would have a tongue and a temper, and make your home twice as doleful as it is now. And then bad times would come—the Clergy would be called on for unlawful concessions—and you would say, 'why really I cannot afford to keep a conscience. Give me a large fat rectory, and I can suffer a little taxing and fining; but what with my four sons (now going on for College) and my five daughters (the youngest turned nine) I cannot stand on punctilios. True it is, this new Bishop Ministers have put in has avowed himself an Unitarian, and I hate his principles, but my family has claims on me' etc etc etc. Now I think, with all your grumbling, you are a happier man now than you would be under such circumstances.

The views you express are in my opinion very good and true—and I should rejoice in having the opportunity of some conversation with you upon them.

As to your leaving the Parish, from thinking you do them no good that must not be. Depend upon it, you do them good, though you do not see it. At all events you fulfil our Lord's charge in preaching—and it does not concern you whether men hear or forbear.

Your question about the Oaths at Institution is a serious one—but I do not yet see that it ought to disquiet any one in the case you mention. Nor do I see how it could affect a person years after he had taken them—but I am open to instruction on the subject.

Really I am very much grieved that we should be so far from each other—I would certainly fulfil my promise of coming to see you, were it not for the expence—that really hinders me.

I trust your Mother is by this time recovered from her accident, which sounded very serious.

Ever Yrs most sincerely John H Newman

P.S. You ever have from me what you ask me to do for you I trust and doubt not you return the kindness.

23

To JOHN WILLIAM BOWDEN

The death of Hurrell Froude

Oriel College March 2 1836

My dear Bowden,

I write in a very great hurry, being just at present quite laden with business. Yesterday morning brought me the news of dear Froude's death—and if I could collect my thoughts at this moment, I would say something to you about him—but scarcely can. He has been so very dear to me, that it is an effort to me to reflect on my own thoughts about him. I can never have a greater loss, looking on for the whole of life—for he was to me, and he was likely to be ever, in the same degree of continual familiarity which I enjoyed with yourself in our Undergraduate days; so much so that I was from time to time confusing him with you and only calling him by his right name and recollecting what belonged to him, what to you, by an act of memory. It would have been a great satisfaction to me had you known him—you once saw him, indeed, but when his health was gone, and when you could have no idea of him. It is very mysterious that anyone so remarkably and variously gifted, and with talents so fitted for these times, should be removed. I never on the whole fell in with so gifted a person—in variety and perfection of gifts I think he far exceeded even Keble—for myself, I cannot describe what I owe to him as regards the intellectual principles of religion and morals. It is useless to go on to speak of him—yet it has pleased God to take him, in mercy to him, but by a very heavy visitation to all who were intimate with him. Yet every thing was so bright and beautiful about him, that to think of him must always be a comfort. The sad feeling I have is, that one cannot retain on one's memory, all one wishes to keep there—and that as year passes after year, the image of him will be fainter and fainter.

I trust you are all recovering your late very great affliction—particularly your Brother. I fear when I saw you in Town, I behaved with very little sympathy—but really, when you and Mrs Bowden spoke to me as you did, why, I felt I had no right to hear such things, said about me—and knowing how very unworthy I am, I could only be quite ashamed, and desirous to disclaim every thing you said—And this, I fear, might seem like not meeting and answering your kindness—and it distressed me very much afterwards.

We are full of our painful controversy here—nothing decisive is done—but the feeling of indignation and apprehension is, I think, growing.

With kindest remembrances to Mrs Bowden
Ever yrs affly John H Newman

24

To MRS JOHN MOZLEY

Family matters, the Influenza and Littlemore parishioners, a reading of 'Emma' and Wesley's Life

Oriel College Jan 19 1837

My dear Jemima,

It is very kind in you and John to be thinking of doing what you mention about Aunt N.—of course I wish to do my part. You say £40 more per annum is requisite. Well—I will do of this whatever you and Frank do not do. Wait and see what F. will do before you say what you will do yourself—or I will arrange it in any other way you like. I should like my Trust money, when it comes into my hands, to be received (i.e. the interest of it) *with yours* by you or John. Then you can pay it over to Aunt as part of what I have to send her. Else the money will have a double journey.

Frank has written me an angry letter lately which has surprised me. It seems he has been all the while fidgeting about my giving a book to his wife. Why not say so then? I am sure it has given me trouble enough. He speaks as if I were treating *her* as I would not *him*, i.e. more kindly. Why I have done everything *through* him, and through delicacy would not even write to her. When the book was received *she* wrote to me and I then answered it—which has excited F's displeasure—I am told that there has been a letter in the Morning Chronicle from Bristol from a person who says he has heard F. say I wrote the article on Dr Wiseman. I do not care who knows it—people are very much out if they think I do—but how did F. know? it is like him to go chattering about, and very decent to have one brother speaking against another in mixed society. If he does it on religious grounds, then I have nothing to say of course, only I should find fault with his taste.

Charles made his appearance here unexpectedly on the Epiphany—he was walking to Town, without clothes. He slept here one night and pursued his journey. He declared he did it for exertion and health, but I thought it foolish this time of year. I fear he must have been laid up of the Influenza in London. I have had the Influenza, and for a week was laid on the shelf. I hope to hear a good account of you all at Derby by James. All the Littlemore people have had it—it has come to them and to me quite suddenly. I had not heard it was about, and would not believe I had a cough; it came so suddenly without preparation or exciting cause. Mrs Birmingham who has been ailing for 6 weeks died last night. Mrs Hedges is dead also, not comfortably. And Mrs (I do not know her name) at Mr Waddle's house of the Influenza.

Tell Miss Mozley that I fear I must decline the place in her poetical collection. I never can write, except in a season of idleness. When I have been doing nothing awhile, poems spring up as weeds in fallow fields.

I have been reading Emma. Everything Miss Austen writes is clever—but I desiderate something. There is a want of body to the story. The action is frittered away in over-little things. There are some beautiful things in it. Emma herself is the most interesting to me of all her heroines. I feel kind to her, whenever I think of her. But Miss Austen has no romance, none at all. What vile creatures her parsons are! She has not a dream of the high catholic ἦθος[1]. That other woman, Fairfax is a dolt—but I like Emma.

I have nearly finished Southey's Wesley, which is a very superficial concern indeed—interesting of course. He does not treat it *historically*, in its connexion with the age—and he cannot treat it theologically, if he would. I do not like Wesley—putting aside his exceeding self confidence, he seems to me to have a black selfwill, a bitterness of religious passion, which is very unamiable. Whitfield seems far better.

My best love to Aunt—thank her for her note—and apologise to her on your own score for having seduced me into filling up this third side to you instead of to her.

Ever yrs affectionately John H Newman

PS The Tract on the breviary has run through 750 copies in the dead time of the year!

PS Thanks for your kind thought of me

25

To MRS JOHN MOZLEY

Should a married lady pay out money to needy relatives?

17 June 1837

My dear Jemima,

Thanks for your tablets which I have already found very useful. You have not told me the name of Mr Mozley's banker, so I assume it is Williams', and have ordered Rivington to pay into his account £100 now, and £100 in about 2 months time—when it is paid, I will ask about the interest of money —It seems to me you are quite right in what you do for Aunt —and I have talked to Aunt about it—and she assents. She would quite assent if left alone—and I think the best way will be to drop the subject till her return. I think she would like this. It is quite preposterous that a married woman should have nothing to spend but on herself (I am taking the lowest ground, as if John were out of the question—though you are a Mozley, you are a Christian). Can any husband, who is good for any thing, like his wife only to have so much as she spends on herself? and if you are bound as a Christian to spend on others as well as yourself, who has claims before Aunt? must we not be just before we are generous? Why even as a Governess, to take the very lowest ground, she has earned from our

justice what she may claim from our gratitude. And when a
certain sum of money has come to you virtually, I cannot see
any impropriety. I am writing abruptly having little room. It
comes to this—are you to give nothing to God of what he has
given you? I think you are quite right.

Ever yrs affly John H Newman

26

To H. E. MANNING

*Manning's wife being seriously ill, he had asked for intercession in
church for her*

Oriel College July 14 1837

My dear Manning,

You and yours have been much in my thoughts lately, and I
have been continually doing that which you ask of me. It has
truly grieved me to hear of the severe trial you are under,
though really such trials are our portion. I think one may say it
without exaggeration, but they who seek God do (as it were)
come for afflictions. It is the way He shows His love, and to
keep from so doing is His exception. I suppose we may consider His words to the Sons of Zebedee addressed to us.[1] It often
strikes me so when I am partaking the Holy Communion that I
am but drinking in (perchance) temporal sorrow, according to
His usual Providence. Hence St. Peter tells us not to think
affliction a strange thing.[2] Let this then, my dear Manning, be
your comfort,—you are called to trouble as we all are, and the
severer the more God loves you. He may mercifully consider
your present distress and suspense sufficient for his unscrutable
purpose—if so it will come to an end with nothing more. But
anyhow be sure He does not willingly afflict us, nor will put a
single grain's weight more of suffering than it is meet and
good for you to bear—and be sure too that with your suffering
your support will grow, and that if in His great wisdom and
love He take away the desire of your eyes, it will only be to
bring her really nearer to you. For those we love are not
nearest to us when in the flesh, but they come into our very

41

hearts as being spiritual beings, when they are removed from us. Alas! it is hard to persuade oneself this, when we have the presence and are without experience of the absence of those we love; yet the absence is often more than the presence, even were this all, that our treasure being removed hence, leads us to think more of Heaven and less of earth.

I know all this is scarcely applicable, since you are in the distressing state of suspense, unable to make up your mind to anything, because nothing is definitely determined for you, yet is it wrong to say that one should contemplate and try to reconcile oneself to the worst, so that if anything happier comes it may be so much gain?

However of course the trial is, when anything like amendment comes or respite, as throwing us out of what we had made up our minds to—May Almighty God be with you.

I do not see at first sight any reason why I should not put up prayers as you suggest, and of course I should like to do so, but will ask or enquire on the subject.

Ever yours affectionately, John H Newman

27

To MRS JOHN MOZLEY

'I am quite worn out with correcting'

O.C. January 29 1838

My dear Jemima,

I have very little to say except to thank you for your letters. Mrs Small is so much better that for weeks she has not been prayed for and I suppose is counted well. The glass in my inner room has stood at 10°, that is 22° below the freezing point. I have never had it so cold for a continuance, or at all, since I have been in them.

As to MRG's [Giberne] MS, since this engagement with the British Critic which has destroyed the possibility of my undertaking anything else I have not (being busy) looked into it.

I am quite sick at the thoughts of having the British Critic—

but there was no-one else, and I did not like so important a work to get into hands I could not trust. I do not begin with it till the July No.

My book on Justification has taken incredible time. I am quite worn out with correcting. I do really think that every correction I make is for the better, and that I am not wasting time in an over-fastidious way, or making it worse than it was —but I can only say the means of correcting are inexhaustible. I write—I write again—I write a third time, in the course of six months. Then I take the third—I literally fill the paper with corrections so that another person could not read it. I then write it out fair for the printer—I put it by—I take it up—I begin to correct again—it will not do—alterations multiply— pages are re-written—little lines sneak in and crawl about—the whole page is disfigured. I write again. I cannot count how many times this process goes on. I can but compare the whole business to a very homely undertaking—perhaps you never had to—washing a sponge of the sea gravel and sea smell. Well —as many fresh waters have I taken to my book. I heartily wish it were done. Seven lectures out of 15 (say) are in the Printer's hands—two more nearly finished. I have to write at the end a sort of Essay as an Appendix on the Formal Cause of Justification which will cost me some thought and reading.

Thank John for his letter. I suppose the first sheet of hymns has passed the press.

Ever Yrs affly JHN

Love to Aunt

28

To A. BELAMY

On the power of newspapers—which should not be overrated

Oriel College. Jan 25. 1839

Dear Sir,

I felt very much obliged by your letter, which I did not answer at once, because I wanted to mention first your suggestion about a Newspaper to a friend. It was not, however, I confess, with any expectation that either of us would look with much hope to any project of the kind. Somehow, it seems to me that time will set a great many matters right, and time only. I do not deny the power of the periodical press, or the duty of making use of it when one can,—and very much obliged of course I must be to such friends as attempt to check its violence against ourselves personally,—but after all I do not hope or fear from it much. The hope of the Church does not lie with Newspaper readers. It lies with thoughtful men, and young men—whether lay or clerical. These are the men who must have weight, and these are the men whom Newspapers do not, for the most part, affect. And they will in their sphere and place spread the truth against the Newspapers; and in the long run be believed against them, as being not anonymous declaimers but men known and valued in their neighbourhoods.

In every thing of the kind there must be misrepresentation at first—and it is a work of time to set it right. Men *will not* be set right at once—they refuse to be—but they right themselves by a natural course. If indeed they could *do* any thing on the spur of the moment, if Convocation was sitting and they could overbear it to pass some stringent articles or turn us out of the Church, then one might feel a call for immediate exertion. We have of late years had several calls in this place for prompt and energetic measures—and have tried to answer them—but I do not feel that this is one—

You must not interpret me to mean that it is not desirable to influence the Periodical Press (as you seem to have been so successful in doing) when we *can*—but that we need not be surprised or frightened at seeing prejudice. We may hope for a reaction; and at least for the gradual growth of better views. What an important book, for instance, is Mr Gladstone's! it outweighs many papers.[1]

Something will appear stitched up in the forth-coming British Magazine, by way of soothing people and strengthening friends.

I am, Dear Sir, Your faithful Servt John H Newman

29

To MRS JOHN MOZLEY

Newman is despondent about the state of the Church of England—but can joke about a friend's mistake with medicine bottles

Feb. 25 1840

My dear Jemima,

I have got very sluggish about writing for various reasons. First I am so busy, next my hand is so tired- and thirdly I am somehow desponding about the state of things, and this disinclines me to exert myself. Every thing is miserable. I expect a great attack upon the Bible (indeed I have long done so)—at the present moment indications of what is coming gather. Those wretched Socialists on the one hand—then Carlisle [sic] on the other, a man of first rate ability, I suppose, and quite fascinating as a writer. His book on the French Revolution is most taking (to me)—I had hoped he might have come round right, for it was easy to see he was not a believer, but they say that he has settled the wrong way. *His* view is that Christianity has good *in* it, or is good *as far as it goes*—which when applied to Scripture is of course a picking and choosing of its contents. Then again you have Arnold's school, such as it is (I do hope he will be frightened back) giving up the inspiration of the Old Testament or of all Scripture (I do not say Arnold himself does). Then you have Milman clenching his History of the Jews by a history of Christianity which they say is worse; and just in the same line. Then you have all your political Economists who *cannot* accept (it is impossible) the Scripture rule about almsgiving, renunciation of wealth, and self denial etc. And then your geologists giving up part of the O.T. All these and many more spirits seem writing and forming into something shocking.

But this is not all—I begin to have serious apprehensions lest any religious body is strong enough to withstand the league of evil, but the Roman Church. At the end of the first Millenary it withstood the fury of Satan—and now the end of a second is drawing on. It has *tried* strength and it *has* endured during these last centuries! and it is stronger than ever. We on the other hand have never been tried and come out of trial without practical concessions. I cannot see that we *can* receive the assault of the foe. We are divided among ourselves, like the Jews in their siege. So that it seems to me as if there were coming on a great encounter between infidelity and Rome, and that we should be smashed between them. Certainly the way that good principles have shot up is wonderful—but I am not clear that they are not tending to Rome—not from any necessity in the principles themselves, but from the much greater proximity between Rome and us than between infidelity and us—and that in a time of trouble we naturally look about for allies. I cannot say enough of the wonderful way in which the waters are rising here—and one should be very thankful. The Heads of Houses promise soon to be fairly carried off their legs, and to be obliged to fast and scourge themselves for good company's sake. All this is a miserable prose, a regular talk worth nothing at all, and soon to be falsified by the event.

I am going up to Littlemore this Easter—while there I may have more time to write to H. and you. Tell her so.

Good accounts of Bowden. I think the *colour* you propose for the altar cloth too light; and meant to have said so. But no matter. It will look very handsome anyhow. I will send you patterns. Bloxam[1] has been called away by his father's illness.

Eden[2] dabbed all through a bottle of salts and senna. His eye at the end of the time being not a bit the better. I suppose you have heard of the whole mishap. He drank up the lotion. They say that if the lotion had been good for anything it ought to have killed him—so that the mediciner was in the dilemma of wishing him poisoned or of stultifying his own mixture. This must not be put abroad however.

In haste

Ever yrs affly JHN

Thanks for your news of dear little Herbert

30

To J. R. BLOXAM

· Thanks for hard work as Curate at Littlemore

Littlemore. March 15/40

Charissime,

I must begin by thanking you, which I cannot do in terms kind and warm enough, for your great services at Littlemore; which I have always partly seen, and always fully believed, but which now I see fully with mine own eyes. What loss I have in you, My dear B! I feel it most acutely, and my only consolation is that you have not laboured for me, but for One who will repay and who has repaid and is repaying it in the minds and conduct of my people themselves. I often think I am more favoured than any one in the whole world, to have so many and such friends. Each has his own place, and does his own work. Williams[1] had done much which he only could do—and you again have done what none but you could do. You have inspired a general reverence for religion and love of the Church, and I see it in more ways than I can name, certainly than I have room to detail in a note like this. It will ever be a mournful pleasure to connect you with this place. I said mournful, because as far as your direct oversight of the place goes, you have put an end to it—but still it is not right so to say, both because I expect you still to give us your presence continually though not your labour, and because what is given to the Great Giver never dies.

I shall long to see you back again—and let me know how matters stand with you at home. For myself, at present I am so drawn to this place, though I have been here but a week, that it will be an effort to go back to St Mary's. How one is pulled in twain! why cannot one be in two spheres at once? however, I have various plans to *effect* this object, of multiplying myself, which when I see you I will detail.

Every thing is so cold at St Mary's—I have felt it for years. I know no one. I have no sympathy. I have many critics and carpers—If it were not for those poor undergraduates, who arc after all *not* my charge, and the Sunday Communions, I should be sorely tempted to pitch my tent here. By the bye, would your Dorchester friend, I forget the worthy man's name, sell me some more ground? Perhaps I might contrive to build a house on it.

The children are vastly improved in singing—and now that the organ is mute, their voices are so thrilling as to make one sick with love. You will think I am in a rapture. I fear I am writing hyperbolically.

There is much to be done at the school certainly. I do not see my way. But I shall take my time.

Your charities shall be attended to. The people mourn after you quite. I trust this will be a most pleasant Lent to me. May it be so! I hope it is not presumptuous thus to write quite in the beginning of it.

I wish I had all *your papers* about the Littlemore people; both your own and those my sister gave you. Should I find them in your rooms?

Ever Yours affly John H Newman

P.S. My Church of the Fathers is out.

31

To MRS JOHN MOZLEY

Teaching the Littlemore schoolchildren

Littlemore April 1 1840

My dear Jemima . . .

I am getting on here, though one only sees the bright side at first. The children are improving in their singing. I have had the audacity to lead them and teach them some new tunes. Also I have rummaged out a violin and strung it, and on Mondays and Thursdays have begun to *lead* with it a party of between 20 and 30, great and little, in the school room. Moreover, I have just begun chanting—and by way of experiment, a Gregorian chant, which the children seem to take to, though they have not learned it yet—for, I see, it makes them smile—though that may be at me.

I am catechising them in Church too, and have got them on so far, that they take *interest* in it. But I am sadly off for girls. I have only one, I suppose, as much as 10—and not two more than 8 or 9, except some Sunday Scholars, who have not time to learn what I would teach them.

As to Mrs W. [Whitman] I have given up the notion of dismissing her from the apparent impracticability of the thing—and shall try to take H's advice, to stimulate some people who have lately come into Mr Costar's house to supervise the school.

I have effected a great reform (for the time) in the girls' hands and faces—lectured with unblushing effrontery on the necessity of their *keeping their work clean* and set them to knit stockings with all their might. Also, I am going to give them some neat white pinafores for Church use, and am going to contrive to make them make them. I saw something of the kind I liked at Bransgore in the Autumn, and have got Mrs H.W. (who is very ill of a fever)[1] to send me a pattern with directions, which it would do your heart good to see, about lappets and pouch sleeves.

Also I have drawn up a sort of liturgy of school prayers varying with the seasons, on a hint I gained from some printed prayers—on pasteboard, done by some ladies in Sussex—and mean to have them hung up in the schoolroom and used according to the day.

I think I shall be a good deal here in future, for it does not do to begin and not go on. If I could get ground, I think I should build on it.

Will you send me with the parcel (I am exceedingly glad of your news of it and hope you are not all overworking yourselves) a dozen or two dozen copies of all H's little poems for the children, and a copy (or tell me the *title* and publisher in London) of Anne Mozley's Selection of Poems. I want to give it away to someone here.

Ever yrs affly J.H. Newman

P.S. Bloxam has lost his father. I expect him here in a day or two.

I live in hopes of your or H's coming through this place in the summer and giving my girls a polishing up.

To R. I. WILBERFORCE

Prayers for Church Unity

Oriel College. May 25/40

My dear Wilberforce,

Some persons here, among whom is Pusey, are very desirous of recommending a practice, which of course prevails considerably already, but which, I suppose, admits of being extended, and certainly of being made more systematic.

The proposal is that as many persons as possible, of all opinions, should be induced to use in private every Friday certain prayers from the Liturgy for the *unity* of our Church, and next for our being all brought into the full truth.

Joint prayer is not contemplated, except so far as friends happen to be staying together, or living together as members of a family.

One should think nothing would tend more than such a practice, especially as being *known to exist*, to allay the violence of party spirit.

At the same time it should be understood that persons who engaged to observe it, should not be in any degree bound to lay aside their present strong advocacy of their own views, or protest or resistance of those who hold opposite views. It being their duty to contend for what they believe to be the truth, they are only called upon to pray that they may know the truth themselves, and that the whole Church may agree together in one doctrine, and live in unity and peace.

Such a plan could not properly be set on foot without the knowledge and permission of the Bishop of the Diocese, which is the first step in bringing it into operation.

Our notion is that two or more persons of different religious sentiments in each diocese should apply to their Bishop for this purpose—not to get his sanction so much, if he scrupled about it, as his leave.

Let me know what you think about it generally

Ever Yrs John H Newman

To MRS THOMAS MOZLEY

*An anecdote suitable for newspapers anxious for
anti-Tractarian gossip.*

July 8 1840

While I was sitting in my surplice at the altar in Margaret
Chapel on Sunday, during the first lesson a large cat fell from
the ceiling, down close at my feet narrowly missing my head.
If I am not mistaken, it fell on its back. Where it came from,
no one I have met can tell. It got up in no time, and was at the
end of the Chapel and back again, before any one knew what
the matter was. Then it lay down thoroughly frightened. I had
heard a mewing since the beginning of the service. Mrs Bowden, who observed a large cat at S. Mary Maggiore at Rome,
suggests that the Record may note it as an additional proof
that, in the Clerk's words, the Chapel in Margaret Street 'goes
as near as ever it can to Roman Catholics.'

34

To W. C. A. MACLAURIN

How to deal with honest indecision about the true church

Derby Oct 8. 1840

My dear Sir,

I have really not known what to say to your last note, because I fear you desire to hear argument, *with a view* to putting
you *out of suspence.*—I do not think a matter such as that which
so painfully distresses you, is to be decided by argument. I
could go on with controversy without ever coming to an end,
or even perhaps being obliged to confess a difficulty, but what
a waste of time is this! I do not think that the truth is so clearly
or demonstrably given us, whether Rome has it or we, to give

you satisfaction at present. On either side you will feel difficulties.

If I might venture to suggest, I would say that, were I in your present most painful state of mind, I think I should give over the *direct inquiry* for several years and give myself to fasting and prayer and practical duties. At the end of that time I trust God would enlighten my judgement—at all events I should be in a better state of mind to judge how my duty lay.

What you say in your last about having come to our Church on your private judgement, does certainly deprive my advice that you should not.go to Rome on your private judgement of some of its force. But I do not think I can be wrong in the suggestions I now make. Anyhow, really I do not think that argument is the mode in which your mind will effectually be relieved.

God does not require of us impossibilities—if we are perplexed, we *are* perplexed—What is our duty *under* the perplexity? Is it not to wait on Him?

Yours very truly John H Newman

35

To J. W. BOWDEN

Trouble over Tract 90

Oriel. March 15/41

My dear Bowden,

The Heads,[1] I believe, have just done a violent act—they have said that my interpretation of the articles is an evasion. Do not think that this will pain me; you see no doctrine is censured, and my shoulders shall manage to bear the charge.

If you knew all, or when you know, you will see that I have asserted a great principle, and I ought to suffer for it—that the articles are to be interpreted, not according to the meaning of the writer, but (as far as the wording will admit) according to the sense of the Catholic Church.

Ever yrs affly J.H.N

36

To MISS M. R. GIBERNE

Plans afoot for residence at Littlemore, no plans for a portrait

Oriel. April 13/42

My dear Miss Giberne

Your letter is very kind and I thank you for it very sincerely
—yet it made me laugh. What a pity it did not come a day
sooner. There was Mr Copeland and my Curate in Cheltenham till this morning, why should not he represent me? I
never have been able to understand, since I could think, what
the connexion is between a man and his name, or a man and
his face—and I really cannot see why every purpose would not
be answered if you got another person to sit instead of me, or
put out a fancy picture. There would be this advantage in the
latter, that you could then flatter me. You talk of scarecrows
—I have not seen them, so my imagination is not affected—
but tastes differ—how do you know that many persons would
not think *me* the scarecrow, and my caricature an improvement? And then again I heard yesterday, truly or not, that a
new sketch of Chaucer's Pilgrimage after Stodart (?) has come
out, and that a good likeness to me figures as the Priest—so
that the kind reason you give does not remain. Besides my
friend Westmacott was flattering enough to take a bust of me,
when I did not know the use he meant to put it to; and I suspect that that is flattered enough for the most indulgent friend.
In truth, were I a person in authority, and did it fairly come to
me to have my portrait taken, I would no more object, (it
would be silly to do so) than to taking my Doctor's degree—
but being what I am, it is just as improper as taking the said
degree, and would make me a sort of Demagogue, Popular
Preacher, Sectarian Leader, and the like—characters which of
all others I most abominate. I am in quite enough in such a
position as it is, much in spite of myself, without taking any
steps of my own. For a step of my own it would be. When a
set of people come forward, and *ask* for a person's portrait, *they*
take the responsibility *off* him—as it is, I should (to the world)

have the whole of it, and did I ever do such a thing, depend on it, would not do it by halves, while I was about it—but should proceed to prefix the said portrait to every one of my books, sermons and all, and would be represented in an elegant dress and attitude, with my hand between the buttons of my waist-coat, or in a new taglioni.[1]

You must not for an instant suppose I do not feel your great kindness; and don't take what I have said as rude, which I trust it is not.

Pray make my best acknowledgments to your kind friends who have so readily seconded your wishes by allowing me to make use of their house, if I came to Cheltenham. This, I fear, is quite impossible. I have been meditating a journey to London for a day ever since Easter, and am under promise to Bowden to go down to him to dinner, but have not been able to manage *it* yet.

The truth is, I am just going to my new abode at Littlemore, and wish to get things into order. The papers give an absurdly exaggerated account of it, as you may suppose. I have long wished to live at Littlemore, and the difficulty has been to get a room for a library. Last Spring the heirs of old Costar turned a granary into a number of cottages, and I offered to rent them, on condition of their turning a stable which adjoined into a room (for books). This is the long and the short of the whole matter. I have taken my books there, and shall care little whether I get other inmates besides myself or not. Perhaps my curate will come—perhaps my school-master—perhaps my Secretary—perhaps some village boy who can be made some-thing of—perhaps one or two pupils—perhaps some Oxford friends—some may stop for a permanence, some for a time. I shall attempt *very* little of a rule at first—though of course I am telling you all this as a secret—Perhaps, engaging every one to get up always at 6 o'clock—not to speak to each other except within certain hours—and perhaps to have but one sit-down meal in the day;—perhaps to pass certain hours in joint-devotion. I shall aim ultimately at dispensing with all servants. But it is all a dream at present. I shall do what I *can*, and I can-not say what I *shall* do, because I do not know what I can . . .

Yours very sincerely John H Newman

37

To S. L. POPE

The distressing state of the Church of England

Littlemore. Sept. 4. 1842

My dear Pope,

I feel quite what you say, and assent to it with all my heart. You have just hit the point. The laity say, *Whom* are we to believe? It is a most distressing state of things for those who *wish* to be quiet and dutiful, and a great triumph to unbelievers and worldly persons. How can that be practically a church, how can it *teach*, which speaks half a dozen things in the same breath? Of course things cannot stand here. What is the *use* of an Establishment, people may well ask, but for the sake of *peace*? We want to be rid of the multitude of opinions—we wish to be spared confusion and discord—You allow yourselves to undertake the office, and you do not fulfil it. What then comes of you?—This is common sense and irresistible—and will be felt more and more. My great hope and belief is, that the so-called Evangelical party is a failing and declining one; so that we may hope that the clamour will be less and less every year. And the very circumstance that there is reason for so thinking is what makes the clamour louder at present. These good people feel and know that they are losing ground, and therefore they cry out so much the louder. They cry while they can.

The rising generation are almost to a man of another way of thinking. Even at Cambridge, where the want of mental discipline is so great that one cannot augur any thing very superfine in time to come, a very much truer view of religious matters is appearing—as even the Camden Society shows in spite of its extravagances. The great point seems to be to stave off any serious collision between the parties for (say) 20 years—by that time the old Protestant generation will be extinct—and one may trust there will be more of unity. But if not, if either zealots force matters on to a collision, or the old party does not disappear in time, our church must inevitably go to pieces. For this reason I am very much against the meeting of Convocation for despatch of business—fearing it would bring on a crisis. The Protestant party would do all in their power to eject their opponents from the church.

I assure you I am in as much despair as yourself as to doing good to my people. What a says, b unsays. No two clergymen, next door to each other, return the same answer to the question 'What shall I do to be saved?'—with this consciousness, with what face can I say, 'Believe the Church, hear the Church'? You recollect the three Lawyers in Terence, and the old man's remark after consulting them 'Incertior sum multo quam ante.'[1]

As you say, this is a great triumph to the Roman Catholics —but not only so, it inclines people to them. Many persons say to themselves 'We are more certain that the discord and variety of opinions which surround us is from beneath, than that the Creed of Pope Pius is not from above.' It needs to be no theologian to be sure that 'a house divided against itself cannot stand.'—My great hope is that the Roman Catholics will turn over a new leaf. By which I do not mean that abuses and excesses will cease among them, any more than among ourselves, who abound in them over and above our theological quarrels. Superstitions will always exist among the multitude. But I wish to see, and trust to see, the ruling power of the Roman Church taking a truer, more manly, more sensible, more Christian line, removing scandals, and unlearning bigotry, and ceasing their vile connexion with liberals and democrats. Meanwhile I can only say that it is lucky for us they are in the deplorably low ethical state, to which I have been alluding, for they would be most formidable opponents, if they were not. Many a perplexed mind is driven by the tumults within us to look abroad for a refuge—but on an examination finds he shall not mend matters by going to Rome.

I cannot describe to you the localities of my Parsonage—but you must come here, and use your eyes. We are very few, and an awkward squad; but we attempt to keep one or two monastic rules; from which, however, you should be quite exempt— with a room to yourself and as many books as you please (including Scott's Novels) to amuse you

Ever Yrs John H Newman

38

To MISS HOLMES

Counsel on spiritual matters

Littlemore. In fest. S. John [27 Dec.] 1842

My dear Miss Holmes,

I was very much interested in your letter and think I quite understand the inconvenience of your present situation. But you must recollect all places have their temptations, nay even the cloister. Our very work here is to overcome ourselves— and to be sensible to our hourly infirmities, to feel them keenly, is but the necessary step towards overcoming them. Never expect to be without such, while life lasts—if these were overcome, you would discover others, and that because your eyes would see your real state of imperfection more clearly than now, and also because they are in great measure a temptation of the Enemy, and he has temptations for all states, all occasions. He can turn whatever we do, whatever we do not do, into a temptation, as a skilled rhetorician turns everything into an argument. It is plain, I am not saying this to make you *acquiesce* in the evils you speak of—if such be the *condition* of this life, to resist them is also its *duty*, and to resist them with success.

Nothing is more painful than that sense of unreality which you describe. I believe one especial remedy of it is to give a certain time of the day to meditation, though the cure is of course very uncertain. However, you should not attempt it without a good deal of consideration and a fair prospect of going on steadily with it. What I mean is, the giving half an hour every morning to the steady contemplation of some *one* sacred subject, I do not know Challoner's Daily Meditations but it is a little book much spoken of, and will explain what I mean. I dare say you know it. You should begin by strongly impressing on your mind that you are in Christ's Presence, and you might (reverently) picture Him to yourself as standing over you with His Saints and Angels. Of course there is the greatest care necessary to do all this with extreme reverence, not as an experiment, or a kind of prescription or charm.

57

I quite enter into the accounts you give me of your visitors etc. You cannot meet the trial, without calling in some such antagonist aid as I have specified. An antagonist principle is what you need.

As for myself, be quite sure that if you saw me again, you would just feel as you did when you saw me before—I am *not* venerable, and nothing can make me so. I am what I am. I am very much like other people, and I do not think it necessary to abstain from the feelings and thoughts, not intrinsically sinful, which other people have. I cannot speak words of wisdom; to some it comes naturally. Do not suffer any illusive notion about me to spring up in your mind. No one ever treats me with deference and respect who knows me—and from my heart I trust and pray that no one ever may. I never have been in office or station; people have never bowed to me—and I could not endure it. I tell you frankly, my infirmity I believe is, always to be rude to persons who are deferential in manner to me. I really do fear it is.

I am much concerned to hear you say what you do about your sister. *Certainly* you should not let her over work herself.

Yrs very sincerely John H Newman

39

To J. F. RUSSELL

Church architecture, church rites should be 'founded on deep inward convictions'

Oriel, College, Decr. 29. 1842

Dear Sir,

I am much obliged to you for the present of your two sermons, and hope they will do all the service to the cause of Catholic Truth which their author intends, and they are calculated to effect

Somehow, I am rather suspicious, or I should say, jealous, of the course of the ecclesiastical movement in some quarters, and not the least in the Ecclesiologist. Of course, I am not so

absurd as to be speaking of its conductors and writers indi-
vidually, of whom I have never heard one of the names, but,
viewing it and other publications in themselves, I cannot but
think them deficient in *inside*, if I may use the word. I think we
are in great danger of becoming, if I may use a harsh word,
theatrical in our Religion. All true attention to rites must be
founded of course on deep inward convictions, and this makes
me dread the fine arts when disjoined from what is practical
and personal. All about the country people are taking up
architecture. I rejoice at it, *if* they take the severer side of Religion as well as the imaginative and beautiful—but no good can
come of all sunshine and no shade. Jonah's gourd will be the
type of our religion in that case.

I have no doubt you, as other thoughtful persons, would
agree with me in these remarks: yet I cannot help making
them, as I have made them to others, from a deep feeling that
our present success is too great,—i.e., more apparent than real.
Perhaps in the over-rulings of Divine Providence the apparent
is to *lead* to the real. It may be so. May it be so!

Yours, my dear Sir, Very Truly, John H Newman

40

To THE BISHOP OF OXFORD

Newman resigns his living at St Mary's

Oriel College Sept, 6. 1843

My dear Lord,

I shall give your Lordship much pain, I fear, by the request
which it is necessary for me to make of your Lordship, before I
proceed to act upon a resolution on which I have made up my
mind for a considerable time. It is to ask your Lordship's permission to resign the living of St Mary's.

If I intended such a step three years since and was only pre-
vented by the advice of a friend, as I have said to your Lordship in print, it is not surprising that I should be determined
on it now, when so many Bishops have said things of me,

and no one has taken my part in respect to that interpretation of the articles under which alone I can subscribe them.

I will not ask your Lordship to put yourself to the pain of replying to this request, but shall interpret your silence as an assent.

Were I writing to any one but your Lordship, it might be presumption to suppose that I should be asked to reconsider the request which I have been making: but kindness like yours may lead you to suspend your permission. If so, I may be allowed perhaps to say, on a matter in which I am able to speak, that I should much deplore such an impediment as probably leading to results which would more than disappoint your Lordship's intention in interposing it. My resolution is already no secret to my friends and others.

Let me heartily thank your Lordship for all your past acts of friendship and favour to one who has been quite unworthy of them, and believe me my Lord to be keenly alive to your anxieties about the state of the church, and to feel great sorrow as far as I am the occasion of them. On the other hand I will say in my own behalf, that I have ever felt great love and devotion towards your Lordship, and have ever wished to please you, that I have honestly tried to bear in mind that I was in a place of high trust in the church, and have laboured hard to uphold and strengthen her and to retain her members. I am not relaxing my zeal, till it has been disowned by her rulers; I have not retired from her service, till I have lost or forfeited her confidence.

That your Lordship's many good words and works for her welfare may receive a blessing in this life and a full reward in the next, is the prayer of your Lordship's

affectionate servant John H Newman.

41

To E. B. PUSEY

Pusey's young daughter is dying

Littlemore. April 10./44

My dear Pusey,

You may fancy what an heart ache your note of to-day has given me. Yet all is well, as you know better than I can say. What would you more than is granted you as regards dear Lucy? She was given to you to be made an heir of Heaven. Have you not been allowed to perform that part towards her? You have done your work—what remains but to present it finished to Him who put it upon you? You are presenting it to Him, you are allowed to do so, in the way most acceptable to Him, as a holy blameless sacrifice, not a sacrifice which the world has sullied, but as if a baptismal offering, perfected by long though kind and gentle sufferings. How fitly do her so touching words which you report to me accord with such thoughts as these! 'Love', which she asks for, is of course the grace which will complete the whole. Do you not bear in mind the opinion of theologians that it is the grace which supplied all things, supersedes all things, and is all in all? I believe they hold, though a dying person were in a desert, without any one at hand, love would be to him every thing. He has in it for-giveness of sins, communion of saints, and the presence of Christ. Dear Lucy has been made His in Baptism, she has been made His in suffering; and now she asks to be made His by love.

Well may you find her sweet countenance pleasant to look upon, when here at a distance I have such pleasure in thinking of her. May we have that great blessedness, when our end comes, (may I especially, who need so to pray more than others,) which is hers, that gift of love which casts out all im-perfections, all doubt, all sorrow!

Should you have a fit time for doing so, pray tell her that she is constantly in my thoughts, and will not, (so be it!) cease to be;—as she, who has gone first,[1] is in my mind day by day, morning and evening, continually.

All blessing on you both, and on your other dear charge[2] at Clifton is the prayer of Yours, my dear Pusey,

Most affectionately but most unworthily, John H Newman

42

To JOHN KEBLE

A long statement of Newman's state of mind and conscience

Littlemore June 8/44

My dear Keble,

Pattison wishes me to tell you that friends of his, a lady and daughter, are going into your Parish . . . . .

I ought to take this opportunity of writing to you a long letter, to which I have a great repugnance because it is about myself—not to say that writing intelligibly makes my hand ache. But you should know my state of mind—and though the disgust of writing, and the thought of the worry and worse that my letters give you, almost deter me, and I don't know how I shall get on, I will attempt to do it.

I have thought much lately of the words of Bishop Andrew's Morning Prayer—Despise not the work of Thine own hands —he repeats it in various forms, as addressed to Each of the Persons of the Most Holy Trinity. May I not take comfort in the plea which they contain? 'Thine Hands have made me and fashioned me.' I look back to past years, or rather to all my years since I was a boy, and I say, 'Is it come to this? had God forgotten to be gracious? would He have led me on so far to cast me off? what have I done to be given over, if it be such, to a spirit of delusion? where is my fault? which has been the false step, if such there be?'

I know He taketh up and setteth down—and of course I know that I have done enough to provoke Him to give me over and to deserve all that is evil. But still such is not His way, and I cannot get myself to believe that He means evil towards me, yet month by month my convictions grow in one direction.

When I was a boy of fifteen, and living a life of sin, with a
very dark conscience and a very profane spirit, He mercifully
touched my heart; and, with innumerable sins, yet I have not
forsaken Him from that time, nor He me. He has upheld me to
this hour, and I have called myself His servant. When I came
up to reside at Trinity, the verse of the Psalms, which was
most in my heart and on my lips, and it has brought tears into
my eyes to think of it, was 'Thou shalt guide me with Thy
counsel,' etc. He brought me through numberless trials safely
and happily on the whole—and why should He now leave me
to a blinded mind? I know I have done enough to provoke
Him;—but will He?

He led me forward by a series of Providences from the age of
19 till 27. I *was* 'the work of His hands,' for He repeatedly and
variously chastised me and at last to wean me from the world,
He took from me a dear sister—and just at the same time He
gave me kind friends to teach me His ways more perfectly.

Time went on, and various things happened by which he
went on training me—but what most impresses itself upon
me, is the strange feelings and convictions about His will towards me which came on me, when I was abroad. When I
went down to Sicily by myself, I had a strong idea that He was
going to effect some purpose by me. And from Rome I wrote
to some one, I think Christie, saying, I thought I was to be
made some thing of in His hands, 'though, if not, the happier
for me.' And when I was in Sicily by myself, it seemed as if
some one were battling against me, and the idea has long been
in my mind, though I cannot say when it came on, that my
enemy was then attempting to destroy me. A number of sins
were involved in the very act of my going down by *myself*—to
say nothing else, I was wilful, and neglected warnings—from
that time every thing went wrong. As I lay ill at Leonforte, before I got to Castro Giovanni, while I was laid up, I felt this
strongly—My servant thought I was dying—but I expected to
recover, and kept saying, as giving the reason, 'I have not sinned against light.' I had the fullest persuasion I should recover,
and think I then gave as the reason, that some work was in
store for me. But any how when I was getting up again, after
it was over, this feeling was strong upon me. I recollect, when
travelling down the country from Castro G. to Palermo, (the

63

ecclesiastical year was on the same days as this year, as the year of my getting in to Oriel, so that Rogers and I were both elected on the 12 of April) it must have been Whit Sunday or Monday morning, sitting on my bed as I was dressing, and crying profusely. My servant, who was obliged to help me from my great weakness (for I could not walk by myself) of course could not think the meaning of it—and I could but say to him, what was quite as unintelligible as my tears, that I thought God had some work for me. And then when I got to England, the very first Sunday after my arrival (July 14) you preached your Sermon on National Apostasy, which was the beginning of the movement.

And now at the end of eleven years from that time, what is my own state? why, that for the last five years (almost) of it, I have had a strong feeling, often rising to an habitual conviction, though in the early portion of it after a while dormant, but very active now for two years and a half, and growing more urgent and imperative continually, that the Roman Communion is the only true Church—and this conviction came upon me while I was reading the Fathers and from the Fathers—and when I was reading them theologically, not ecclesiastically, in that particular line of study, that of the ancient heresies, to which circumstances, external to myself, had led me fourteen years ago, before the movement began.

And when this trial came upon me, I told only two persons with whom I happened to be at the time—and set myself to resist the impression. As you know, I wrote against it, and I am not aware in what respect I have indulged it. And I have attempted to live a stricter life. Every Lent since it first came to me, I have spent up here, except such necessary returns to Oxford in the course of the week as Oxford duties made necessary—and for the last two years I have been here almost entirely. And I have made great efforts to keep others from moving in the direction of Rome also.

Of course there is no fear of your supposing me not to be conscious of innumerable weaknesses and errors in my heart and conduct—but I cannot help trusting they need not come into account here. Or, even though there has been at times sin more than ordinary, I trust it is not being laid to my charge.

Moreover I certainly think I may say, that in many respects

my heart and conduct have improved in the course of this five years, and that, in respects in which I have prayed for improvement. Then the question comes upon me, why should Providence have granted my prayers in these respects, and not when I have prayed for light and guidance?

And then, as far as I see, all inducements and temptations are for remaining quiet, and against moving. The loss of friends what a great evil is this! the loss of position, of name, of esteem—such a stultification of myself—such a triumph to others. It is no proud thing to unsay what I have said, to pull down what I have attempted to build up. And again, what quite pierces me, the disturbance of mind which a change on my part would cause to so many—the casting adrift, to the loss both of religious stability and comfort—the temptation to which many would be exposed of scepticism, indifference, and even infidelity.

These last considerations are so serious, in the standard of reason as well as in the way of inducement, that, if it were not for antagonist difficulties, I don't see how I could ever overcome them. But it does strike me on the other side, 'what if you are the cause of souls dying out of the communion of Rome, who have had a *call* to join it, which you have repressed? What, if this has happened already?' Surely time enough has been allowed me for wavering and preparation—I have fought against these feelings in myself and others long enough. And then another terrible thought strikes me. We hear of physicians, thinking they have cured a complaint, when they have but thrown their patient into a contrary one—and enough has happened to make me fear greatly, lest a sort of latitudinarianism and liberalism *may* be the end of those (though forbid it!) whom I am keeping from Rome. I am quite sure there is this *danger*. I dread it in particular persons. The time may even come, when I shall beg them to join the Church of Rome and they will refuse. Indeed I sometimes feel uncomfortable about myself—a sceptical, unrealizing temper is far from unnatural to me—and I may be suffered to relapse into it as a judgement.

What then is the will of Providence about me? The time for argument is past. I have been in one settled conviction for so long a time, which every new thought seems to strengthen. When I fall in with friends who think differently, the temptation to remain quiet becomes stronger, very strong—but I really do not think my conviction is a bit shaken. So then I end as I began—Am I in a delusion, given over to believe a lie? am I deceiving myself and thinking myself convinced when I am not? Does any subtle feeling or temptation, which I cannot detect, govern me, and bias my judgement?—But is it possible that Divine Mercy should not wish me, if so, to discover and escape it? Has He led me thus far to destroy me in the wilderness?

Really I dread what would be the consequence if any intimate friend of mine joined the Church of Rome. Might I not feel it impossible to disobey what seemed a warning to me, whatever trial and pain of mind it involved?

How this letter will distress you! I am ever thinking of you, my dear Keble,

Yours affly JHN

43

To ELIZABETH NEWMAN

A visit to the house that was his grandmother's

Roehampton. St James's day [25 July] 1844

My dear Aunt,

Having a quarter of an hour before I am summoned to administer the Holy Communion to dear Bowden (for this is the reason of my frequent journeys here—I come in the evening and go away next morning) I will begin to tell you what in fact there is nothing, (as it turns out), to tell about—but it is this.

You know Roehampton is a bad place for coaches, and yesterday was not the first time I have felt the want. I had to walk the whole way with my luggage, which considering the glass had been 80 or 84 in the shade (I believe 86) and that it was a vigil, and that I had walked from Littlemore to the Oxford station with my luggage, and had walked and rode for 2 hours and a half about town, was a good day's work.

Well, when I got to Fulham, I thought I would make an excuse of taking a dose of quinine, to have a peep at my Grandmother's house which I recollected forty years before, or at least 39—for I think you left in 1805. (I recollect your leaving, or at least mine, quite well. I went in one of those long coaches which were like the modern omnibusses.) You know I told you some time ago that part of the front of the house is turned into a chemist's shop.

I wanted to have a peep at the house, but the good chemist, civil as he was, did not take my hints—so I saw nothing, except the hall through the door. I saw too the staircase which I had forgotten. But I described to him the lie of the house, which he confirmed. I told him where the kitchen was, where I recollect you going to superintend the making of apple puffs. And the room opening on the garden where were the two card-racks with a lion (I think) on them; and the pictures of the prodigal son, and giving alms to the poor, and the unjust steward, or some one or other paying a number of people. There you used to breakfast—at least I recollect coming down in the morning and seeing the breakfast things looking bright and still—and I have some vague reminiscence of dry toast. And I have a sort of dream of my father and mother coming one day to call, and the room being crowded.

I told the worthy man also where the drawing room was—and I spoke of a sort of loft above, in which I have a dim vision of apples on the floor and a mangle. And of the garden—the summerhouse, he said was gone, but the drying ground behind it remained;—By this time my quinine was compounded and swallowed, and so I came away.

How strange it is, I wish I could describe it, to stand in a house which was so much to me, as that house was, and it so different, and I so different! Whatever good there is in me, I owe, under grace, to the time I spent in that house, and to you and my dear Grandmother, its inhabitants. I do not forget her Bible and the prints in it. Alas, my dear Aunt, I am but a sorry bargain, and perhaps if you knew all about me, you would hardly think me now worth claiming; still I cannot help it—I am what I am—and I have grown into what I am from that time at Fulham.

What a strange change forty years makes. How little did the little child whom you used to fondle, think of what he thinks now! He had no thoughts. There is a poem of mine in the Lyra, 'Did we but see, when life first opened, how our journey lay' etc) which applies to one at any two periods—but how strangely does it apply to me then and now! I know not now of course what is before me, before my end comes—still more strange may be the contrast—but it is very touching and sub-duing as it is.

I think I had more to say on the subject, but it has gone from me.

May we all meet again in peace, when this troublesome world and its many contentions are over. I really do think I love peace, yet I am destined to be 'a man of strife.' I am talk-ing a great deal of myself, but, if anyone will pardon it, you will, my dear Aunt, from

Your affectionate Nephew, John H Newman

P.S. Love to Harriett, Jemima, their husbands, and the chil-dren, and kind thoughts to every one else who will re-ceive them from my worthless self. Only think of my likeness having been taken by Richmond for Henry Wil-berforce!

44

To MRS JOHN MOZLEY

Loss and change

Temple, London Aug 13/44

My dear Jemima,

Here I am waiting for a London dinner hour, thinking six would be a probable time for a lawyer, but he does not come home till seven. So I take up my pen.

I have seen Bowden for a quarter of an hour. This damp day tries him sadly. He goes down to Clifton in a few days—and I suppose I shall be able to go to him there as here—the distance and expence is about the same. But, as you may suppose, both the loss of time and the expence are serious matters, great as is the pleasure. But it is a case, when, I suppose, I may without blame lose both time and money. It is of course quite an event in my life, and cannot happen again. My oldest friend—whom I knew for as much as nine years before I knew dear Froude—and whom a habit of affection has made part of my life, though I cannot realize things yet. Do not think because I speak thus selfishly, that his wife and children do not come into my thoughts. They do indeed.

It is my lot, (and suppose it is the lot of all persons who live) to lose one friend after another, in one way or another. Or rather I should say, it is God's most gracious and undeserved blessing upon me to give me so many kind friends, that it would be a miracle if the ordinary course of life did not separate from me one or other of them. And it may be His blessed will, in this way to prepare me for separations on a larger scale and still more painful. It is certainly strange Bowden's state just now—and seems to cut me off from Oxford.

I do fancy I am getting changed. I go into Oxford and find myself out of place. Every thing seems to say to me, this is not your home. The College seems strange to me, and even the College servants seem to look as if I were getting strange to them. I cannot tell whether it is a fancy or not, but to myself I seem changing. I am so much more easily touched than I used to be. Reading St Wulstan's Life just now almost brought tears into my eyes. What a very mysterious thing the mind is! Yet nothing that my feelings suggest to me is different from what has been engraven more or less strongly on my reason long ago.

Now I dare say that if I kept this a day or two, it would seem unreal, and I could not bear to send it—and yet I do think there is truth in it—making allowance for accidental feeling . . .

Do not be discomposed by this dismal letter

Ever Yrs affly JHN

P.S. Do not suppose that I am not quite well. I am and every one compliments me. Did they tell you at Tooting and in Finsbury Circus that I was looking fat and grey? . . .

To RICHARD WESTMACOTT

*Reasons for becoming a Catholic—and reasons for reserve with some
people*

Littlemore. July 11 1845

My dear Westmacott,

It was very kind in you at the present time going into my
matters. I suppose I may now tell you, that it is morally certain
I shall join the R.C. Church, though I don't wish this *told* from
me. It has been the conviction of six years—from which I have
never receded. It was gained while outward circumstances
were promising all around us, and every thing spoke of hope. I
told my feeling to one or two persons who were about me in
the autumn of 1839. I have waited patiently a long time.

My conviction has nothing whatever to do with events of
the day. It is founded on my study of early Church history. I
think the Church of Rome in every respect the continuation of
the early Church. I think she is the early Church *in* these times,
and the early Church is she *in* these times. They differ in
doctrine and discipline as child and grown man differ, not
otherwise. I do not see any medium between disowning
Christianity, and taking the Church of Rome.

This being the ground of my conviction, I have at various
times been reluctant to tell it to you—and I dare say seemed to
you either reserved or afraid to argue. It was the latter—I was
afraid. I will be frank with you, and tell you why. It was
because I had got a notion that you had been inclined to scepticism—and it seemed a most serious thing to tell a person so
inclined that one's own conviction was that he must believe
every thing or nothing. You have been so kindly persevering,
from the interest you take in me, that I am forced to tell you
my ground of conviction; and besides, I think you are stronger
now than to be put out by such an avowal on my part. But for
myself I say fairly, that I cannot believe only just as much as
our Reformers out of their own heads have chosen we should
believe—I must believe less or more. If Christianity is one and

the same at all times, then I must believe, not what the Reformers have carved out of it, but what the Catholic Church holds.

I do not agree with Ward and Oakeley in their ground,[1] but think you are hard on them. You call them disingenuous in trying to *stretch* the articles of our Church. Well then, do you wish them to *leave* our Church? that I suppose would not please you better. You abuse them for staying—you remonstrate with me for going. What middle course is there? I suppose, going into 'lay communion', giving up preferment etc and remaining quiet. This might be very well for a middle-aged, indolent person like myself—but do you really mean that a number of active, able men between 23 and 40, can think it their duty to waste their prime in doing nothing? Is it not a more fantastic idea than turning Mormonite or Jumper?

I am amused at your calling me 'cloistered—' it is true—but I am a sharper fellow than you think.

Ever Yrs affectly J H Newman

46

To MRS JOHN MOZLEY

News that Newman is to be received into the Catholic Church

Littlemore. Oct. 8 1845

My dear Jemima,

I must tell you, what will pain you greatly, but I will make it as short as you would wish me to do.

This night Father Dominic the Passionist, sleeps here. He does not know of my intention, but I shall ask him to receive me into what I believe to be the One Fold of the Redeemer.

This will not go, till all is over.

Ever Yours affectly John H Newman

71

To MRS J. W. BOWDEN

The same news, and a description of Father Dominic Barberi

Littlemore Oct. 8. 1845

My dear Mrs Bowden,

I am this night expecting Father Dominic the Passionist, in his way from Aston in Staffordshire to Belgium, where he goes to attend a Chapter of his Order, and he, please God, will admit me tomorrow or Friday into what I believe to be the one true Fold of Christ. Two more of our party, Bowles and Stanton, are to be received with me. Christie, if you know him by name, who has been here all the Vacation, is to go, as today, to a Priest in London. These coincident movements are through sympathy more than anything else.

For myself, I found my work almost finished, and the printing going on slow, and some friends objected both to Christmas and to Advent, as times when they would rather not be unsettled, so I determined to act at once. And since I had all along been obliged to act from my own sense of right, I was not sorry that an external call, as it might seem, should come, and cut short my time, and remind me of the sudden summons of St Matthew or St Peter, and of the awful suddenness of the Judgment. So when Dalgairns, whom he admitted, asked Father Dominic here for a night on his way, I determined to avail myself of his coming. He does not yet know of my intention.

I have seen the Padre once, on St John Baptist's Day last year, when I showed him the Chapel here. He was a poor boy, who (I believe) kept sheep near Rome and from his youth his thoughts have been most singularly and distinctly turned to the conversion of England. He is a shrewd clever man, but as unaffected and simple as a child; and most singularly kind in his thoughts of religious persons in our communion. I wish all persons were as charitable as I know him to be. After waiting near 30 years, suddenly his Superiors sent him to England, without any act of his own. However, he has not laboured in conversions, but confined himself to missions and retreats among his own people. I believe him to be a very holy man.

I have so many letters to write, that I must break off. I shall not send this till it is all over.

With most affectionate thoughts of all of you, My dear Mrs Bowden. Most sincerely Yours

John H Newman

P.S. I have written a line to Henry, but am not sure of his direction. Will you kindly let me know.

48

To JOHN KEBLE

A message of gratitude and a farewell

Littlemore. November 14 1845

May the Holy Trinity,
Father, Son, and Spirit,
return to you sevenfold, My dear Keble, all the good, of which you have been the instrument towards me, since I first knew you. To you I owe it, humanly speaking, that I am what and where I am. Others have helped me in various ways, but no one can I name but you, among those I ever knew, except one who is gone, who has had any part in setting my face in that special direction which has led me to my present inestimable gain.

Do not let me pain you, My dear Keble, by saying this. Let me not seem rude. Let it be your comfort, when you are troubled, to think that there is one who feels that he owes all to you, and who, though, alas, now cut off from you, is a faithful assiduous friend unseen.

Ever Yours very affectionately John H Newman

To J. SPENCER NORTHCOTE

Reasons for becoming a Catholic? 'You cannot buy them for a crown piece'

Littlemore February 8 1846

My dear Northcote,

It is unreasonable in any one to object that the grounds a
. person gives for his conversion cannot be expressed in a formula, but require some little time and consideration to master;
which seems to be your correspondent's complaint of my
Volume. If I could express them in a formula, they could not
really be the more intelligible or comprehensible—indeed to
show this as a general principle is the main object of the
Essay.[1] Catholicism is a deep matter—you cannot take it up in
a teacup.

Any dogmatic or sententious proposition would too surely be misunderstood. If I said, for instance, 'I have become a
Catholic, because I must be either a Catholic or an infidel' men
would cry out 'So he has flung himself into the Catholic
Church to escape infidelity,' whereas I should only mean that
Catholicism and Christianity had in my mind become identi-
cal, so that to give up the one was to give up the other.

I do not know how to do justice to my reasons for becoming
a Catholic in ever so many words—but if I attempted to do so
in few, and that in print, I should wantonly expose myself and
my cause to the hasty and prejudiced criticisms of opponents.
This I will not do. People shall not say 'We have now got his
reasons, and know their worth' No, you have not got them,
you cannot get them, except at the cost of some portion of the
trouble I have been at myself. You cannot buy them for a
crown piece—You cannot take them in your hand at your will,
and toss them about. You must consent to think—and you
must exercise such resignation to the Divine Hand which leads
you, as to follow it any whither. I am not assuming that my
reasons are sufficient or unanswerable, when I say this—but
describing the way in which alone our intellect can be success-

fully exercised on the great subject in question, if the intellect is to be the instrument of conversion. Moral proofs are grown into, not learnt by heart.

I wish however to say something in answer to your friend's question—let me refer then to p 138 of my Essay, where I state my conviction that were St. Athanasius and St Ambrose now to come to Oxford, they would go to Mass in St Clement's.

And in proof of this position, I should refer to Chapters iv and v pp 204–317, which your correspondent might read without troubling himself with the rest of the Essay. The argument of those Chapters is this: that the general type of Christendom, and the relation of part with part, in early times and in the present is one and the same—that the Catholic Church and sects and heresies then, correspond to the Roman, Protestant, and other communions now—and in particular that the Anglican Church corresponds to the Semi-arian body, or the Nestorian, or the Monophysite.

With kind remembrances to your circle, I am Very

sincerely Yours John H Newman

50

To J. B. MORRIS

Morris, one of the community at Maryvale, was convalescing at Oscott after mumps

Mary Vale. May 8/46

My dear Morris,

One is so seldom able in the common course of things to hear from others what concerns oneself, that I cannot bring myself to let slip the opportunity which now offers of begging you to hear me say about you what will be painful to me as well as to you, yet acceptable to you, I am sure, notwithstanding. Nay I feel confident, that, even though you should not see the justice of some things I am going to say, you will on the whole thank me still, from the chance of your learning something or other about yourself amid whatever I may say irrelevant or erroneous. Angel visits are said to be 'few and far between'; and speaking as I wish to do in Christian charity, I know, my dear Morris, you will pay me back that charity, and consider my words, in spite of their infirmity, as almost an Angel's, and a blessing.

Nor am I unmindful, as I do trust, of what may be the beam in my own eye while I venture to speak of the mote in another's; nor again do I forget the weakness of your general health, which may seem to account for the points which I am to notice. And here I am brought at once to my subject.

Weak health certainly has a tendency to make us selfish, unless we are watchful; and though I dare not use so hard a word of so good a person as you, yet I do think it has made you your own centre, more than is expedient, to the disparagement of the Scripture exhortations of yielding to one another, consulting for each other, and bearing one another's burdens.

And now, My dear Morris, comes my great difficulty, how to bring this home to you; for at first you will not see things in my light. And again, the evidence of it depends on a number of very small details which it is difficult, and almost frivolous to set down on paper. Each by itself may be explained away, whatever be the cumulative force of all together. Accordingly I shall give up absolutely any attempt to prove to you my impression; I shall but seek to convey it, by means of instances, which, however minute, nay though exaggerated, distorted, or unfounded here or there, and though abrupt in their sound, may on the whole gradually let you into my meaning on reflection. And now I begin.

Your first object apparently when you came here, was to get suitable rooms for yourself, and you have got such as no one else has. You wanted your books brought upstairs—several men cheerfully undertook at once what was a considerable labour. You took their services as a matter of course; you did not thank them, or feel that they were working for you. Then you set about carpentering for yourself; not for the house, except in one or two matters when you were directly asked, such as nailing down the parlour carpet. Then you ordered wood in my name at Mr Grove's; with my consent indeed, but you used it for yourself, not for the house. When we said you should be carpenter, you took the office, not as a duty towards the house, but as a sort of privilege. You kept the keys of the shop from us, while you made use of the shop only for yourself.

As you suffered your books to be brought up to you, so did you let us sweep your room, and attend to you when indisposed, as a matter of course, not showing that you felt the kindness. Each of us took his turn in the routine house business as Septenarius; it seemed never to occur to you that you ought to have a week too. I took yours for you during Lent thinking you would be less wearied when Easter came. At Easter you were surprised to hear that you were to have two weeks together, nay that you were to have any week at all. You did not attend to either of them as a matter of duty. You went up to Oscott, leaving others to do your work, without asking them.

Instead of living with us, you have kept your own room. Nay you grudged us your company for any time however short, for a quarter of an hour after dinner, though you could go up to Oscott for the whole of Sunday. You could give us nothing of you, and nothing struck you but surprise that others did not leave the house on Sundays too. In consequence you knew nothing of our plans and rules, or what was going on among us and when you made suggestions, they were out of place, from your not knowing how things stood with us. How could you, who never were with us but at meals? At breakfast and supper your one object was to make your own cocoa or tea, and get your meal. When you were septenarius, you thought it enough to engage another to make the coffee instead of you. Then you had the matter off your hands, and might sit down to your cocoa; as to standing by him, assisting him, doing what you could since you could not do all, seeing that every one was helped though you did not help them, in a word cultivating the spirit of ministration, as it may be called, it does not appear to have entered your mind.

These are illustrations, my dear Morris, of what I mean to point out to you; and it distresses me to pursue the tokens of a similar habit of mind into other matters. I am reluctantly led to think that you like your way, more than you ought, generally. You have before now done serious things which ever seemed to me to be marks of something faulty in you, and for which I have not been able to account. I refer especially to that old matter, the letters in the English Churchman about the Vice Chancellor's election, as to which it avails very little to say that you consulted another person. You are apt too, without knowing it, to set up your own views as a standard, in indifferent matters, so as even to smile on those who measure things differently. You would be surprised to be made aware how frequent the word 'I' is in your mouth. E.g. your first remark on a book being mentioned is, 'This is a book I have never read' though it is nihil ad rem to say so; or 'I have read part of that book,' or 'that is a book I don't think much of.' And as perhaps one remembers best, what has been personal to oneself, I will add my feeling, that you have been bent, more than you are aware of, on forcing your own judgement on me in my matters. E.g. in the case of the new bookshelves in the small library, you insisted that they should be grooved in at Birmingham, though you knew my own contrary view on starting, and I could hardly bring you to end the discussion. So again you took a view that I ought to go up to Oscott for the functions, which was no concern of yours. This made you insist on the Bishop's wish that we should be all there on Palm Sunday; and you told someone most erroneously that he was 'cut up' by my absence on Maundy Thursday.

And now, My dear Morris, I beg your pardon if I have not written this as kindly as I might have done. I have been anxious to do it well, and have written it more than once over; but I know well that had I more of the spirit of love, I should have written it better. While then I am giving you pain, I am not without some feelings of humiliation myself. That our most Merciful Father and Guide may ever be with you, show you His will, and direct you in your vocation is the earnest prayer of

Your affte Friend John H Newman

51

To HENRY WILBERFORCE

From Milan, on the way to study at Rome

Milan. Sept. 24/46

My dearest H W

I wish very much to write to you, though I have very little to say. But somehow I was left with a painful impression on my mind after seeing you that I had, not knowing how very much depressed you were, been in a former letter inconsiderate towards you. In writing as I did in an apparently offhand manner, I acted as I thought rightly—because I did not wish to say what I had to say seriously—but, when I saw you, I fully saw that you were too sad to be able to bear what would at other times have been the natural tone for me to write to you in—so forgive me.

We are most happy here. We arrived here on Sunday morning in time for Mass—and after all the troubles of our journey, the heat, the tight confinement in diligences, the dust, the smoking, the strange faces and the uncatholic bearing of fellow-travellers, and the long spells of journeying, night as well as day, and then again the discomforts of an hotel, we are quite in harbour. An Abate, to whom Hope gave me an introduction, has got us most excellent rooms, lofty, cool and quiet in the heart of Milan. They form a part of the Priests' house of S.Fidelis, and are reserved for the missioners who come to give retreats in Lent. We can get into the Church without going through the street , so it is like a private Chapel. It belonged to the Jesuits before their suppression, having been given to them by the great St Charles. It is like a Jesuit Church, Grecian or Palladian—but I cannot deny, that, however my reason may go with Gothic, my heart has ever gone with Grecian. I loved Trinity Chapel at Oxford more than any other building. There is in the Italian style such a simplicity, purity, elegance, beauty, brightness, which, I suppose the word 'classical' implies, that it seems to befit the notion of an Angel or Saint. The Gothic style does not seem to me to typify the sanctity or innocence of

79

the Blessed Virgin, or St Gabriel, or the lightness, grace, and sweet cheerfulness of the elect as the Grecian does. I could go into this beautiful church, with its polished tall pillars and its smiling winning altar, all day long without tiring. And it is so calm, as it happens, (for it is not one of the more popular Churches,) that it is always a rest to the mind to enter it. Nothing moves there but the distant glittering Lamp which betokens the Presence of our Undying Life, hidden but ever working, for us, though He has entered into His rest.

It is really most wonderful to see this Divine Presence looking out almost into the open streets from the various Churches, so that at St Laurence's we saw the people take off their hats from the other side of the street as they passed along;—no one to guard It, but perhaps an old woman who sits at work before the Church door, or has some wares to sell. And then to go into St Ambrose's Church—where the body of the Saint lies—and to kneel at those relics, which have been so powerful, and whom I have heard and read of more than other Saints from a boy. It is 30 years this very month, as I may say, since God made me religious, and St Ambrose in Milner's history was one of the first objects of my veneration. And St Augustine too—and *here* he was converted! and here came St Monica seeking him. Here too came the great Athanasius to meet the Emperor, in his exile. I never have been in a city, which moved me more—not even Rome—I do not know whether it will, but I have not the history of Rome enough at my fingers' ends to be so intimately affected by it. We shall be here, I suppose three weeks, or a month—how sorry I shall be to go!

I have said not a word about that overpowering place, the Duomo. It has moved me more than St Peter's did—but then, I studiously abstained from all services etc. when I was at Rome and now of course I have gone when they were going on and have entered into them. And, as I have said for months past that I never knew what worship was, as an objective fact, till I entered the Catholic Church, and was partaker in its offices of devotion, so now I say the same on the view of its cathedral assemblages. I have expressed myself so badly that I doubt if you will understand me; but a Catholic Cathedral is a sort of world, every one going about his own business, but that business a religious one; groups of worshippers, and solitary ones—kneeling, standing—some at shrines, some at altars—hearing Mass and communicating—currents of worshippers intercepting and passing by each other—altar after altar lit up for worship, like stars in the firmament—or the bell giving notice of what is going on in parts you do not see—and all the while the canons in the choir going through their hours matins and lauds or Vespers, and at the end of it the incense rolling up from the high altar, and all this is one of the most wonderful buildings in the world and every day—lastly, all of this without any show or effort, but what every one is used to—everyone at his own work, and leaving every one else to his.

My best love attend you, your wife and children—in which St John joins

Ever Yrs Charissime, most affectionately J H N

52

To MRS J. W. BOWDEN

The decision to be Oratorians

Collegio di Propaganda Febr. 21. 1847

My dear Mrs Bowden,

My first business this morning is to write to you—and you will be glad to be told, that, not only the day leads me to do so, but that, as it happens, this very evening Mgr Brunelli (the Secretary of Propaganda) is to go to the Pope to gain his approbation to what I suppose is to be henceforth our calling. So many things succeed, one the other, in a place like this, that all this cannot but be abrupt to you—and I cannot in a few words explain all about it. I suppose we shall be *Oratorians*, that is, of the Congregation of St Philip Neri—we shall try to pass some time as Novices here in Italy; and if we can, we shall bring back a Father with us. Certain it is, we shall do our best to import a tradition, not to set up something for ourselves, which to me is very unpleasant. I still hope to be back at the time originally proposed—Dr Wiseman is very anxious for it—but I must leave all this in the hands of others. I shall keep this letter to tell you of Mgr's interview with the Pope. He proposes to get a Brief from him with such alterations of the Rule as will be necessary for England. I do not doubt we shall be backed up with all the Holy See can possibly do for us—and that (what is most anxious to say) all will depend on ourselves. In the Rule of St Philip this is especially the case—for as there are no vows, there is nothing to fall back on, but the personal religiousness and mutual love of the members, for the well-being of the body. I wish (but perhaps it is not right to wish) I had more confidence in myself—but I seem to have none. I cannot realize to myself that my time is not past—I may be of use by past recollections of me and by personal influence, to bring and keep others together—but that I shall be able to *do* any thing by myself, beyond being this bond of union, I do not feel. Indeed I do need the prayers of all friends, and you must all of you bear me in mind.

You will be disappointed, I fear, to be told what our duty will be—it will be to plant ourselves in a large town, say Birmingham, and attempt to get hold of those classes which at present are any thing or nothing, members of clubs, mechanics-institutes etc etc. Not that this is not a great object, but perhaps you would not wish it for me. But it has great recommendations for me personally—It gives me what I want, active work, yet as much or as little as I wish—time for reading and writing—and a rule without being a very severe one. It will associate also together persons of very different tastes—as we want to argue, to preach, to sing and play, and to train young people. I trust we are doing what is intended for us. I have so many letters to write, that I shall make this a short one. Our mind has been made up ourselves sometime, but we have waited for letters from England. They came last Tuesday—since then, Mgr B. has wished to push the matter on. Love to the children.

Ever Yrs affly John H Newman

No, perhaps you had better not say it, beyond the children.
Feb. 23. The Pope has taken us up most warmly—offered us a house here for a noviciate, proposed others joining us here—and our going back together to England. I trust this plan would not keep us beyond the Autumn. It is no secret we are

to be Oratorians—but matters of detail I don't wish mentioned. Will you kindly send the inclosed to the Post.

53

To AMBROSE ST JOHN

The responsibility of being the head of a community

Maryvale July 12/48

Charissime

My head is so stupid today that I take up my pen, as the only thing I can do, even if that. I have a little cold, but, independent of that, my head has been worse since you left. I took to my medicine and got better, and have no fear, but it is a nuisance at the time. It makes me languid and drowsy, and then I can't do my duties, and people think me reserved etc when I don't mean to be.

At times the sense of weight (of responsibility) and of desolateness has come on me so strongly, that I could fancy it might grow equal to any pain; and I thought what this Pope must suffer. It is useless to tell you on paper all the little trials which constitute all this—and it is ungrateful in me not to be more cheered with the improvement of things in some quarters. My great trouble is some of the giovani[1]—not that any thing new has occurred, but they have so repelled any thing between us but what is external, shown so little kindness when I have done things for them, treated me with so little confidence, as to throw me back upon myself—And now I quite dread the fortnightly chapter day, when I have to make them a little address, as being something so very external, when I have no means to know what is going on in their minds. In consequence I feel as if I was not doing my duty by them, yet without any fault. I don't know what influence I am exerting over them. It is as if my time of work were gone by. Except that one has been led step by step to where one is, beginning in 1841 with going to Littlemore, one is tempted to say, 'How much happier for me to have no liabilities (so to speak) but to be a single unfettered convert—'but if this had

83

been so, I should not have known you, Charissime—so good and evil go together.

The above I wrote before dinner—and suddenly during dinner my deafness etc went away completely on my taking some cayenne pepper, which I had speculated upon using for some hours before—and for the time I am better than I have been for a fortnight past—how odd it is—whether nervous, or what?

I grieve for your troubles at home[2], though I have been talking only of my own. Don't take them to heart. Hansom has been here to-day. We shall decide finally on Friday[3]—so think of us—we know your opinion and shall make it count

Love from all Ever Yrs Affly John H Newman

54

To MISS MUNRO

'I have nothing of a Saint about me'

Oy Bm Feb 11/50

My dear Miss Munro

If I understand a passage in your letter, it simply shocks me. It is to the effect that you have been allowed by a director to take a vow of obedience to him! I doubt its legality, and, without of course compromising you at all, shall inquire generally.

We think it best to introduce a religious body, if we can get one—and then get you to join it. So we shall not expect you in Lent—but we shall think of you.

I return you Miss Moore's letter. You must undeceive her about me, though I suppose she uses words in a general sense. I have nothing of a Saint about me as every one knows, and it is a severe (and salutary) mortification to be thought next door to one. I may have a high view of many things, but it is the consequence of education and of a peculiar cast of intellect—but this is very different from *being* what I admire. I have no tendency to be a saint—it is a sad thing to say. Saints are not literary men, they do not love the classics, they do not write Tales. I may be well enough in my way, but it is not the 'high

84

line'. People ought to feel this, most people do. But those who are at a distance have fee-fa-fum notions about one. It is enough for me to black the saints' shoes—if St Philip uses blacking, in heaven.

Ever Yours affectly John H Newman Cong. Orat.

55

To MISS HOLMES

On Pugin, who identified religious orthodoxy with a love of Gothic architecture

Oratory, Birmingham April 7 1850

What Mr Pugin writes I do not know, and do not much interest myself about—because he does not talk or write like a sensible man. He puts down to people what they never have said or thought of. For myself, no one here has ever written one line of discussion, criticism or correspondence in the *Rambler*—so I speak as a simple looker-on, who never has been able to bear extreme views or bigots; and I see that he is a bigot or will not understand or admit anything but his own narrow view of things, and misrepresents all who differ from him— e.g. who ever dreamed of that Byzantine Church in the Rambler being a model church? it was sent by the architect as *one out of other cheap* forms of Churches[1].

I suppose from what you say he has led you to suppose that the Rambler advocates 'operatic music', 'dandified Priests,' 'neglect of Functions,' and 'every thing poetical or solemn.'

Now is not a *dome beautiful,* 'poetical and solemn?' Is not a row of pillars beautiful? By my taste they are as beautiful, nay more so, than any thing in Gothic. But it is enough that they *are* beautiful. Now Gothic does not admit them. No fault to Gothic—but it just shows so much, that Gothic does not gather up into itself *all* the elements of fine architecture, or exhaust the beautiful;—and therefore any one who says that it does, is narrow minded and a bigot—for he excludes things which *are* beautiful.

85

This Pugin carries so far, as to call *heresy, not* to be intolerant of domes and rows of pillars.

This is a fresh and more grievous fault I find in him—that he *identifies* love of Gothic art with orthodoxy, and love of classical or ancient Italian art with heresy. He has even said that the sight of Rome is a *trial* to a neophyte. What a very objectionable sentiment! it does not do to joke on such subjects—He who makes orthodoxy consist in any thing but truth in *faith* and *morals*, or thinks that there is exclusive truth, necessary for us, except in faith and morals, goes far towards being a heretic himself—and I have no confidence *whatever* in such theorists. I am not speaking against Pugin himself, observe, but against the temper of mind which he represents, and is encouraging. It tends to heresy.

And, begging his pardon, it is *antecedently* a great *paradox*. If there was a nation, who by universal consent excelled in perception of the *beautiful*, it was the Greek. Say their architecture *is irreligious* if you will,—say that it does not typify Christian ideas—say that its specimens in detail are immoral— but do not go to the length of saying that classical architecture is synonymous with 'paltriness, want of education,' and absence of 'the poetical', as you say.

The truth is this—Catholics have been under-educated. They are waking up—and the first beautiful thing that they meet with is Gothic architecture. So they take it, and fall into raptures (as they well *may*), and, it being the only thing they know or have heard of, they ride it like a hobby. When I hear of a thorough Puginian, I am sure he is a 'dandified,' under-educated man;—always excepting Miss Holmes, and dear Mr Phillips[2] who is by nature an enthusiast.

In saying this, I still firmly admit, or rather maintain, that Gothic is on the whole a far *more* beautiful idea in architecture than Grecian—far more fruitful, elastic, and ready.

But there is something higher than architecture—and that is the ecclesiastical ritual—and Puginism exalts architecture to the profanation of higher things. Pugin cares nothing for Rubrics—to him they do not exist—the Sacred Congregation of Rites is almost one of the stumbling blocks of Rome in his eyes. We used to laugh at Protestants for putting their Pulpit in *the centre* of the Church to hide the Altar. Puginism has returned to that exploded idea. Not only the screen, but especially the high eagle-reading desk, effect this. I was in a church the other day, and there was a high eagle with the large cross on it inside the Rail, immediately before the Altar—who could see the priest or the Blessed Sacrament at the elevation? what is the *meaning* of elevation, but to *exhibit* the Blessed Sacrament? We hear of the *Exposition* of the Blessed Sacrament. How is this done in a Puginian Church? The throne is atop of the Tabernacle, and the top of the Tabernacle is on a level with one's eyes, (standing at the Altar); a small chance has such an Exposition of fulfilling its name, *through* Eagle, skreen and the Arches and thick buttresses of the nave.

Now if the rites of the Church have *changed*, let the architecture *develop*—let it modify and improve itself to meet them. No, says Mr Pugin, though the 13th century was *changed* into the 14th, and the 14th to the 15th, architecture shall stay—what it was then. 'The living spirit shall expand, the outward material case shall not; I will adore mullions of tracery more than the Blessed Sacrament;—thus the architectural movement is reduced to a sort of antiquarianism, or dillettante unpractical affair for Puseyites, poets, and dreamers, who have no religious earnestness. But my paper is out.

Yours affectly John H Newman

56

To MISS HOLMES

'When men get old then they see how little grace is in them'

Oratory Birmingham July 31/50

My dear Miss Holmes

I have been from home which will account for my silence. Else I should certainly have answered you sooner . . .

Never be afraid, my dear child, of telling any weakness to me, because we all have our faults, and those who take confessions of course hear many . . .

Do not be disheartened by these inconsistencies, whatever

they may be, for your dear Lord will give you grace to over-come them.

As time goes on you will know yourself better and better. Time does that for us, not only by the increase of experience, but by the withdrawal of those natural assistances to devotion and selfsurrender which youth furnishes. When the spirits are high and the mind fervent, though we may have waywardnes-ses and perverseness which we have not afterwards, yet we have something to battle against them. But when men get old, as I do, then they see how little grace is in them, and how much what seemed grace was but nature. Then the soul is left to lassitude, torpor, dejection, and coldness which is its real state, with no natural impulses affections or imaginations to rouse it, and things which in youth seemed easy then become difficult. Then it finds how little self command it has, and how little it can throw off the tempter when he comes behind and places it in a certain direction or position, or throws it down, or places his foot upon it. Then it understands at length its own nothingness, and that it has less grace than it had but it has nothing but grace to aid it. It is the sign of a saint to *grow*; common minds, even though they are in the grace of God, dwindle, (i.e. seem to do so) as times goes on. The energy of grace alone can make a soul strong in age.

Do not then be cast down, if you though not *very* aged feel less fervent than you did ten years since—only let it be a call on you to seek grace to supply nature, as well as to overcome it. Put yourself ever fully and utterly into Mary's hands, and she will nurse you and bring you forward. She will watch over you as a mother over a sick child . . .

57

To GEORGE RYDER

The Christian's rule of life

Oy Bm Dec 2/50

My dear George

I am very glad to find you think you can keep your boys with you this winter. You can't do better, they will get good from being with you, and you will have companions. Give them my love.

I would not have you go to any mortifications. I will tell you what is the greatest—viz to do well the ordinary duties of the day. Determine to rise at a certain hour—to go through certain devotions—to give certain hours to your boys—Don't oppress yourself with them, but keep to your rules—and you will find it a sufficient trial.

Our Blessed Lady be with you whose great feast is coming, and all Saints and Angels

Ever Yrs affectly in Xt John H Newman Congr. Orat.

•P.S. I received Mr Bastard of Devonshire yesterday.

58

To THE EDITOR OF THE *MORNING CHRONICLE*

During the No Popery agitations, strange rumours were circulating about the new Birmingham Oratory

Oratory, Birmingham, May 15 1851

Sir,

The *Times* newspaper has just been brought me, and I see in it a report of Mr Spooner's speech on the Religious Houses Bill. A passage in it runs as follows:

'It was not usual for a coroner to *hold an inquest*, unless when a rumour had got abroad that there was a necessity for one, and how was a rumour to come from the *underground cells* of the convents. Yes, he repeated, *underground cells*, and he would tell honourable members something about such places. At this moment, in the Parish of Edgebaston, within the borough of Birmingham, there was a large convent of some kind or other being erected, and the whole of the *underground* was fitted up with *cells*; and *what were those cells for*? (hear, hear).'

The house alluded to in this extract is one which I am building for the Congregation of the Oratory of St Philip Neri, of which I am Superior. I myself am under no other Superior elsewhere.

The underground cells, to which Mr Spooner refers, have been devised in order to economize space for offices commonly attached to a large house. I think they are five in number, but I cannot be certain. They run under the kitchen and its neighbourhood. One is to be a larder, another is to be a coal-hole; beer, perhaps wine, may occupy a third. As to the rest, Mr Spooner ought to know that we have had ideas of baking and brewing; but I cannot pledge myself to him, that such will be their ultimate destination.

Larger subterraneans commonly run under gentlemen's houses in London; but I have never, in thought or word, connected them with practices of cruelty and with inquests, and never asked their owners what use they made of them.

Where is this inquisition into the private matters of Catholics to end?

Your obedient servant, John H Newman

59

To WILLIAM FROUDE

The correspondent, near Catholicism, needs to see how it is lived

Oratory Bm August 11/51

Charissime,

I should have written to you by the first post, after the receipt of your letter from Mrs Ward, were I not in such suffocation of business, from the lectures I am delivering. And now I cannot say much more than express my thankfulness to Him Who has brought you so far, and will surely bring you on still. Your ideas about confession are most unreal and romantic. The Priest is nothing—God is everything. They are the greatest friends who know each other most intimately. The Confessor's sympathy so flows out upon a penitent that it is as if he were making, not hearing a Confession. I can only repeat, you are making bugbears.

What I should *like* would be, if you could come and live with us for a week, pledged to nothing. You would see Catholicism to a disadvantage so much as this, that we profess nothing. We have nothing high about us—you would be sharp enough to see this—we do not profess it—what we profess is to do hard work for the sake of Xt—to be busy, and to be cheerful. You might see things to shock you—never mind. I want nothing hid from you. It would try you—if you overcame it, it would be a test for you, where your heart lay and what was God's will. If your romantic idea continued, charissime, I would not quarrel with it—but send you up, if you were disposed, to the Cistercian Convent at Mount St Bernard, where every one wears a white habit, and fasts till 12 or 3 in the day—and whom you need never see again. Charissime, pardon and forget it, if I seem to be light. Here am I, worked beyond my powers, just now; but if you would bring work, you could mix with us naturally, tho' no one has time on his hands. On Friday or Saturday comes a French architect with suggestions for a Basilica, and our own architect who is of your own trade, being the Engineer on the Blackburn Rail. Tres faciunt Collegium. We should be sure to have a good plan, if you joined them.

Write to me, please, and say you forgive me, if I have written freely

Ever Yrs affectionately John H Newman Congr. Orat.

P.S. I said Mass for you directly your letter came.

60

To CHARLES NEWSHAM

First steps have been taken to try Newman for libelling Achilli

Oratory Birmingham Nov. 26 1851

My dear Dr Newsham,

I have been exceedingly touched by your kind letter just received. O what a surpassing compensation will it be for any trouble which may come on me of this world, if I have the masses, the prayers, and sympathy of brethren, of whom I am so unworthy! As to this trial, certainly it is likely to be severe—but 'they who play at bowls, must expect rubbers-' I deserve it, and shall have strength (I trust) given me to bear any thing. I have looked forward to it, since the middle of August, and said with St Andrew, O bona Crux, diu desiderata[1]—and now with St Andrew's day it comes—for I am told that the day after, the first steps are to be taken for the trial.

I took advice, and thought a good deal before I put out the passage which has been laid hold of. I ought to have reflected that a man guilty of what I laid to his charge, was not likely to scruple at an additional sin—He has sworn, not only that each fact is false, which I have stated, but that he never committed any such sins any where or at any time. When he has once got himself to do this, justification is exceedingly difficult, for one must get oaths to refute his oath, and that on the part of persons who know as much about each case as he knows.

I am perfectly clear, that, if trouble is to come on me, it is for some greater good in a higher order. May I continue prepared for any thing! and I shall, if you support me with your prayers. Give my most sincere thanks to your kind friends and pupils at Ushaw who are at present assisting me—and to the good nuns too—My enemies will be doing me abundant good, where they meant harm—and accept yourself the most heartfelt acknowledgement of

Yours affectly in Xt John H Newman Congr. Orat.

P.S. I am attempting a compromise (not of course on the ground of denying what I have said) but of suppressing the passage. If you have any thing to remark on it, will you drop me a line at once to 24 *King William Street, Strand, London* If the matter goes on, I suppose I shall have, not only to suppress it, but to be imprisoned.

92

61

To ANTHONY HUTCHISON

Miss Giberne to go to Italy to find women seduced by Achilli and bring them back as witnesses

Dec. 4/51

My dear F Anthony

Can you set any one to get me information, (if possible, by return of post) what is the best way for an unprotected female to go to Rome by? Will she be made a barricade of in Paris just now?[1] Or can she get through the snows of Germany which the papers speak of?—In short how should she go? And if she must go thro' Germany, can you send me a small foreign Rail road book?

I *do not wish it known*—for we must be quite secret in all our movements—but Miss Giberne is on the point of setting out for Italy—she is to pounce on one woman at Naples, another at Viterbo, and forthwith to return with one in each hand.

Ever Yrs affly JHN . . .

62

To F. W. FABER

A rebuke to Faber who was putting zeal before obedience and care of his health

Oy Bm Dec 30/51

My dear F Wilfred,

I am going to write you a very ungracious letter, that is, to express my *sorrow* at your return.

The truth is, I have been fuming ever since you went, at the way you have been going on. I wrote to Malta to protest against your preaching—the letter missed you, and next I heard of you as lecturing an Orat. Parv.[1] in Italian. The tone of your letter from Palermo pleased me not at all—I had no con-

93

fidence in your sudden restoration, and I thought your letter excited. Then suddenly you were making for Rome, which was *forbidden* you—and before a letter could hit you, you are, against all medical orders, in England.

St Philip used to obey his physician. Have you taken one of the few opportunities a Father Superior has for obedience? I saw his letter—he prescribed six months for you.

You are *not* recovered—the very impatience with which you have come back shows it. As far as I can see, you are still bound to obey your medical adviser, and explere numerum. Your life is precious.

This, I know, is very ungracious but I am bound to say it.

Ever Yrs affly JHN

P.S. As *I* am like to have to submit to 'Ανάγκη² so must you

63

To MISS M. R. GIBERNE

The difficulties of coaxing the female witnesses (and one husband) to England

Oy Bm Jany 23/52

My dear Miss Giberne,

A letter, which I have opened, has just come for you, forwarded from Rome, from Mr Harting under date of Naples January 7, to the effect that he had two, perhaps four, more women for you. It amuses me that you should be thought capable of such a tail. They must come as they can. FF Joseph and Vincent must bring them. You have done quite right in setting off. To secure *one*, and that from Viterbo, is the great thing. There is all the difference between one and none—far more than between 4 or 5 and one. To get 5 is to increase in *quantity* –but by securing at least one, you altered the *quality* of the evidence. And then again, *supposing* you *had* brought Naples and Capua, *they* may come as it is—whereas you might have lost Viterbo altogether. So that I think you and Mgr Talbot judged right.

We think you don't allow Gippina's husband cigars enough —let him have an unlimited supply. Let him have any thing else he takes to—perhaps he would get tired if he rode in legno every day—but is there nothing else?[1] is there no equestrial exhibition? no harmless play? no giant or dwarf? no panorama, cosmorama, diorama, dissolving views, steam incubation of chickens, or *menagerie* (the jardin des plants!) which he would like to see. Surely beasts are just the thing for him. I wonder he has no taste for a review. I should not *ask* him, but I should *take* him to the jardin des plants, as if I wished to see them myself.

I shall send, if all is well, F Ambrose to see you soon. Did I tell you we are in an anxious crisis! Achilli is trying to find a flaw in our pleas—so that, as he got rid of the process of affidavit by finding fault with my affidavit, so by finding fault with the Pleas, he is attempting to get rid of our witnesses, now we have been at the trouble to get them, and wishes to get me condemned without coming into court!

Lady Olivia is rather better.[2] We talk of beginning our Church directly.

Ever Yrs affly JHN

64

To AUSTIN MILLS

Newman was having problems with his Irish housekeeper

16 Harcourt Street Dublin June 3 1852

My dear F Austin,

I fear this won't get to you in time. It struck me that, tho' I only spoke to the Bishop about the tonsure for our two novices, he might mean minor orders. If so, they must go up Friday night to Oscott. But it is useless writing now, when I have missed the post.

Tell F Nicholas I have made a great mistake about the size of my room. It is not more than 30 feet long at most—but it is certainly 17 or 18 feet high—and a fair width. It is, bating the wind which may come in at the window, the warmest room I could desire. The size precludes draughts, and the doors are all double with an interval between them.

When I got here, I found that the house-keeper, who would not let any other of the servants do it, had arranged, not only my clothes, but all my papers for me. I had put my letters in various compartments according to my relations towards them—and my Discourse papers, according as I had done with them or not. She had mixed every thing, laying them most neatly according to their *size*. To this moment I have not had courage to attempt to set them right—and one bit, which was to have come in, I have from despair not even looked for. And so of my linen; I had put the linen in wear separate from the linen in reserve. All was revolutionized. I could find nothing of any kind. Pencils, pens, pen knife, tooth brush, boots, 'twas a new world—the only thing left, I suppose from a certain awe, was, (woe's me,) my discipline. Mind, everything was closed up, as far as they could be without lock and key, which I had not. She then came in to make an apology, but was so much amused at her own mischief, as to show she had no deep sense of its enormity.

I have found all sorts of useful books in the Bookcase—two copies of Shakespeare, Mitford's Greece, Aristotle's Ethics, Crabbe, Scott, Dryden, Wordsworth, Swift, Berkeley, Waverley Novels, Blackstone, Blair, Ovid, and Gibbon

Ever Yrs affly JHN

65

To F. W. FABER

Two letters at the conclusion of the Achilli Trial: Newman has been convicted

Edgbaston, Birmingham June 25/52

My dear Father Supr

I almost stole away like a thief last night—but since I must go to Ireland I wished to be some little time here first. I intend to go tomorrow—

It strikes me to say, *you must none of you be doleful*. We are floored, if we think ourselves floored. Of course we *are* floored, whether we think ourselves so or not, *in a worldly standard*—but we must steadily recollect that we are above the world, above human law, above the feelings of society—and therefore must cultivate a lightness of heart and elasticity of feeling, which, while deeply based on faith, looks at first sight to others as mere good spirits. Mere good spirits are not enough—but bad spirits will be a positive hallucination. We are done if we feel beaten. We must have no indignation against Judge and Jury, or any thing else—they act according to their nature—and accomplish according to God's will. Poor shadows, what are they to us! You must make your Brothers meditate on the nothingness of the world unless the subject be too intellectual . . .

Ever Yrs affly in Mary & Philip

JHN

P.S. You must bear this in mind, viz that we *always*
thought the verdict would be unfavourable—
and relied on the *moral effect* of the evidence—
now the article in today's Times[1] is sufficient to prove
that we have attained the *moral effect*.

66

To J. M. CAPES

Edgbaston Bm July 4/52

My dear Capes

I have been thinking of you for a long time past, and meant to write to you the first thing when this affair was over—but have been busy in Ireland since.

Suspence is the trial, not certainty—to have one's thoughts, prayers, masses occupied for months, without definite prospect of being released—to be on an ocean of expence and responsibility with a receding horizon, this is a trial—but certainty is, comparatively speaking, no trial.

I have continually had in my thoughts, I trust not impatiently or in complaint, that *suspence* was a trial which our Lord did not bear for us, of which He (apparently) made no experiment.

I ought to be very thankful the end has come, when it might have been protracted on another six months. Could I have fancies last August, that I had to go on in suspence till the end of June, how could I have borne it! The ignorance which was the cause of the suspence, was also its alleviation—So all is well.

I have been very anxious to hear how you are. I shall say Mass for you and Mrs Capes every Tuesday between this and the Assumption.

I suppose you do not leave home—else, you should come and see our new House.

I have not a dream who the writer of the Times article is. He speaks the feeling of the common sense of London.

My proofs against Achilli *were* wonderful. The prayers of my friends have gained, 1. evidence. 2. keeping it together for 6 months—3. its lucid and orderly production in Court, 'without a flaw', as the lawyers said. 4. the conviction of the public by means of it. 5. and mostly, (what under the circumstances is a gain, because the stultification of Judge and Jury,) my condemnation.

Ever Yrs affly in Xt John H Newman of the Oratory

67

To JOHN JOSEPH GORDON

A visit to Abbotsford, the home of his friend James Hope, the former home of Sir Walter Scott

January 7/53

My dearest F Joseph
(Private)

Badeley, who has been here since Christmas Eve, goes tomorrow—and it came upon me with such a thrill of horror that I might have cried out before every one when I heard it, 'O that I were going with you.'

Every one is as kind and considerate as possible, and I have quite my own way. Hope is most vigilant in seeing I am quite at ease; he is ever eager to get me out, ever careful to guard me from wind and wet. The consequence is that various expeditions have been projected, but the upshot has been one walk to Galashiels, and one to Thomas the Rhymer's glen, which is in the Abbotsford domain. Sometimes there is a fair morning, and we all take advantage of it—or an hour or two after lunch. Under such favorable circumstances, we go out two and two, Hope and his wife and Lord and Lady A[1]. first with outriders in the form of Lady Victoria or little Henry, and I and Badeley to bring up the rear. We are able to go down the Terraces to the walk by the Tweed; or we attempt the Terrace through the plantation, which is always tolerably dry. Sudden storms come on, however, and make the neighbourhood of the house an advantage.

The House itself is dark and the rooms low. The first floor passage is not so broad (not above half) as the 'Newman Alley', leading to my room from our corridor. Very dark withal, and winding. I could shake hands with the nursery maids in the rooms opposite me, without leaving my own room—and sometimes of a morning or evening in going down stairs, seeing nothing, I hear a step approaching, and am obliged to stand still where I am, for fear of consequences, and then a little light figure shoots past me on the right or left, she having better eyes than I. Once there was an awful moral stoppage, neither daring to move. Every other day is stormy, and I have found the Tablet of great use in acting as a blower to my grate—where a portion of it has remained steadily for hours till it was fairly crumbled into tinder. The rooms are small; I am surprised there is not more draught than there is; but as for light, it was not much after ½ past 3 one day that I left off attempting to employ the sun's light. The House is lighted with gas, even in the bedrooms it is very good gas, but I burn a candle a good deal.

From 10 till 2, and from 3 till 7, I sit in my room—except what time I am in chapel. The post goes at a little past noon, and you get a letter then posted in the evening of the next day—It comes in at 7, and brings me your letters of the evening before.

I dare say, when you see me, you will see that the change of air has freshened my face. Otherwise I have no reason to think I am better—I have the anxiety of being from home—and now this Achilli business, like a bad tooth which for a while has ceased to ache, is making itself felt again. It will come on some time or other between next Tuesday and the end of the month.

Hope anticipates every want of mine—gives me the easiest seat, and has not listened to the notion of my preaching, since he heard the Fathers were against it. Never was a party which got on so well together, yet even here there is considerable cause for anxiety, and I am not at ease. It is from no over fidget, that I am led to recollect the proverb, 'Familiarity breeds contempt.' The very absoluteness with which I feel at home is certainly dangerous—and I have ever to be on my guard lest I go too far. I am in danger of arguing too much, or of laughing too much—and, though I ought not personally to care that persons should go away with a lower and truer notion of me, the thought of giving scandal comes before me, and annoys me. I very much doubt whether it is good, i.e. expedient, for a person like me to be in a house like this with others, however kind and friendly.

Certainly very inexpedient, were they any persons but the Hopes and Arundels, but really the As (to say nothing of the Hopes) are quite Saints. I do not know which of them is in the Chapel most. I suppose they are ordinarily there at four stated times of the day (including Mass) and for a good long space each time. Indeed it is impossible to be in a more simply religious house, which was not a convent. Some of the servants, I see, come in to visit the Blessed Sacrament and the communions have been very good during the Christmas season.

I have not noticed this great compensation of my banishment, which I could hardly have expected any where, an altar, nay the Blessed Sacrament in the House. I had no hope of the Blessed Sacrament and was taken quite by surprise, when I heard it—and every thing is as it should be for the service of the Altar. And, when I once get on the staircase, (there are two capes to pass first) it is straight down stairs without any trouble to get at. There is a fire in the chapel all day. I have been able to go to confession four times, and might have gone a fifth.

Is it not mysterious, that, considering I have so soon to go to

Ireland, I should thus be kept from home apparently for nothing at all, except St Philip's wish to mortify me? I do not allow myself to think of any thing—but go on at a jog trot through the day, seeming very merry and cheerful to every one, but with an aching heart.

Every one here is so truly kind and good, that I should be pierced at what I have said to you getting known *even to our Fathers*—but you may show this to F. Ambrose.

Evers Yrs affly in Mary & Philip

JHN

68

To HENRY WILBERFORCE

Reminiscences of childhood at Ham

Edgbaston July 13/53

My dear Henry . . .

I have seen our house at Ham once in 1813, in the Holydays, when my Father, brother, and myself rode there from Norwood—and the gardener (Taylor) gave us three apricots—and my Father telling me to choose, I took the largest, a thing which still distresses me, whenever I think of it.

And once again on January 23–1836, when I walked there with Bowden and his wife. It was then, I believe, a school—and the fine trees, which were upon the lawn, were cut down—there used to be on the lawn a large plane, a dozen of *tree-acacias*, with rough barks, as high as the plane—a Spanish chestnut, a larch. A large magnolia, flowering (in June I think) went up the House, and the mower's scythe, cutting the lawn, used to sound so sweetly as I lay in a crib, in a front room (garden front) at top.

To find it, you must go down Ham walk with your back to Lord Dysart's House, towards Ham common—On your right hand, some way down, is a lane called 'Sandy lane'—our house lay on one side (the *further* side left side, as you went up it) of that lane, which formed a boundary, first of the lawn and shrubbery (which tapered out almost to a point, between the lane and the paddock,) and then of the kitchen garden. Hence some people got over the wall, and stole grapes. There was no hot house, but there was a small green house in the kitchen garden, against the said wall, over which was a poor billiard room. There I learned to play billiards, having never seen the game played since.[1]

I left the place in September 1807. I recollect the morning we left; and taking leave of it. My Mother, my brother Charles, Harriett and I in the carriage—going to Brighton—with my Father's horses (Their names were Trusty and Gazer) as far as Ewell (? is there such a place?) and then posting (I think there were 4 stages—the last Cuckfield or the like) How odd one's memory is! I could tell you, I suppose a hundred times as much about Ham.

Ever Yrs affly JHN

P.S. I hope next month *certainly* to go to Ireland.

P.S. I will tell you an odd thing about memory. Lately (since my Aunt's death) the Bible I read at Fulham when a child was sent me at my wish. I looked over the pictures, and when I came to the *Angel* inflicting the pestilence on David and his people, I recollect I used to say 'That's like Mr Owen'. This must have been *dormant* 46 years in my mind...[2]

69

To AUSTIN MILLS

An account of travels in Ireland

Cork, February 22. 1854
(I shall not put this into the post for a day or two)

My dear Austin,

Though you are not Secretary, yet as Fr Edward is a new hand, perhaps you will inform him how best to bring the following before the Congregatio Deputata.[1] I submit part of a sketch of a *new work*, which must be submitted to *two Fathers*; I propose to call it 'The doleful disasters and curious catastrophes of a traveller in the wilds of the west.' I have sketched five chapters as below.

1. The first will contain a series of varied and brilliant illustrations of the old proverb, 'more know Tom Fool than Tom Fool knows.'

2. The second will relate how at Carlow a large party of priests was asked to meet the author at dinner, after which the said author, being fatigued with the day, went to sleep—and was awakened from a refreshing repose by his next neighbour on the right shouting in his ear, 'Gentlemen, Dr N is about to explain to you the plan he proposes for establishing the new University,' an announcement, which the said Dr N. does aver most solemnly took him utterly by surprise, and he cannot think what he could have said in his sleep which could have been understood to mean something so altogether foreign to his intentions and his habits. However, upon this announcement, how the author was obliged to speak and answer questions, in which process he made mistakes and contradicted himself, to the clear consciousness and extreme disgust of the said author.

3. Chapter third will detail the merry conceit of the Paddy who drove him from the Kilkenny station, and who, instead of taking him to the Catholic Bishop's, took him to the Protestant Superintendant's palace, a certain O Brien, who now for 15 years past has been writing against the author and calling him hard names—and how the said carman deposited him at the door of the Protestant palace, and drove away, and how he kept ringing and no one came—and how at last he ventured to attempt and open the hall door without leave, and found himself inside the house, and made a noise in vain—and how, when his patience was exhausted, he advanced further in, and went up some steps and looked about him, and still found no one at all—all along thinking it the house of the true Bishop, and a very fine one too. And how at last he ventured to knock at a room door, and how at length out came a scullery maid, and assured him that the Bishop was in London—whereupon gradually the true state of the case unfolded itself to his mind, and he began to think that, had that Protestant Superintendant been at home, a servant would have answered the bell, and he

should have sent in his card or cartel with his own name upon it, for the inspection of the said Superintendant.

4. And the fourth chapter of the work will go on to relate how the Bishop of Ossory pleasantly suggested when he heard of the above, that the carman's mistake was caused by a certain shepherd's plaid which the author had upon his shoulders, by reason of which he, the author might be mistaken for a Protestant parson. And this remark will introduce the history of the said plaid, and how the author went to F. Stanislas Flanagan's friend, Mr Geoghegan, in Sackville Street, and asked for a clerical wrapper, on which the said plaid was shown him. And he objecting to it as not clerical, the shop man on the contrary assured him it was. Whereupon in his simplicity he bought the said plaid, and took it with him on his travels, and left behind him his good Propaganda cloke; and how now he does not know what to do, for he is wandering over the wide world, in a fantastic dress, like a merry andrew, yet with a Roman collar on.

5. And the fifth chapter will narrate his misadventure at Waterford—how he went to the Ursuline Convent there, and the acting Superior determined he should see all the young ladies of the school to the number of 70, all dressed in blue, with medals on, some blue, some green, some red; and how he found he had to make them a speech, and how he puzzled and fussed himself what on earth he should say impromptu to a parcel of school girls—and how in his distress he did make what he considered his best speech—and how, when it was ended, the Mother Schoolmistress did not know he had made it, or even begun it, and still asked for his speech. And how he would not, because he could not make a second speech; and how, to make it up, he asked for a holiday for the girls, and how the Mother Schoolmistress flatly refused him, by reason (as he verily believes) because she would not recognise and accept his speech, and wanted another, and thought she had dressed up her girls for nothing—and how he nevertheless drank her rasberry's vinegar [sic], which much resembles a nun's anger, being a sweet acid and how he thought to himself, it being his birthday, that he was full old to be forgiven if he would not at a moment act the spiritual jack pudding to a girl's school.

This is as much as I have to send you—Would you kindly add your own criticisms on those of the two Fathers? Love to all.

Ever Yrs affly J H N

70

To F. W. FABER·

Everyone thought that Newman would be made a bishop—The London Oratory offered him mitres

16 Harcourt Street, Dublin April 26/54

My dear Fr Wilfrid,

I am only too happy to have any such memorial as you offer me from your Fathers and youths of the London House. At the same time I hope the very fact of their offer is a proof that I shall be securing as *cheap* mitres as possible. I mean, not only, as they will know well, that as much love goes with the gift of a cheap mitre as a grand one, but really for my own comfort let me not have about me more precious things than I absolutely *need*. 'The abundance of the rich, says Ecclesiastes (at least in the Protestant version) does not suffer him to sleep.'[1] At present I sleep in a rail-carriage or a steam boat tolerably well— but, if I know that in the van behind I have a lot of precious things to lug about with me, which I must be seeing after, with no 'Newman' (such as the Cardinal's) to be my cad,[2] why all I can say is, it is next door to travelling with nursery maids, and their paraphernalia, and a worse penance than St Philip's cat, or 'cruel scourge of human minds'.[3]

Your letter has come to me from Birmingham, or I would have replied sooner—but I am sorry to say, that, even as it is, I have delayed a post

Ever Yrs most affectly JHN

To EDWARD CASWALL·

Lay brothers should not be treated as servants waiting on gentlemen

Mount Salus Dalkey Oct 4. 1854

My dearest Edward

I have to tell you in *strict confidence* that Frederic is going to leave the Oratory.

The reason he gives is, that you have treated him like a servant.

You said to him something like this; that the Brothers were like Servants waiting on Gentlemen.

I do not write to you, however, about him but merely to say, that I think you will find it your wisdom, as I have found it mine, *not to interfere with the brothers*. Leave them to the Father Minister. *I* do not interfere with the Brothers' work at all—If I did, they would have *two* masters, the Minister and me.

Therefore I should recommend you to have nothing whatever to do with the Brothers, as such, except as *a private Father*—nothing as Rector.

I have already heard you had some words with John who is gone—who, though not a brother, was in loco fratris. I have serious anxiety lest you should hurt *Laurence's* vocation on his return.

All this makes me say, Leave the brothers to the Fr Minister.

I am somewhat pained, my dear Edward, to hear you speak of us as 'Gentlemen—' We are not Gentlemen in contradistinction to the Brothers—they are Gentlemen too, by which I mean, not only a Catholic, but a polished refined Catholic. The Brothers are our equals in the same sense in which a Priest is a Bishop's equal. The Bishop is above the Priest ecclesiastically—but they are both sacred ministers. The Father is above the Brother sacerdotically—but in the Oratory they are equal.

Excuse this hint, my dearest Edward, and forgive me, and believe me Ever Yours affly in St Philip

JHN

72

To MRS WILLIAM FROUDE

The Crimean War—and the question of extravagant devotions

The Oratory. Hagley Road Bm Jan 2/55

My dear Mrs Froude

The best wishes of the new year to all of you. I am so full on [sic] the subject of the war, that I cannot tell *what* I said to you—but I know well, not a tenth of what I feel. War is not *necessary*, till we have attempted to keep peace—and that we did not. The very opponents of government only complain that we did not threaten the Russians soon enough. The Russians threw out plans of accommodation and compromise—we would not even entertain them. And, whereas Turkey lies below water mark, and that water is the great ravening empire of Russia, we have attempted, not like Mrs Partington with a broom, but by mounds and dykes, to keep the ocean out.[1] Turkey must go; yet we have attempted to set Humpty Dumpty on the wall again—and have enveloped ourselves in illusions and shams, as John Bull always does, instead of looking at things as they are, and having the manliness to confess the truth. And then, having resolved that the Turk shall be alive, when he is dead, we next resolve that Russia shall be a contemptible enemy, when she is a most formidable one—and we cheer Lord John when he has the grave inconsiderateness to declare that we are undertaking only a little war. Three years before we had undertaken the Pope, whose arms are spiritual—we go on to the Czar, whose arms are fleshly—Perhaps the second blunder is the punishment of the first.

Well—but as to your question. I answer thus:-

There is a marked contrast in Catholicity between the views presented to us by doctrine and devotion respectively. Doctrines never change, devotions vary with each individual. Catholics allow each other, accordingly, the greatest licence, and are, if I may so speak, utter liberals, as regards devotions, whereas they are most sensitive about doctrine. That Mary is the Mother of God is a point of faith—that Mary is to be honoured and exalted in this or that way is a point of devotion. The latter is the consequence indeed of the former, but a consequence which follows with various intensity, in various degrees and in various modes, in various minds. We know from the first that St Joseph was our Lord's foster father and the guardian of Mary—we know nothing more now than was known by St Irenaeus and St Cyprian—yet till two or three centuries ago the devotion of St Joseph was almost unknown in the Church; now it is one of the dearest devotions, and closely connected with the affections and enshrined in the hearts, of myriads. It is not to the purpose here to inquire the philosophy of this—but so it is, we live in devotions to which our next door neighbours are dead; we do not find fault with them, nor they with us. Fr Spencer comes to me, and preaches at me for not taking up his particular devotions of Prayers for England—I say, 'Well, mine at present is that of Prayers for the souls of the dying and the dead in this terrible war.' I feel my own most keenly—I am not denying his—the duty of prayers for England, and for the dying and the dead, we both admit,—and practice; but when it takes the shape of a devotion, one takes one, another another.

As far as I can make out from history and from documents St Chrysostom had not the devotion to Mary, which St Buonaventura had or St Alfonso—but they agreed together most simply and absolutely that she was the Mother of God. And in like manner, while you and I admit this doctrine, and while we both admit and maintain that God is to be worship [sic] with an honor of His own, infinitely distinct from any honor we give His creatures, even Mary, the first of them, I shall not quarrel with any form of words *you* use about her, or to her, so that it *does not state some untruth*, and shall expect *you* not to quarrel with *me*, who refuse to use your forms and devotions.

'We praise thee, O Mary; we acknowledge thee, to be our Lady'. Is it the doctrine, or the taste of this, to which you object? I expect, the taste. You mean, 'the words in themselves are not strong—but it is exceedingly indecorous, it is a mere parody, a profane parody, thus to parallel the Te Deum.'

Well. I turn to the Anglican service for the 30th of January—and read 'The people stood up, and the rulers took counsel together, against the Lord and against His anointed.' That is, against Charles the first—here is not even a parody—but *the very words* are used, which belong to our Lord.

The non-conformist is furious with you—and he calls the service blasphemy. And so on, 'The *breath of our nostrils*, the *anointed* of *the Lord*, was taken in their pits: of whom we said, UNDER HIS SHADOW (!) we shall be safe.'

Now what do you say in answer? You say this—'My good friend, you are quite ignorant of the whole structure of Scripture. It is founded on the principle of mystical interpretation. Every sentence has a score of meanings—one under another—one above and through another. I suppose, originally and primarily, the 'anointed of the Lord' meant David. David was a type or shadow of Christ—and so was King Charles. You may dispute this *doctrine*, that Kings are Christ's Vicegerents—but they who hold it, are committing no blasphemy in using words of King Charles, which have a higher meaning, unless the inspired writer committed blasphemy, in uniting in one sense Christ and David. Moreover, what applies to Kings, applies to all Christians—we are all Christs—we are all 'gods—' there is no attribute of the Supreme God, which He has not in His love communicated, in the way of grace, to us.'

Now all this is *our* explanation also. If even Anglicans use the mystical interpretation, we do still more freely. He who called judges 'gods', is our warrant for applying all that is included in the idea of God, and all that is said of God, to the regenerate, and especially to its higher specimens, though in what is called an 'improper' sense. The Breviary is full of such adaptations, E.g. on a Bishop's festival. 'Thou art a priest for ever, after the order of Melchisedech.' In Compline office 'He shall give His angels charge concerning thee, to keep thee in all thy ways.' etc etc.

I really do think then, no objection can be made to 'We praise thee O Mary—etc' except that it is 'very bad taste.' And if this is all, let us recollect that, using our own judgement, we should call the Orientalisms of Scripture 'very bad taste'. Every nation and age has its own taste—and though there are invariable principles, we must allow a great latitude for such accidents. Think of the condescension of Almighty God comparing Himself to an eagle, with His Saints between His shoulders etc etc.—There is no end of this, if you go on. Use your own taste, and let me use mine.

To answer then your question precisely, I say, that the Church has not expressly *authorized* the formularies of devotions you speak of, but, as far as I know, she has not interfered with them

Ever Yrs affly JHN

73

To SIR JOHN ACTON

How should a young Catholic nobleman celebrate his coming of age?

The Oratory Birmingham Jany 7. 1855

My dear Sir John Acton

I am so busy to day that I much fear I shall not get this off by the post this evening—but I have set about it without delay.

It is very difficult to answer your question without some considerable knowledge of the circumstances of your place. My first impression is, that it would be best to avoid the subject of religion altogether—or at least to speak of it as little as possible—and in the most general terms. Kind mutual feeling makes way for the introduction of religion—but this is the work of time. It would seem most natural to introduce yourself in that character only or mainly, which gives occasion to the festivities. The other is sure to follow in proportion as you are known.

As to the Queen, every one must respect her private conduct. There is but one opinion as to the excellent way in which she brings up her family—and she is the keystone of the social fabric—so that all our political happiness is bound up in her welfare. Moreover, as being a lady, it is right to have certain chivalrous feelings about her. Yet I doubt whether I could be enthusiastic in her favor, knowing how opposed she is to the Catholic religion. I agree with you that it would have a bad effect for the priest and the Protestant clergyman to divide the grace between them.

Excuse this hasty letter. I have not given myself time to wish you and your place joy on the event, which I do most sincerely.

I hope it will not be taking a liberty to say Mass for you on Tuesday morning.

I am, My dear Sir John, Very truly Yours in Xt
John H Newman of the Oratory

74

To MRS J.W. BOWDEN

A modest account of himself as Rector of the Catholic University

The Oratory Hagley Road Bm. August 31/55

My dear Mrs Bowden,

I have just felt like you—wishing to write and having nothing to say. We must remember each other at holy times and seasons the more. What I heard from Henry Bowden, that you were troubled with rheumatism, annoyed me, because I really feel you do not take care of yourself, as you should.

We are getting on with the University as well as we possibly can. It is swimming against the stream, to move at all—still we are in motion. The great point is *to set up* things—That we are doing. The medical schools will begin in October—the Church is building—and an Institution for Physical Science in course of formation. It will be years before the system takes root, but my work will be ended when I have made a beginning. Four years are now gone since I have been engaged upon it—the Holy Father has given me leave for two years more—and, as you may think, I shall be heartily glad when they are at an end. A Rector ought to be a more showy, bustling man than I am, in order to impress the world that we are great people. This is one of our great wants. I feel it vividly—but it is difficult to find the man who is this with other qualifications too. Do you recollect how we used to laugh at poor Goldsmith's 'My Lord Archbishop' uttered from one extremity of a long room, crowded and in hubbub, to the other?—that voice is the symbol of what we want in Dublin. I ought to dine out every day, and of course I don't dine out at all. I ought to mix in literary society and talk about new gasses and the price of labour—whereas I can't recollect what I once knew, much less get up a whole lot of new subjects—I ought to behave condescendingly, whereas they are condescending to me—And I ought above all to be 20 years younger, and take it up as the work of my life. But since my qualifications are not those, all I can do is attempt to get together a number of clever men, and set them to do what is not in my own line. I think of St Gregory of Nazianzus at Constantinople, and see, that at least I resemble him in his deficiencies.

My best love to dear Emily Ever Yours affectly in Xt

John H Newman of the Oratory

75

To AMBROSE ST JOHN

A strange dream

6 Harcourt Street Nov 24/55

My dear Ambrose

I got here with a good passage, and slept the greater part of the way from Bm [Birmingham] to Kingstown. My dreams were wonderful—Think of a Parson getting into my birth [sic], and threatening my face with his feet; and my resolving to convert him; and choosing as my instrument a glass jar of large preserved gooseberries; and failing, because he found them undeniably full of large maggots! . . . .

Ever Yrs affly J H N

76

To JOHN STANISLAS FLANAGAN

How to treat two novices

6 Harcourt Street Febry 22/57

My dear S

I really did not, and do not, wish you to take my remarks
for more than they are worth, for more than prima facie impressions of another person.[1] It would be a shame to come
down with offhand criticisms on a plan which has cost you
much thought, if the criticisms meant any thing more
than this. I don't wish you to alter any thing on the ground
of what I have said, but to look at such things for a second
time.

Directly that you tell me that you mean to feel your way before imposing this or that rule, or that you have already done
so, I am quite content. I knew the energy and heart with which
you take up things and I thought there might be a chance of
your beginning abruptly in some matters.

I am very sorry and disappointed to find that they have not a
habit of punctuality and precision—but it is plainly necessary
for them, as a very beginning.

As to Harry, I don't expect much from black doses—they
only augment the evil.[2] There are mild and alterative medicines, which succeed much better. One suits one person, one
another. I, who am troubled in the same way myself, find nothing better than some lemon juice squeezed in my tea every
night (there must be plenty of sugar, and no milk.)—Milk
of sulphur, or Sulphur lotum, a spoonfull in milk suits
others. And so on—but he ought to be free in his communication with you on this point as a matter of duty. I dare
say a very little blue pill and extract of colocynth, now and
then, would be good for him. But I protest against salts and
senna.

Keep the 'whistling' prohibition by all means. Don't alter
any thing except with your own judgment.

I have just preached what, if not my last sermon, is my last for a long while. I am sadly overcome with R W's (Wilberforce) death—it seems to show me I ought to be preparing for mine.

Ever Yrs affly J H N

77

To JOHN WALLIS

The Editor of the 'Tablet' wished Newman to start a new periodical after the 'Rambler' affair

The Oratory Bm May 24/59

Confidential
My dear Wallis,

Thank you for your valuable letter. I tell you in confidence that I give up the Rambler after next Number. I only engaged to take it till Christmas, and our Bishop came up to me on Sunday and expressed a wish that I should give it up at once, which I am doing.

What you say is good, true, and important—but does not apply. Nothing, except a command, which it would be a duty to obey, would make me set up a review or a magazine—the idea of it! I have no love for the thing—and, at my time of life, I feel it a departure from that seemliness which ought to accompany all our actions.

You will say, to *take* up and *continue* a review or magazine is still less seemly—but I suppose it would be allowable in a fire, old as one was, or dignified, to throw off one's coat, tuck up one's shirt sleeves, and work at the pump. And then, if a fireman came and said, 'My good old boy, you are doing your best, but don't you see you are doing nothing but drowning all your friends in your ill directed attempts,' I should with the best heart in the world say, I take your hint, and leave the management of the fire and its extinction to others.

This does not apply in all its parts to the state of the case— but it will do something to show you why I have not any

114

dream of undertaking a new magazine, why I attempt the Rambler, and how with the greatest possible joy I relinquish it.

Ever Yours most sincerely John H Newman

J.E. Wallis Esqr

78

To HENRY WILBERFORCE

Newman gives up the 'Rambler' prepared to wait for time to justify his views

The Oratory Bm July 17. 1859

My dear H.W

I shall have the greatest pleasure in having your boys here— You shall have the refusal of room—I asked whether there were still vacancies—and Fr Darnell tells me there are, but he cannot tell how long they will be. I am thankful to say that to all appearance we are prospering very much. Your boys will be a great charge, but Mrs Wootten[1] is only too careful for her own strength. I live in continual fear lest she should overdo herself. We hope to have a second house when this is full—so that any how we should have room, but I had rather the dear boys were with Mrs W. We have another Lady, who will help us, when we take a second house.

Did I tell you that I have given up the Rambler? As I think I told you, I only took it *till the end of the year*, and this was perfectly understood, but, when I got it, I found I *must* do *every thing*. The July number is nearly entirely written by me. Some Numbers would have been necessary, before I *could* let it out of my hands. However, the *labour* was not the cause of my resigning it. Our Bishop interfered immediately after the May Number and asked me to resign it, which I at once promised him I would do. I could tell you a great deal why I took it, if I saw you. I did all I could to ascertain God's will, and that being the case, I am sure good will come of my taking it—I am of opinion that the Bishops see only one side of things, and I have a mission, as far as my own internal feelings go, against

115

evils which I see. On the other hand, I have always preached that things which are *really* useful, still are done, according to God's will, at one time, not at another—and that, if you attempt at a wrong time, what in itself is right, you perhaps become a heretic or schismatic. What I may aim at may be real and good, but it may be God's will it should be done a hundred years later. What an illustration is poor Gioberti! He actually advocated the Italian Confederacy with the Pope at the head, in his book (I think) called Il Primato. He *pressed* it unreasonably and died, I fear, out of the Church.[2] When I am gone, it will be seen perhaps that persons stopped me from doing a work which I might have done. God overrules all things. Of course it is discouraging to be out of joint with the time, and to be snubbed and stopped as soon as I begin to act.

Every Yrs affly John H Newman

P.S. I wish you would come down for the day

79

To ELEANOR BRETHERTON

Eleanor, at her convent school at Stone, was 'Lady Abbess' for the festivities on Holy Innocents' Day

The Oratory, Birmingham. Innocents Day [28 Dec.] 1859

My dear Lady Abbess,

I wish your Venerableness as many returns of the duties and honors of this day as is good for your said V's soul and body, for honors sometimes turn the head, and duties sometimes distract the brain.

Also I hope you have grown well into your monastic habit, and that it fits you, and that you move easy in it.

I hope too you can give a good account of 2 young nuns or novices, who belong to your community, and who, I have reason to hope, do not give you much trouble, but on the contrary by their gravity and exactness are a consolation to your Venerableness. Especially take care that they are very tidy. And, in consequence of the great austerity of life which you commonly practise, allow yourself in some indulgence in this festive season, and do not scruple to eat a small piece of Christmas pudding, or other good things which come in your way —for Christmas comes but once a year—

Accept the assurance of my distinguished consideration,

Yours most politely, John H. Newman..

80

To MISS M.R. GIBERNE

She was about to enter the Visitation Convent at Westbury

The Oratory Bm Dec 29/59

My dear Miss Giberne,

I should speak, instead of writing, did it not hurt me to use my voice.

Written words are harsher than spoken, so you must make allowances as you read on. Please to bear, what will give you pain; and invoke the Blessed Virgin.

The truth is, your conversation the other day about Westbury quite frightens me. Your dispositions towards the place are not the right ones. Change them, or do not attempt what will infallibly be a failure, entailing pain on yourself and others.

St Philip tells us that the razionale[1] is the source of all evil. Now, that you should fancy yourself interrogating and flooring your Mother Superior, is portentous. I think you must clean wipe out from your heart, as a sin, any intention to allow yourself even in *inward* criticism, or you had better not go.

I think deliberately, that, as a Catholic represses thoughts against *faith*, so a novice represses all *criticism*, if she be a good and true novice. As you would not allow yourself to tax our Lord with inconsistency, after the manner of unbelievers, so neither must you consent to any mental questionings of the acts of those, under whom you are voluntarily placing yourself. You must put down every such thought, every such imagination, by an act of the will.

117

Such strict and stern suppression of criticism is as much involved in the vow of obedience, as is the extermination of all light thoughts by the vow of chastity. It would be more wicked indeed, but not more inconsistent, for a profligate unbelieving woman, some French novelist, or Italian red-republicaness, to go to the Visitation, than for you, as you showed your feeling the other day.

I think it is your duty to promise this mortification of your natural reason to our Lord, and to go to communion upon the promise, or not to attempt to be a nun.

You are making a *sacrifice*:—who obliges you to make it? don't promise all, and give but half. 'Whiles it remained, was it not thine own? after it is sold (now, that is, when you have committed yourself,) is it not in your own power?'[2]

All this is very severe—but charity is sometimes greatest, when it is severest.

I shall say Mass for you tomorrow morning.

Ever Yrs affly J H N

81

To EDWARD BADELEY

On the warmth of friendship and on the lay address to the Pope protesting at the loss of papal states.

The Oratory, Bm Jany 13/60

My dear Badeley,

It would be well, if the same custom prevailed among us, as in some foreign countries, when the beginning of the New Year is the occasion of friends knowing from each other that they are alive and well. For myself, I have not been in London since the end of May, when I called on you and luckily caught you.

What have you been doing since? (besides Law, you know) —Did you travel in October? or were you with Hope Scott? Tell me something of him on some vacant Sunday half hour—and about yourself.

There is some thing awful in the silent resistless sweep of time—and, as years go on, and friends are taken away, one draws the thought of those who remain about one, as in cold weather one buttons up great coats and capes, for protection.

I want to know so many things which a letter cannot tell me, though a letter does a good deal. I don't know how people think on ecclesiastical matters. I see Hope Scott signed the lay declaration—but I don't see the Duke of Norfolk's name. I thought Mónsell's address a good one, and Dr Moriarty's speech, but they neither were so definite as the lay Address. And then how is the Pope ever to get back the Romagna, however we speak, address, and declare? Such speeches, however, I suppose have their fruit in the effect they have on those who speak and those who hear them.

Wishing you with all my heart a happy new year, I am, My dear Badeley

Yours affly in Xt John H Newman

E Badeley Esqr

82

To FRANCIS WILLIAM NEWMAN

Holyoake, an atheist lecturer, has been reading Newman's work with admiration.

The Oratory, Birmingham Jan: 18. 1860

My dear Frank,

I assure you I do not at all undervalue the interest which Mr Holyoake may take in my writings—More than most people have I had lessons through my life to 'Cast my bread upon the waters', and 'not to observe the winds'.[1] You may understand, that my Creed leads me to feel less surprise at an Atheist than a Protestant feels. In truth, I think that *logically* there is *no* middle point *between* Catholicism and Atheism—At the same time, holding this, I hold of course also, that numbers of men are logically inconsistent; and as I think many a Protestant has principles in him which ought to make him a Catholic, if he followed them out, so I think of an Atheist also—And, while you are wondering how I can be a Catholic, I on my own side may think that both you and (from what you say) Mr Holyoake may cherish that in your hearts, of which Catholicism alone is the full account. So far from thinking it little to advance him and his friends a step, I should think it a great favour shown me by Almighty God to be made the instrument of doing so—I should consider, that, as his disciples go further in the right direction than he, so their disciples again will go further than they, and so on; just as the lava of Vesuvius, after cooling is first covered with an almost invisible lichen, which becomes the mould of some higher vegetation, and that again of higher, till step by step we arrive at last to that rich fine soil which produces the lacryma.[2].

I have a nasty husky cough, quite unusual to me, which I cannot get rid of

Ever yours affecly John H Newman

83

To CARDINAL WISEMAN·

*Newman was in trouble with the authorities in Rome about his article
'On Consulting The Faithful in Matters of Doctrine'*

The Oratory Birmingham January 19 1860

(Copy)
My dear Lord Cardinal

Our Bishop tells me, that my name has been mentioned at Rome in connexion with an Article in the Rambler, which has by an English Bishop been formally brought before Propaganda,[1] as containing unsound doctrine. And our Bishop says that your Eminence has spoken so kindly about me, as to encourage me to write to you on the subject.

I have not yet been asked from Propaganda whether I am the author of the Article, or otherwise responsible for it; and, though I am ready to answer the question when it is put to me, I do not consider it a duty to volunteer the information, till your Eminence advises it.

However, I am ready, without the question being asked of me, to explain the Article as if it were mine.

I will request then of your Eminence's kindness three things:—

1. The passages of the Article, on which the Cardinal Prefect of Propaganda desires an explanation.

2. A copy of the translations, in which His Eminence has read them.

3. The dogmatic propositions, which they have been represented as infringing or otherwise impairing.

If your Eminence does this for me, I will engage, with the blessing of God, in the course of a month from the receipt of the information.

1. to accept and profess ex animo in their fulness and integrity the dogmatic propositions implicated.

2. to explain the animus and argument of the writer of the Article in strict accordance with those propositions.

3. to show that the English text and context of the Article itself are absolutely consistent with them.

I marvel, but I do not complain, that, after many years of patient and self denying labour in the cause of Catholicity, the one appropriate acknowledgment in my old age should be considered to consist in taking advantage against me of what is at worst a slip of the pen in an anonymous un-theological paper. But I suppose it is a law of the world, that those who toil much and say little, are little thought of.

One great favour I ask your Eminence to obtain for me, viz that I may not be sent to Rome. A journey would seriously impair my health and strength and would create great confusion.

Kissing the sacred purple, I am, My dear Lord Cardinal, Yr faithful & affte Servt in Xt

(signed) John H Newman of the Oratory

The Cardinal Archbishop of Westminster.

84

To JOHN BRAMSTON

*Renewal of a friendship when Newman returned a book borrowed
thirty years earlier*

The Oratory, Birmingham, March 25 1860

My dear Bramston

I have just received your most kind and touching letter. Ever
since the day when you first introduced yourself to me, at the
Provost's, when, a poor Probationer Fellow, I dare scarely
look around me in the middle of Gentlemen Commoners and
recherché wines, and you sat next to me and took pity on me, I
have ever thought of you with feelings of special affection.
And I recollect the last time I saw you in 1843 or 44, for a
moment at the carriage door of a Great Western and North
Western train.

And therefore I have been unwilling to return your book,
which I took from you at Great Baddow in 1834, though it has
stared me in the face day by day, raising in my mind mixed
feelings of you as a dear friend, and of myself as an impenitent
thief.

Well, at last, I determined to make restitution of stolen property. I had written in it your name, lest I should die with it in
my possession—but still my conscience smote me, unwilling
as I was to part with it—and it lay on my table days done up in
its cover, before I could make up my mind to send it to the
post. And, had I had a dream that you would know my hand
writing, I should not have directed it myself, for what excuse
could I make for keeping it so long?

But now, you see, your letter and not less, your recollection
of my hand writing have led me to a courage which I ought to
have shown towards you without such aids. But in this shift-
ing state of things, though I have my own feelings, I have
sometimes found out I did not know those of others: and I am
obliged to lock up in my heart what, if put out to view, might
come to harm.

And now, praying God to reward you for your kindness to me, I am,

My dear Bramston Yrs very affectionately John H Newman

85

To HENRY WILBERFORCE

Of money matters, of the Wilberforce boys, and of the possibility that Lord Calthorpe would sell land next to the Oratory garden

The Oratory, Bm. April 4. 1861

My dear H

I was very much concerned to read your letter. To me one of the greatest worldly anxieties is suspense as to money matters. As a youth, I experienced it—but at that time the sanguine temper, which one starts with in life, carried me on—but even then it was a heavy cross. But I have felt it lately in the Achilli matter—it was the only, but a cruel trouble, which that affair caused me—To be in a whirlpool, spending hundreds every week, then thousands, then the delay of the trial, with the prospect of additional thousands, till the whole amounted to above £10,000! I wonder it did not turn my brain. It was the immense mercy of the Providence which brought me through it, mind, body, and estate. Haud ignara mali,[1] etc. So I mean, please God, if all is well, to say a weekly Mass for your intention, till I hear from you again on the subject.

It was a great disappointment to me, that you did not set your Patriarchal Tent in motion as you proposed. And then, I meant to have urged you to come at least for St Philip's day, about Trinity Sunday, when the Rt Revd Monsignor preaches for us. But I must suspend the thought at present, I suppose.

I hope you are pleased with your boys. My private (quite private) information says that Wilfrid has seemed much happier, but that Harry has been somewhat giddy.

You have done us a real act of friendship in speaking to Lord Calthorpe. If he wants to do an undeserved act of kindness to me personally, he will 'pity the sorrows of a poor old man,' and give a place of exercise, when I have none, and when daily exercise, gentle and not laborious or public, is really necessary for my health. But why should he wish me to live long?

Ever Yours affly John H Newman of the Oratory

Best Easter wishes to you and all yours

86

To SIR JOHN ACTON

Views on the 'Rambler' and on the character of Simpson

The Oratory Bm July 5/61

My dear Sir John

I don't like writing in a hurry, when I ought to write with care—but then I don't like to delay. So I must do my best.

I did not mean to differ from you (nor do I) in any principle, but in a fact. The Rambler certainly does seem to me ever nibbling at theological questions. It seems to me in its discussions to come under the jurisdiction of the ecclesiastical power; and therefore I think the ecclesiastical power ought to be deferred to.

If it advocated homeopathy, or the broad gauge—and the Bishops of England said any thing in discouragement of such conduct, I don't see how it could be bound to defer to the Bishops.

If it said that the Classics ought to be taught to laymen, and the Bishops said that Prudentius was far better poetry than Virgil, and, in order to the cultivation of poetical taste, insisted on the Rambler being silent in its praises of Virgil, I do not see that the Rambler need be silent.

But this is not the fact. The Bishops have a direct jurisdiction in the education of the clergy for the ministry—they act under an Ecumenical Council. To discuss the question of the education of the clergy does seem to be entering on a question under their jurisdiction. This the Rambler has done. It has not itself given judgement, but it has discussed at length, through its correspondents, the question. I cannot tell you how this dis-

124

cussion has annoyed me, not only for the sake of the Rambler, but in itself.

The Article on Campion again—no one surely can say that a Life of Campion was *obliged* to come out with the statement of insinuation that St Pius preferred to maintain untenable claims to retaining England in the Church; no reader surely but was surprised that it came into the narration. Such matters should not be dealt a back handed blow—it was not a history of St Pius, or of his times—even then, a Saint surely is not to be approached as a common man. If the Ecclesiastical Power makes saints, it requires that they, as well as their images, should receive the 'debitum honorem et venerationem.'[1] The historical character of St Pius, as it seems to me, was treated very much as if, in showing a Church, the Sacristan were to take an axe and knock off a piece of an Altar—and then, when called to account, were to say that the Altar was about to be removed, as it was in the way, and he was only by his act beginning the intended reforms.

Rednall. July 6

Then again, in the Article on Ward's Philosophy, I think the Reviewer spoke of the highest ecclesiastical courts of the Church having for two centuries impeded in Italy the advance of science—or something of the kind. Now, however true this may be, was it necessary to say it *there*? and was it not any how an attack upon the said courts? I don't see that those courts went beyond their *powers* in the bare fact of their impeding science. They thought science interfered with religion, and no one can say that they had not a prima facie case in their favor—and they had the community (I suppose) with them. But whether this be so or not, is not the point—What I would insist on is, that it is not wonderful, if a writer in the Rambler attacks those courts, the representatives of those courts will attack him—and, (without saying that the prima facie view of the matter in the eyes of the public will be in their favor, if he is writing *ex professo* on the subject and they come in his way,) yet I think, if a writer, reviewing Ward, has a sudden side blow at them, the good sense of the public will side with *them*, if they in turn inflict some severe stroke upon their assailant.

I am saying all this by way of explaining what I meant by saying that the Rambler now is in a false position, if authority speaks against it. It has been sufficiently theological and ecclesiastical, to impress the world with the idea that it comes under an ecclesiastical censor, and if it caught it for tilting against Inquisitors, Ecumenical Councils, and Saints, the world would be apt to say 'Serve him right'. This is how it appears to me.

And further, I must, though it will pain you, speak out. I DESPAIR of Simpson[2] being other than he is—he will always be clever, amusing, brilliant, and *suggestive*. He will always be flicking his whip at Bishops, cutting them in tender places, throwing stones at sacred Congregations, and, as he rides along the high road, discharging pea shooters at Cardinals who happen by bad luck to look out of window. I fear I must say I despair of any periodical in which he has a part. I grieve to say it—but I have not said it till the whole world says it. I have, I assure you, defended him to others—and it is not many weeks, I may almost say, days, since I was accused of 'solidarity with the Rambler'. But what is the good of going on hoping against hope, to the loss of union among ourselves, and the injury of great interests? For me,—I am bound to state my convictions, when I have them; and I have them now.

You will act with true sincerity of intention and with full deliberation, whatever conclusion you come to about the Rambler—but I don't think Protestants ought to say that an independent organ of opinion is silenced, but one that loved to assail, and to go out of his way to assail what was authoritative and venerable.

Ever Yrs most sincerely John H Newman

87

To HENRY BITTLESTON

An account of a holiday in Cambridge

Cambridge July 29/61

My dear Henry,

Knowing your disputatious power, I am not sure you will not be able to deny that I *am* in Cambridge, in spite of the post mark—but you must let me assume that I am there, and it shall be a reserved point to discuss when I see you again.

On Friday, after seeing Badeley, whose torments seem to have been extraordinary, we caught the train to Hampton Court, where we slept. Of course I am not going to write descriptions, but I will say that we were both enchanted with the place, and thought how great her majesty must be to have palaces such, as to enable her to chuck Wolsey's building to her servants and pensioners.

Well—I thought we should enjoy our incognito, and so we did during good part of 24 hours—but at length we fell on Platner who is so mighty in words, that I simply fell—and William making an excuse that just now I was unable to talk, picked me up and carried me off.

Forthwith we fled; whither was a secondary question. We rowed to Kingston—the weather has been, and is , sometimes lovely, sometimes splendid. Then, after dining, we set off for Richmond through Ham. Thence at once by train to London, musing all the way where we should find ourselves at night fall. On getting to Waterloo Station we made for King's Cross, and by half past 9 PM behold us at Cambridge.

I have been here once before, for a quarter of a day, in 1832. Then, I recollect, my allegiance to Oxford was shaken by the extreme beauty of the place. I had forgotten this—but a second sight has revived the impression. Certainly it is exquisitely beautiful.

We weathered Mr Q. though we were so near capzising [sic], as to be asked by him to change our place, because we were in the way of his Confessional—And, as there was but one person, a stranger, at the Bull in the Coffee Room, we have been quite comfortable.

He has a strange distrait manner, and I took him for some enthusiastic parson, say a Drummondite or the like. I said but a few words to him, but he seemed absent—but, as he fidgetted about, and went in and out of the room, read the Bible, then sat where he could see me say office, and certainly followed our movements, we migrated to the other end of the room.

This was no annoyance to us; but what did annoy us was, that when we were into King's College Chapel to hear the chanting and see the place, a little man at once fastened his eyes

127

on us, whom William instantly jaloused as having been at the Oratory. William, who acts as a sort of Guardian Angel or Homeric god, instantly enveloped me in darkness, rustling with his wings, and flapping about with a vigor which for the time was very successful. But, alas, all through the day, wherever we were, this little man haunted us. He seemed to take no meals, to say no prayers, or elsewhere to know our times for these exercises with a preternatural exactness. William was ever saying, whether we were here or there, in garden or in cloister—'Don't look that way—turn this way—there's the little man again.' His anxiety led him to make matters worse, for he boldly approximated him to be sure of the individual, but with too little caution, for the little man caught his hand and asked him how he was. However, his generalship kept me out of harm's way, and we dined peaceably at six. There was then no further danger—we lounged out at seven, and were tempted, by the merest accident to turn aside into PeterHouse. We were not two seconds in the Court, when William cried out, 'There's the little man—don't look.' But it would not do—he pounced upon his prey, and William turned quite red, whipping his finger as if it had been stung. He most civilly asked us, if we should like to see the Munich painted glass in the Chapel, and went at once for the Porter. Then he vanished—but William is now out paying him a call with my card; and I should certainly have done the same but that I am far from well this morning, very weak, because I have not had any sleep (from distress, it is not so much as pain) since 3. I heard 3 strike and every hour till I got up.

I have been hardly able to speak, certainly not to converse, with our fellow occupant in the Coffee Room, who has left for the North just now—having never seen Cambridge before, and, like ourselves, having run down for the Sunday. He began talking this morning about Cambridge, which I agreed with him was most beautiful. He said he had been into the University Church for the evening service—and, after a word or two between us, he suddenly said 'I think I have heard *you* in the pulpit of St Mary's Oxford some thirty years ago.' 'Well', I answered rather bluntly, 'how *could* you know me? for my friends, who have seen me only half that time ago, don't know me, they think me so much changed.'

This led to some conversation, when at length we got on the Essays and Reviews. After which I started, proprio motu, a new subject, that of the movement for the alteration of the Liturgy. He said that was a religious movement, very different in spirit from the other. I agreed, but I said I have been much struck with the account of the effect, which I heard was produced by a book written by a lawyer, a Mr Fisher, whom the Bishops had noticed in their charges. His book, they said, was a logical, candid work; but it was removing the veil from the eyes of a number of evangelicals, showing them that they could not honestly use the baptismal service, and demanding in consequence its alteration. I said, I thought this a remarkable movement and would gather strength. So we shook hands and parted.

I came down again, and he was not gone. It seemed to me rude not to have asked his name—So I said to him, 'Since you know me, pray do not let us part without my having the satisfaction of knowing with whom I have been conversing.'

He looked nervous, and distrait—and then said 'I am the Mr Fisher, of whom you have been talking'

Ever Yrs affly J H N

88

To THE DUCHESS OF NORFOLK

A School Report

The Oratory Bm April 16/62

My dear Duchess,

I suppose Henry has already shown you his Prizes. They were well won. And they show what he *can* do. He said Wordsworth's Happy Warrior, right off, very fluently. Another boy did so also. They both got a prize. No other boy came near them. His other prize was for writing out passages of Shakespeare on dictation. There was no one came near him; but what made a doubt for a moment, was his spelling 'Thou' several times, 'Thow', and another false spelling.

I hope we shall rouse him to exert himself in other things, and these prizes may encourage him. He has fits of negligence when every thing goes wrong, and then we are perplexed with the number of impositions which fall upon him from every quarter—and we have to release him from the weight of them, as best we may.

There are boys who do him harm by encouraging him to make game of these magisterial corrections—and he sometimes comes up for the imposition, as if it were good fun. (Pray, do not hint this to him.) He will become more manly in a little time. I think on the whole he is better in getting up—but here too he has fits of dawdling.

In spite of all this, he is exact and methodical in his habits—and it is amusing to see how well he keeps. his books and clothes.

He has a great deal to do in arithmetic and grammar.

As to ourselves, the only fear is that, from extreme anxiety about him, we should meddle with him too much, and make too much of little things.

Easter is not come yet—but I will ask leave to anticipate my best Easter Greetings for you and yours. Do be so kind as to say a good prayer for me in turn, for we have heavy crosses. Meanwhile, St Philip certainly has done wonders for us this Term.

Yours, My dear Duchess, Most sincerely in Xt
John H Newman of the Oratory

89

To THE EDITOR OF THE *GLOBE*

A public refutation of statements that Newman was about to return to the Church of England

The Oratory, Birmingham, June 28, 1862

Sir,

A friend has sent me word of a paragraph about me, which appeared in your paper of yesterday, to the effect that 'I have left, or am about to leave, my Oratory at Brompton, of which I have been for several years the head, as a preliminary, in the expectation of my private friends, to my return to the Church of England.

I consider that you have transferred this statement into your columns from those of a contemporary, in order to give me the opportunity of denying it, if I am able to do so. Accordingly I lose not an hour in addressing these lines to you, which I shall be obliged by your giving at once to the public.

The paragraph is utterly unfounded in every portion of it.

1. For the last thirteen years I have been head of the Birmingham Oratory. I am head still; and I have no reason to suppose that I shall cease to be head, unless advancing years should incapacitate me for the duties of my station.

2. On the other hand, from the time that I founded the London Oratory, now at Brompton, twelve years ago, I have had no jurisdiction over it whatever; and so far from being its head, it so happens I have not been within its walls for the last seven years.

3. I have not had one moment's wavering of trust in the Catholic Church ever since I was received into her fold, and ever have held, that her Sovereign Pontiff is the centre of unity and the Vicar of Christ. And I ever have had, and have still, an unclouded faith in her creed in all its articles; a supreme satisfaction in her worship, discipline, and teaching; and an eager longing and a hope against hope that the many dear friends whom I have left in Protestantism may be partakers of my happiness.

4. This being my state of mind, to add, as I hereby go on to do, that I have no intention, and never have had any intention, of leaving the Catholic Church and becoming a Protestant again, would be superfluous, except that Protestants are always on the look-out for some loophole or evasion in a Catholic's statement of fact. Therefore, in order to give them full satisfaction, if I can, I do hereby profess *ex animo*, with an absolute internal assent and consent, that Protestantism is the dreariest of possible religions; that the thought of the Anglican service makes me shiver, and the thought of the Thirty-nine Articles makes me shudder. Return to the Church of England! no; 'the net is broken, and we are delivered.' I should be a consummate

fool (to use a mild term) if in my old age I left 'the land flow-ing with milk and honey' for the city of confusion and the house of bondage.

I am, Sir, your obedient servant, John H. Newman

90

To WILLIAM NEVILLE

A holiday in Deal

43 Walmer Road Deal Oct 13 1862

My dear Wm

I certainly am not comfortable—but what weighs on my mind is, that I suppose I shall have altogether muddled away close upon £5 a week here. A first rate hotel, such as Rich-mond or the Isle of Wight (*they* were the places) would not have cost more. You see I was right in my original view before starting, but it is so difficult to carry it out. I was not able at Deal—for there is no good Hotel. Three days I have fed on an expensive old tough gander—never making a meal. Yesterday I attempted veal cutlets—they were made up of stringy, gris-tly, and sinewy meat, parts not quite done. I am now wild how to get a dinner. I am told there is an Hotel here better than the Clarendon, which was hardly better than a pothouse. My first entrance into the Coffee Room was attended by the simul-taneous exit from it of two girls running, apparently from a young gentleman who was over his wine and walnuts. I shall go and try the Royal Hotel, though with sad trepidation. Another scheme I have is to go over to Ramsgate. It is a nice morning, and a return ticket is only 3 shillings. I can look about for lodgings. You see, I had laid in a stock of wine, and I did not know what to do with it. Else, I should have gone off to an Hotel at Ramsgate or Dover for the week till Austin [Mills] came. Now I have been drinking it against time. I hope I shall not make myself drunk. Why has not one a bag like the Camel to keep wine in?—then, it would be laying in a stock for next week.

Please ask Ambrose what he thinks I ought to give the man and his wife here for three weeks. It seems they are put in to keep the house. I have no fault to find with them—they are tidy, quiet, and civil. *For three weeks*, I shall leave behind me 10 or 11 bottles (pint) of porter, very good too, judging by the bottle I opened.

My rheumatism is nearly gone—but it has kept me from bathing the last week . . .

The fineness of the day is very tempting—but I have so many letters to write.

Ever Yrs affly J.H.N.

You must answer my question about what I am to give for attendance by return of post.

91

To HENRY BITTLESTON

Better lodgings in Ramsgate

Ramsgate Oct 19 1862

My dear Henry . . .

Austin is better, but the weather has changed for cold, the very day we came here, and the glass is falling. Never mind, we are very comfortable, are waited on by an Oxford scout (who showed me his testimonials—very flattering ones) and have very good feeds. We had prime fillet of veal yesterday preceded by an excellent codling (not an apple) and I eat so much that I thought I was going to be ill. The bathing is cheaper than Deal, and far better—the circulating library is far better supplied with books, and the water of the harbour is only 15 feet, as the crow flies, from our windows, both sitting room and bed room. We have been obliged to take to fires, to my disgust, but they have thawed Austin's leg and my brain— I don't get quite as much sleep at night as I could wish. Wonderful wicket doors to Pugin's Church—about as high as the entrance to a kennel—simply wonderful—say three feet six high

Love to all Ever Yrs affly J H N . . .

92

To MRS JOHN MOZLEY

The value of letters as biography

The Oratory, Bm. May 18. 1863

My dear Jemima

I take advantage of the recurrence of the 19th, of which I trust and pray you may have many happy returns, to get you to tell me how you are. Alas! as life goes on, one understands that it is almost a mockery to talk of many happy returns, if by 'happy' is meant as is commonly meant something temporal and external; for, if there are many returns, they cannot be happy ones. ·

I had looked out for you my letters from abroad in 1832–3, as you wished; when the friend, to whom I am to leave all my papers, happening to see them spread out, protested, on the ground that they contained the originals of my Poems in the Lyra Apostolica, and were intimately connected with the rise of the Oxford movement. The obvious solution of the difficulty would be to get copies made of them; but I doubt if you think them worth so much fuss. However, I will gladly do so, if you wish it, and you shall have the autographs. Any how, I should like, some time, to see the letters, which during the same expedition, I wrote to *you*.

I wish I had any thing else to offer you instead. I would propose yours and my Mother's letters to me, if they were not of an ephemeral character necessarily, consisting of reference to what was going on either in the public or in their own world, or of matters of business. To be sure, they would vividly bring before you times gone by; yet to my own feelings the most pleasant memories of the past are painful. What one should like would be that a selection of some of them or parts of them could be made, which would interest a girl like Jane in her mother's early life and in her grandmother. I have often regretted that I never asked my Mother any thing about her early life, her father of whom she was so fond, and her connections. Jane may be one day a grandmother herself; and, could any thing be preserved of my mother of a tangible nature, would thus be able to connect five generations, being the centre of them herself.

But I fear it is too probable that the warm affections and charities of the human heart, of which correspondence is both the stimulant and the expression, are evanescent in their exhibition, and fade away from the gaze of men as the ink in which they are recorded. Thackeray's Virginians opens very beautifully with a reference to a supposed collection of such letters, though he professes to have made a story out of them. And so too I was reading, a few days since, as for a last revision, my own books of Extracts, made in 1825, of my Letters received by me between 1804 and 1824; and it certainly reads like an interesting tale, with perfect unity of plot, yet sufficient variety of digression. But then, I am the hero of it; and moreover can from memory fill out and colour the outlines of which it is made up;—what would be *another's* judgement of it? Perhaps there are not half a dozen letters in the whole collection that are of any permanent value; yet I cannot tell myself, nor can any one else perhaps just now, what portions are important, and what are not; and under such circumstances I suppose I must leave it, as it stands, for the judgement of those who come after me.

What I really should covet, though I dare say it would give you much trouble, or rather would be impossible in you to grant till your strength is restored to you, would be the loan of my own letters to you between 1833 and 1845. If you numbered them, you should have them all back safely. It has ever been a hobby of mine (unless it be a truism, not a hobby) that a man's life lies in his letters. This is why Hurrell Froude published St Thomas à Beckett's Letters, with nothing of his own except what was necessary for illustration or connection of parts. It is the principle, I suppose, of the interest which attaches to such novels as Clarissa Harlowe, Evelina etc. And it is exemplified in one of the popular novels of the day, the Woman in White, in which I cannot detect any merit except what lies in the narrative being a living development of events as exhibited in supposed letters, memoranda, and quasi-legal depositions.

A much higher desideratum than interest in Biography is

met by the method, (as it may be called,) of Correspondence. Biographers varnish; they assign motives; they conjecture feelings; they interpret Lord Burleigh's nods; they palliate or defend. For myself, I sincerely wish to seem neither better nor worse than I am. I detest suppression; and here is the great difficulty. It may be said that to ask a biographer to edit letters is like putting salt on the bird's tail. How can you secure his fidelity? He must take care not to hurt people, make mischief, or get into controversy. Hence men, like Talleyrand, have forbade the publication of their correspondence till a thirty years have passed since their death, that the existing generation may have fairly died out. But party interests and party feelings never die out; and how can one promise oneself that men thirty years hence, whom one has never seen, into whose hands one's MSS come, will be above the influence of party motives, at a time when personal delicacies and difficulties are in their graves? It is very seldom that correspondence can be given *in extenso*, by reason of its prolixity. There must necessarily be a selection of passages; sometimes one half sentence alone is valuable in a whole letter, and that, very valuable: but it may tell on this side a controversy, or on that: and whether it sees the light or not will depend upon the perspicacity or straightforwardness of an Editor.

However, I did not intend any such disquisition on biographical literature, when I began to write. The subject comes before me by fits and starts. When I have a little leisure, I recur to my pigeon-holes of letters, where they stand year by year from 1836 down to this date. I have digested them up to the former year. Thus from time to time I do a little work in the way of sifting, sorting, preserving, or burning. By the bye, one ought to write on good paper; some of my Mother's of 30 years since break under my hands like tinder, on the very opening of them.

Ever Yours affectly John H Newman

Mrs John Mozley

P.S. I have found one or two child's letters of Herbert's— which I send you as a not unwelcome birthday gift. You will not treat them as before now other people have done, to whom I have sent letters I have found of theirs and have got, not only no thanks, but no answer to show that they had arrived safely.

93

To EMILY BOWLES

A 'growl' and an account of past slights and difficulties

The Oratory Bm May 19 1863

MOST PRIVATE

My dear Miss Bowles

Thank you for your most affectionate letter. What you tell me is utter news to me. *I* never had any message from Fr St John. *I* never knew you had sent me a book. There is another thing which I do know, and perhaps you don't; that in a most cruel correspondence which we had in 1860, a letter of mine to you, perhaps a concluding one, was, as we found, mysteriously lost—I don't think *here*—but it was put into the post box, and did not get to you. I have so washed away the whole matter from my mind, that I know nothing but this fact. Perhaps its absence may have had some bearing on your impressions about my feelings, and have served (untruly) as a key to interpret other acts or non-acts of mine by.

Don't think about *me*—God uses his instruments as he will. Hunc humiliat et hunc exaltat.[1] To myself I feel as full of thought and life as ever I was—but a certain invisible chain impedes me, or bar stops me, when I attempt to do any thing—and the only reason why I do not *enjoy* the happiness of being out of conflict is, because I feel to myself I could do much in it. But in fact I could not do much in it. I should come into collision with every one I met—I should be treading on every one's toes. From the very first an effort has been successfully made to separate all converts from me, and they are the only persons who would be likely to move aside of me without jostling. You told me that the Cardinal said that he had asked me to go to live in London. I said he never did. After you were gone, I asked Fr St John whether I could have forgotten it—but he answered with a distinctness and force which I did not use in

137

speaking to you; 'No, no he never did' (By the bye the last day or two Fr St John was in London, and tried to get at you, but could not get the time.) Well, I know what the Cardinal did say to Fr Faber, and what Fr Faber said to the world, viz 'that I had put myself on the shelf, and there was no help for it.'

But now to go to the root of the matter. This country is under Propaganda, and Propaganda is too shallow to have the wish to use such as me. It is rather afraid of such. If I know myself, no one can have been more loyal to the Holy See than I am. I love the Pope personally into the bargain. But Propaganda is a quasi-military power, extraordinary, for missionary countries, rough and ready. It does not understand an intellectual movement. It likes quick results—scalps from beaten foes by the hundred. Our Bishop once on his return from Rome, said pointedly to me what I am sure came as a quasi message from Propaganda, that at Rome 'they liked good news'.

True, the words were said with an implied antithesis—for I had lately been to Rome to complain. I suppose the issue of the Achilli matter must have made them despise me at Rome— but, whatever the cause of it was, two years after, Propaganda, without saying a word to me, appointed three Bishops to examine and report to it whether the Rule of the Birmingham Oratory could be, on a certain point, suspended to advantage. The news broke upon us in a message to the effect that a *Rescript* (which one, who was in the plot, said it would be mortal sin to disobey) was on the road from Rome, embodying the change. You may fancy the commotion it excited among us. Our Fathers wrote to me in Dublin, conjuring me to do something. I wrote an urgent letter to the Cardinal. He left it unanswered for a month. I wrote again, and then went up to London from Dublin—but effected nothing. Then, our Fathers prevailed on me to go to Rome about it. When I got there, I found to my great relief and gratitude, that at the last moment the dear Pope, when the matter necessarily came before him, simply asked 'Has Dr Newman been consulted?' and would not give his assent to the act. Then, when I saw him, he asked me, *why* I wished to get him to make me head or general of the two Oratories! of which not even a dream had come into our minds here, more than that of making you a Father General of us; showing what hidden tales against me were going on.

When we saw Mgr. Barnabò, he was very cross, and asked me why I had come to Rome, when if I had remained quiet at home, the Pope would, as it turned out, have acted for me. When Monsell went to Rome shortly after, he came back with the remark that I had no friend at Rome. It was true:—but what had I *done*? *this* I had *not* done, and there was the rub. I had not preached sermons, made speeches, fussed about, and reported all my proceeding to Propaganda. I had been working away very hard in Ireland at the University, and saying nothing about it.

Well, immediately my Dublin engagement was over, at the Cardinal's and our Bishop's direct sollicitation, I interfered in the Rambler matter—and found myself in consequence, to my surprise and disgust, compelled to take the Editorship on myself. I not only made the best of it, but I really determined to make it *my work*. All those questions of the day which make so much noise now, Faith and Reason, Inspiration, etc etc would have been, according to my ability, worked out or fairly opened. Of course I required elbow room—but this was *impossible*. Our good Bishop, who has ever acted as a true friend, came after the publication of the first number, and advised me to give up the Editorship. He said I had caused dissatisfaction. I only edited two numbers; but I wrote enough to cause one of our Bishops formally to denounce one of the articles to Propaganda. What did Propaganda know of the niceties of the English language? yet a message came (not a formal one) asking explanations, and on the other hand dangling before my eyes the vision of a Bishoprick, if I explained well. It seems they fancied that I was soured because a Bishoprick was to be given me in 1854 (six years before) and Dr Cullen had stopped it. How little they knew of me! but I suppose they have to deal with low minded men. As what was said to me was very indirect and required no answer, I kept silence and the whole matter was hushed up. I suppose so—for I have heard no more of it—but I suppose it might (nel bisogno)[2] be revived at any time.

Don't you see that this, if nothing else, puts a great obex to my writing? This age of the Church is peculiar—in former times, primitive and medieval, there was not the extreme centralization which now is in use. If a private theologian said any thing free, another answered him. If the controversy grew, then it went to a Bishop, a theological faculty, or to some foreign University. The Holy See was but the court of ultimate appeal. *Now*, if I, as a private priest, put any thing into print, *Propaganda* answers me at once. How can I fight with such a chain on my arm? It is like the Persians driven on to fight *under the lash*. There was true private judgement in the primitive and medieval schools—there are no schools now, no private judgement (in the *religious* sense of the phrase,) no freedom, that is, of opinion. That is, no exercise of the intellect of former times. This is a way of things which, in God's own time, will work its own cure, of necessity; nor need we fret under a state of things, much as we may feel it, which is incomparably less painful than the state of the Church before Hildebrand and again in the fifteenth century.

I am only speaking of it in its bearing on myself. There was some talk when the Bishop put in his plea against me, of calling me to Rome. Call to Rome! What does that mean? It means to sever an old man from his Home, to subject him to intercourse with persons whose languages are strange to him; it means to bring him to a climate, which is unhealthy to him— to food, and to floors, which are almost starvation on one hand, and invite restless days and nights on the other—it means to oblige him to dance attendance on Propaganda week after week and month after month—it means his death. (It was the punishment on Dr Baines in 1840–1 to keep him at the door of Propaganda for a year.)

This is the prospect which I cannot but feel probable, did I say any thing, which one bishop in England chose to speak against and report. Others have been killed there before me. Lucas went of his own accord indeed—but when he got there, oh how much did he, as loyal a son of the Church and Holy See as ever was, what did he suffer because Dr Cullen was against him! He wandered, (as Dr Cullen said in a letter he published in a sort of triumph,) he wandered from Church to Church without a friend, and hardly got an audience from the Pope. And I too should go from St Philip to our Lady, and to St Peter and St Paul, and to St Laurence and to St Cecilia, and if it happened to me, as to Lucas, should come back to die.

We are not better than our Fathers. Think of St Joseph Calasanctius, or of Blessed Paul of the Cross, or of St Alfonso—or of my own St Philip, how they were misunderstood by the authorities at Rome. The Cardinal Vicar called Philip, to his face and in public, an ambitious party man, and suspended his faculties. It is by bearing these things that we gain merit, but has one a right to *bring it on one?*

I never wrote such a letter to any one yet, and I shall think twice before I send you the whole of it

Ever Yrs affly John H Newman

94

To CHARLOTTE BOWDEN

Thanks for a present of cakes

May 26. 1863

Who is it that moulds and makes
Round, and crisp, and fragrant cakes?
Makes them with a kind intent,
As a welcome compliment,
And the best that she can send
To a venerable friend
One it is, for whom I pray,
On St Philip's festal day,
With a loving heart that she
Perfect as her cakes may be,
Full and faithful in the round
Of her duties ever found
Where a trial comes, between
Truth and falsehood cutting keen;
Yet that keenness and completeness
Tempering with a winning sweetness.
Here's a rhyming letter, Chat,
Gift for a gift, and tit for tat.

JHN

95

To WILLIAM MONSELL

*Questions were being raised in Parliament about the treatment of
Spanish Protestants*

Rednall. June 17 1863

My dear Monsell

As to the question of the Spanish Protestants, of course you
must take me as speaking under the reserves and protestations
with which I began my letter yesterday.

I do not know whether the friend you speak of, who is to introduce the subject, will touch upon the question of doctrine,
but you (I think) can have nothing to do with it. Whether the
Church has the power, or has not, to punish heresy, is beyond
the mark. I take it, the question is not so much an ecclesiastical
one, or a political or legal or constitutional one in *Spain*, but a
social one. Surely Members of Parliament have abundance of
evidence on this point. Why is Lord E. Howard the only
Catholic in the House?[1] not because Church or State or Laws
forbid more, but because the people won't have us. Now, I do
not of course *know* the fact in Spain—but, were I an M.P., I
should say that I wish *no where* that the Government should
impose a faith on its subjects—it ought to follow the popular
voice. I suppose the Spanish laws are Anti-protestant, because
the people is such. How different from Ireland, where the laws
are Protestant because the people are *not* such, and to *make*
them such! Well then, government must best know what it can
do, and what it cannot. Do we not hear continually that the Spanish Government is more liberal than the people, just as our
ministries have been more liberal, and our representatives, than
the constituency? As then our Government cannot do much for
Catholics which they would do if they had their will, so if the
Spanish Government does not do more for Protestants than it
does, [it] may be because it can't; and I really do not know
how we can hope to change the popular feeling in Spain, by
any thing that can be said in our Parliament. I should say the
same about Sweden: if the Government and legislature, in up-

holding Protestantism, is doing so in a hostile spirit towards Catholicism, I think it might be remonstrated with: but if the people were furiously Anti-catholic, I don't see how we could interfere. Particular cases of wrong whether in Spain or Sweden of course stand on their own ground.

So far perhaps I should not agree with your friend, that is, *supposing* I have stated the facts truly; but in another respect I should warmly side with him. *As a fact*, persecution does not answer. It does against men's feelings; the feelings of the age are as strongly against it as they were once for it. The age is such, that we must go by reason, not by force. I am not at all sure that it would not be better for the Catholic religion every where, if it had no very different status from that which it has in England. There is so much corruption, so much deadness, so much hypocrisy, so much infidelity, when a dogmatic faith is imposed on a nation by law, that I like freedom better. I think Italy will be more religious, that is, there will be more true religion in it, when the Church has to fight for its supremacy, than when that supremacy depends on the provisions of courts, and police, and territorial claims. I could *not bear* to pull it down (to put things at the lowest point of view,) or rather who could take the responsibility of doing so? but we see every where a new state of things coming in, and it is pleasant to believe one has reasons not to fear it, but to be hopeful about it, as regards the prospects of religion. It is pleasant not to be obliged to resist a movement, which is so characteristic of the age; and with these feelings one may concur with Protestants in no small measure in such proceedings as that which has been the occasion of your question.

But I have said nothing which has not already suggested itself to you, and I have said enough to show you what suggests itself to me, on the subject

Ever Yours affectly John H Newman

The Rt Honble Wm Monsell M P

96

To AMBROSE ST JOHN

On holiday at Ostend

Ostend Sunday Augst 9/63

My dear Ambrose

We are very happy here, and our only drawback is that you are not here to enjoy the rest after the turmoil of travelling. There are shoals of people here; it seems to be the yearly meeting of all well-to-do Belgians, when their King's presence makes the season. It lasts six weeks, is the harvest time of hotels and lodging-letters, after which the place relapses into deadness and desolation. I have here just what I like: a great crowd of people with utter incognito; there hardly seems an Englishman here.

We have had our troubles and anxieties. The Hotel Fontaine is a disappointing place. Not only has it no view of the sea, which hardly a house here has; or can have, for the fortifications; but it is not first rate. We had two bed rooms, one of which was large enough to be a sitting room too; they opened into each other; so far well; but they wanted to charge us 15 francs a day, even though we stopped for a time. Why, at the first rate Hotel d'Europe we paid but 16 for the superb room with its look out and three bed rooms, four rooms instead of two. So we had in our bill, and found that, though we had had no dinner, we had in the course of 12 or 14 hours to pay 30 francs.

We determined to go, whatever came of it; to England, alas, we could not go—there was no steamer on the Saturday—but, at least we could pass Sunday (to day) at Bruges. We went about to other hotels. They were not only full, but the people told us we could not get any lodgings, and sent us in one case, as a favor, to some miserable ones, which we were almost tempted to take, because there seemed no chance of better, at 4 francs a day. However, we would not be hasty, though the people at the Fontaine professed to wish us out of our rooms at once—and on going about, we were surprised at the number of notices in the windows of Lodgings to let. After several essays, we chose our present, No 2 Rue de la Chapelle, which we have taken for a week, at 5 francs a day. They are on the seconde—very clean and neat—and the people give us breakfast at 60 centimes.

We enjoyed ourselves yesterday after our troubles, which lasted up to 2 P M. We then went on the splendid pier, which was full of people all the day—The sun, as at Rednall, was behind us, and in consequence the sea had a beauty it cannot have in England. There is no shipping, but the objects, both land and amphibious, are most varied and brilliant. A vast hard dry expanse of sand—lots of children making castles on it. Bathing machines without end, and bathing all day—a continual landing, more or less dexterous, of the clumsy machines, drawn by clumsier horses scarcely in harness, from the pier into the level sea-line of deep ploughed-up sand—hosts of donkey boys stretched at full length, with their donkeys not knowing what to think of it—an awning over head, and a restorateur at our backs—where we had a good dinner at 4 francs, and a military band. Here we remained till sunset—William's quick eyes discovered on the edge of the water the royal carriage, and sure enough the King[1] passed close to us—then the Duke of Brabant with his wife—and after some hours, the two grandchildren walking up from the sands. As the sun was setting, William [Neville] said, why 'here's the King again.' He was walking this time, and knowing how ill he had been, I was surprised to see how well and long he walked. At the moment, there were few people where we were—he walked right past us, and I had a good view of him—he was with his daughter in law—and some gentlemen behind. After a while he turned, and came past us again. We were quite by ourselves, and received a gracious bow. He is rather weak on his legs, and in consequence struts a little, but I was surprised at his young appearance. The last time I saw him was at the Coronation of George the iv, July 1821! What a time he has been before the world! since 1816, nearly 50 years—a man who has born arms against the first Napoleon, and the husband of a lady who has long and long become simply historical! Of course he is some years older than I am, but still to persons of my age he is a sort of compendium of the whole political history of their times. I am trying to think where he was, and what he did, between 1817 and 1830—and cannot make out—he was, I think, at Clermont—but what a strange inactive interval of 13 years in a busy life.

William is bathing just now—as he did yesterday and means to do every day. He is enjoying himself much. He presses me to bathe, but my arm is not well enough, I think, for it.[2] It was worse and worse, and very uncomfortable, when I got here—but by a bright thought I put that elastic belt, which I used for my skirt, round me under my arms, and it just confines tight those muscles, which pained me when I coughed, sneezed, laughed, or even spoke. However, last night when I took it off, my arm seemed no better. I think it is a strain from the fall —Recollect, I had a parcel in each hand before I dropped the one in the right, I fancy I must have got a strain from it.

My kindest remembrances to your hosts. Don't forget to report to Hope Scott the health and condition of Charley.[3]

Viva valeque Ever Yours affly John H Newman of the Oratory

97

To MESSRS MACMILLAN AND CO.

The beginning of the controversy which led to the writing of the 'Apologia'

The Oratory, Dec. 30, 1863

Gentlemen,

I do not write to you with any controversial purpose, which would be preposterous; but I address you simply because of your special interest in a Magazine which bears your name.

That highly respected name you have associated with a Magazine, of which the January number has been sent to me by this morning's post, with a pencil mark calling my attention to page 217.

There, apropos of Queen Elizabeth, I read as follows:—

'Truth, for its own sake, had never been a virtue with the Roman clergy. Father Newman informs us that it need not, and on the whole ought not to be; that cunning is the weapon which Heaven has given to the saints wherewith to withstand the brute male force of the wicked world which marries and is given in marriage. Whether his notion be doctrinally correct or not, it is at least historically so.'

There is no reference at the foot of the page to any words of mine, much less any quotation from my writings, in justification of this statement.

I should not dream of expostulating with the writer of such a passage, nor with the editor who could insert it without appending evidence of proof of its allegations. Nor do I want any reparation from either of them. I neither complain of them for their act, nor should I thank them if they reversed it. Nor do I even write to you with any desire of troubling you to send me an answer. I do but wish to draw the attention of yourselves, as gentlemen, to a grave and gratuitous slander, with which I feel confidence you will be sorry to find associated a name so eminent as yours.

I am, Gentlemen, Your obedient Servant, John H Newman

98

To MRS T. W. ALLIES

An account of his busy life at the Oratory

The Oratory Bm Jan. 18/64

My dear Mrs Allies,

Your kind letter made me smile, I have not had one day's holiday, nor am likely to have. I can only thank the good God who *enables* me to work. I feel quite what you say. I am likely to lose my manners, likely to get a great reluctance to stir from home, especially if my health gets weaker, but what can I do? I am over oppressed with a thousand little works, and when I have an hour or two for anything else, I have not vigour enough to use them.

We are fewer in number than we were, and, independently of this, our work is *absolutely* far greater than it ever was. Fancẏ! I am *sacristan*, and though I cannot move platforms or decorate cribs, yet it involves a good deal of little work, and little teasing sollicitudes, things to remember, órders to give. I have had to write to all the parents of the boys, as usual at the end of the half year, and my hand does not run so fast as it once did, and it sooner gets tired. I have had to have my eye upon the Terminal accounts, have had a number of petty school matters, which only can be attended to in the Vacation, and which make Vacation a busier time to me, as regards the School, than Term. I have had to go through and arrange the past years bills as regards sacristy, church decoration, and my private expenses. I have had to balance payments and receipts by banker's books. I have my share in church spiritual duties. I have a great lot of teasing controversy, with friends, with opponents, barren letters which take time, and which I may or may not have to publish, but which must be written with the caution which the chance of publishing requires. I have a good deal of private correspondence. I have community duties, meetings of the congregation, and the ordinary observances of the day, which cut up my time. I am printing an expurgated edition of Terence's Phormio for boys. I am on the point of taking some of Arnold's classes in the School, on the boys' return, since he has had scarlet fever and is away.

And your husband asks me if I am writing on Nature and Grace and you ask me what bones I am cracking? the bones of old jackalls and hyenas, of foxes, rats, and mice, in some ancient palaeòntological cave. What can I do? If you can tell me how to better myself, I will make you (as St Philip says) a very handsome present.

Ever yours affectly in Xt
John H Newman of the Oratory

99

To MRS JOHN MOZLEY

Keeping warm and well when old age draws on

The Oratory, Bm Febry 23/64

My dear Jemima,

Thank you for your affectionate letter. I have now passed my great climacteric, and am older than my Mother when she died. Hitherto old age has come on me like the falling snow, so gently that I cannot realize it. I am better now than I have been for years, judging by any phenomena which I can detect. That I am getting thinner and thinner, is the exception, its outward indication, if it be one. I get up earlier than I used to do at Oxford—earlier perhaps than any time of my life, except when I was a boy at Alton, and used to read every morning at a spell from 5 till 9. The last two years I have, at my own suggestion, taken to the shower bath, which I used in Oriel—When I was an undergraduate, I used to bathe through the winter in the cold baths at Holywell—and indeed no medicine is like it. It requires indeed to be well to be able to stand it—that I am able to use the shower bath now, is a proof how substantially strong I am. I take it not later than six o'clock, and this is the second winter which I have gone through with it. It has done me wonderful good in various ways; and among others in preserving me from cold. I do not know whether you recollect, that, when I was young, I never used a great coat in winter, and used to go up to London outside the coach with nothing but my ordinary coat on. I could not do that now—I am very warmly clad from head to foot. There is a lady, whom I have never seen, who is ever throwing flannels and silks at me, in spite of my protesting, and sometimes sending them back[1] I could not carry more clothes, without becoming a beast of burden, nor could I do with less. I go as far as I can go without passing the line of demarcation. Slender clothing then is not my boast—but the shower bath has wonderfully kept me from colds. I have not had a really bad one for all but two years—though I have had several bad threatenings and need to be very careful. I wish I heard from you a better account of yourself.

Ever Yrs affly J H N

100

To SISTER MARY GABRIEL DU BOULAY

The pressures that attended the writing of the 'Apologia'

Rednal. June 25/64

. My dear Child,

You must not suppose I did not in my heart thank you for your letter though I could not answer you. We all said Mass for you all on St Catherine's day. I never had such a time of it. When I was at Oxford, I have twice written a pamphlet in a night, and once in a day—but now I had writing and printing upon me at once, and I have done a book of 562 pages, all at a heat; but with so much suffering, such profuse crying, such long spells of work, sometimes 16 hours, once 22 hours at once, that it is a prodigious awful marvel that I have got through it, and that I am not simply knocked up by it. I am sure it is the prayers of my friends, which have sustained me, and you must go on praying that I may not feel the bad effects of such a strain on me afterwards.

And now excuse a short letter for my hand is tired and believe me to be

Ever yrs affectionately in Xt
John H. Newman of the Oratory

101

To AMBROSE ST JOHN

The visit of Monsignor Talbot

The Oy Bm July 25/64

My dear A

I shall transcribe for your benefit some sentences of my letter to Henry. I tell him the wind here is like March, and the heat of the sun makes it worse. Certainly this climate is most unlucky for nearly all of us. I caught a bad cold as soon as I came near it. A mile or two from Birmingham I had to put the glasses up, and I wish I had put on warmer clothing at once. I have been lying in bed this morning. The house is quite cold and the wind comes in gust down my chimney.

Mgr Talbot came on Saturday before I returned. Only Austin saw him. William was sulky at his name. Edward[1] said, when told, that he would not go to any of those bumptious Romans. He sat and talked with Austin in the Boys' Refectory. He asked what I thought of Catholic boys going to Oxford— *he* was against it— but the Catholic gentry, he feared were 'worldly'. He wished me to preach some Lent Sermons at Rome—and said that the Pope was pleased at the idea. Austin said I preached *here*—but he said 'ah, but this would be a very different thing—educated people etc etc'. It puts me in mind of the story of the two Smiths, when they suddenly became famous in 1812 by their Rejected Addresses. Albina Countess of Buckingham the famous blue, asked them to some conversazione. They answered that they were sorry that 'Mr Horace was engaged that evening to be Clown at Saddler's Wells and Mr James to play the part of the Yellow Dwarf in the Pantomime.' What is Brummagem to Mgr Talbot but a region of snobs. Yet souls are souls, your Rt reverence. He went on to ask what I *did*—did I read? Austin said he did not know—but he saw me take out books from the library. (the German flute!)[2] . . .

Ever Yrs affly JHN

102

To GEORGE TALBOT

Refusing an offer of a preaching engagement in Rome

July 25. 1864

Dear Monsignor Talbot,

I have received your letter, inviting me to preach next Lent in your Church at Rome, to 'an audience of Protestants more educated than could ever be the case in England.'

However, Birmingham people have souls; and I have neither taste nor talent for the sort of work, which you cut out for me: and I beg to decline your offer.

I am &c JHN

103

To ROBERT WHITTY

Newman's life is bitterly frustrating but friends need not worry

The Oratory Birmingham March 19, 1865

My dear Fr Whitty,

I thank you very much for your most kind letter; and thank you heartily for your prayers, which I value very much. It is very kind in you to be anxious about me, but, thank God, you have no need. Of course it is a constant source of sadness to me that I have done so little for Him during a long twenty years—but then I think, and with some comfort, that I have ever tried to act, as others told me—and if I have not done more, it has been because I have not been put to do more, or have been stopped when I attempted more.

The Cardinal brought me from Littlemore to Oscott—he sent me to Rome—he stationed and left me in Birmingham. When the Holy Father wished me to begin the Dublin Catholic University, I did so at once. When the Synod of Oscott gave me to do the new translation of Scripture, I began it without a word. When the Cardinal asked me to interfere in the matter of the Rambler, I took on myself, to my sore disgust, a great trouble and trial. Lately when my Bishop, proprio motu, asked me to undertake the Mission of Oxford, I at once committed myself to a very expensive purchase of land and began, as he wished me, to collect money for a Church. In all these matters I think (in spite of many incidental mistakes) I should, on the whole, have done a work, had I been allowed or aided to go on with them—but it has been God's Blessed Will that I should have been stopped.

If I could get out of my mind the notion, that I could do some thing and am not doing it, nothing could be happier, more peaceful, or more to my taste, than the life I lead.

Though I have left the notice of the Catechism to the end of the letter, be sure I value it in itself and as coming from you. Mr Pope will be very glad to hear the Author of it.

Ever Yrs affly in Xt John H Newman

104

To EMILY BOWLES

'What a laity must be in the 19th century'

The Oratory Bm May 1/65

My dear Child

I enclose a post office order for £5. If you think Miss S. *ought* to have £2 be so good as to ask her to accept it, according to her letter. As to the rest I wish it to go in a special kind of charity, viz in the instrumenta, as I may call them, and operative methods, of your own good works—that is, not in meat and drink, and physic, or clothing of the needy, but (if you will not be angry with me) in *your* charitable cabs, charitable umbrellas, charitable boots, and all the wear and tear of a charitable person who without such wear and tear cannot do her charity.

As to Catholic matters, there is nothing like the logic of facts. This is what I look to—it is a sad consolation—but Catholics won't stand such standing still for ever. And then, when much mischief is done, and more is feared, something will be attempted in high quarters. Do you see what is said to be going on at Rome? Since they find that Louis Napoleon is in earnest, they are beginning to draw towards Victor Emmanuel.[1] A great Prelate said to me years ago, when I said that the laity needed instruction, guidance, tenderness, consideration etc etc, 'You do not know them, Dr N. Our laity are a peaceable body—they are peaceable.' I understand him to mean 'They are grossly ignorant and unintellectual—and we need not consult or consult for them at all.' Don't repeat this—and at Rome they treat them according to the tradition of the Middle Ages, as, in Harold the Dauntless, the Abbot of Durham treated Count Wittikin.[2] Well, facts alone will slowly make them recognise the fact of what a laity must be in the 19th century, even if it is not, if it is to cope with Protestantism

Ever Yours affectionately, John H Newman

105

To R. W. CHURCH

Thanks for the gift of a fiddle

July 11 (1865)

My dear Church

I have delayed thanking you for your great kindness in uniting with Rogers in giving me a fiddle, till I could report upon the fiddle itself. The Warehouse sent me three to choose out of—and I chose with trepidation, as fearing I was hardly up to choosing well. And then my fingers have been in such a state, as being cut by the strings, that up to Saturday last I had sticking plaster upon their ends—and therefore was in no condition to bring out a good tune from the strings and so to return good for evil. But on Saturday I had a good bout at Beethoven's Quartetts—which I used to play with poor Blanco White—and thought them more exquisite than ever—so that I was obliged to lay down the instrument and literally cry out with delight. However, what is more to the point, I was able to ascertain that I had got a very beautiful fiddle—such as I never had before. Think of my not having a good one till I was between sixty and seventy—and beginning to learn it when I was ten! However, I really think it will add to my power of working, and the length of my life. I never wrote more than when I played the fiddle. I always sleep better after music. There must be some electric current passing from the strings through the fingers into the brain and down the spinal marrow. Perhaps thought is music.

I hope to send you the 'Phormio' almost at once.

Ever yrs affly, John H Newman

106

To MRS WILLIAM FROUDE

Keble, Newman, and Pusey meet after many years

The Oratory Bm. Oct. 16/65

My dear Mrs Froude

I have had so much to do in various ways since I have been back that I have not had time to tell you, as I hoped to do, of my visit to Keble. It was not much of a visit, for first he was obliged to put me off on account of Mrs K's illness. This kept me here and at Rednall, in suspense—Then, when she got better and they returned home, Pusey wrote me word, he too was going to Keble at the very same time—And, to complete the mischance when I got to Hursley, she had just been taken ill again and poor Keble was obliged to be in and out of the room, and out of the room in mind, when he was in it. I did not stop above five hours, and retreated to the Isle of Wight, where, at H Bowden's and Sir J. Simeon's, I waited for her recovery. But when a week had past and Keble wrote me word she was not well enough for me to return, I set off to receive two or three persons of some name and position in Kent—and thence home. But I am too old to travel, and I am only now recovering the fatigue.

When I got to Keble's door, he happened to be at it, but we

did not know each other, and I was obliged to show him my
card. Is not this strange? it is imagination mastering reason. He
indeed thought, since Pusey was coming, I should not come
that day—but I knew beyond doubt that I was at his house—
Yet I dared not presume it was he—but, after he began to talk,
the old Keble, that is, the young, came out from his eyes and
his features, and I dare say, if I saw him once or twice, I should
be unable to see much difference between his present face and
his face of past days. As Mrs Keble was ill, we three dined
together tête a tête—a thing we never perhaps had done before—there was something awful in three men meeting in old
age who had worked together in their best days. Vanity of
vanities, in all is vanity, was the sad burden of the whole—
once so united, now so broken up, so counter to each other—
though neither of them of course would quite allow it—Keble
has since written me, 'When shall we three meet again?...
when the hurly burley's done.'

Keble is deaf—but, what is worse, his speech is much im-
paired—and I think he *thinks* more slowly. Pusey was full of
plans, full of meetings. He has since made an important speech
at Norwich on the interpretation of Scripture, which will do
good, and of this he was full. Then, he was just on publishing
his book which he calls an Irenicon, and he was full of it,
though he was cautious of letting out all that was in it. Have
you seen it? It is anything but an Irenicon—it is likely to make
Catholics very angry—and justly angry.

Ever Yrs affectly John H Newman

107

To W. G. WARD

On differences between Catholics

The Oratory Bm Febry 18 1866

My dear Ward,

I thank you very much for the present of your volume, and
for your kind letter—but far more of course for your prayers. I

do not feel our differences to be such a trouble, as you do; for such differences always have been, always will be, in the Church, and Christians would have ceased to have spiritual and intellectual life, if such differences did not exist. It is part of their militant state. No human power can hinder it; nor, if it attempted it, could do more than make a solitude and call it peace. And, thus thinking that man cannot hinder it, however much he try, I have no great anxiety or trouble. Man cannot, and God will not. He means such differences to be an exercise of charity. Of course I wish as much as possible to agree with all my friends; but, if, in spite of my utmost efforts, they go beyond me or come short of me, I can't help it, and take it easy.

As to writing a volume on the Pope's infallibility, it never so much as entered into my thoughts. I am a controversialist, not a theologian. And I should have nothing to say about it. I have ever thought it likely to be true, never thought it certain. I think too, its definition inexpedient and unlikely; but I should have no difficulty in accepting it, were it made. And I don't think my reason will ever go forward or backward in the matter.

If I wrote another pamphlet about Pusey, I should be obliged to have a few sentences to the effect that the Pope's infallibility was not a point of faith—that would be all.

Ever Yours affectly in Xt
John H Newman of the Oratory

108

To EMILY BOWLES

No more theological writing; the death of Keble

The Oratory Bm April 16 1866

My dear Child,

You don't say how you are. I am afraid not well.

As to myself, you don't consider that I am an old man and must husband my strength. When I passed my Letter[1] through the Press and wrote my notes, I was confined to my bed, or barely sitting up. I had a most serious attack—it might have been far worse. I did not know how much worse till (through God's mercy) it was all over. It would have been very imprudent to have done more. Nor *would* I write more, hastily. I should have much to read for it. Recollect, to write theology is like dancing on the tight rope some hundred feet above the ground. It is hard to keep from falling, and the fall is great. Ladies can't be in the position to try. The questions are so subtle, the distinctions so fine, and critical jealous eyes so many. Such critics would be worth nothing, if they had not the power of writing to Rome, now that communication is made so easy—and you may get into hot water, before you know where you are. The necessity of defending myself at Rome would almost kill me with the fidget. You don't know me, when you suppose I 'take heed of the motley flock of fools'.[2] No—it is *authority* that I fear. Di me terrent, et Jupiter hostis.[3] I have had great work to write even what I have written—and I ought to be most deeply thankful that I have so wonderfully succeeded. Two Bishops, one my own, have spontaneously, and generously, come forward. Why cannot you believe that letter of mine, in which I said I did not write more because I was 'tired'? This was the real reason, then others came in. The subject I had to write upon opened, and I found I had a great deal to read, before I could write. Next, I felt I had irritated many good people, and I wished the waves to subside, before I began to play the Aeolus[4] a second time. Morever, I was intending to make a great change. I thought at length my time had come. I had introduced the narrow end of the wedge—and made a split—I feared it would split fiercely and irregularly—and I thought by withdrawing the wedge,—the split might be left at present more naturally to increase *itself*. Every thing I see confirms me in my view. I have various letters from all parts of the country approving of what I have already done. There are just two or three cliques in London who are the other way. The less I do myself, the more others will do. It is not well to put oneself too forward. Englishmen don't like to be driven. I am sure it is good policy to be quiet just now.

I have long said 'the night cometh etc,'[5] but that does not make it right to act in a hurry. Better not do a thing than do it badly. I must be patient and wait on God. If it is His will I should do more, He will give me time. I am not serving Him, by blundering.

You will be glad to know, (*what (at present) is a great secret*) that we are likely to have a house at Oxford after all. Be patient, and all will be well.

As to dear Keble, I have lent a letter about him, or I would send it you. It is grievous that people are so hard. In converts it is inexcusable; it is a miserable spirit in them. Keble was told his wife could not live many hours. He had borne up, in spite of his great infirmities, longer than I had supposed possible. He was seized with fainting fits. His friends took him from her room. When he got into his own, he fancied it a Church. He knelt down, and said the Lord's Prayer. Then he began a Latin Hymn—they could not make out what. Those were his last words. Thus he ended with the prayer which he first said on his knees as a little child.

Ever Yours affly in Xt John H Newman of the Oratory

109

To MARIANNE FRANCES BOWDEN

Counsel to a girl who could not see her path in life

The Oratory Birmingham June 5 1866

My dear Child,

Fanny told me about you, as doubtless she has told you. I will not forget the Masses—they will help you, and you must simply put yourself into God's hands. As I understood F. you have no call on you to do any thing, or to decide on doing any thing, at this moment, Do you know, though this is of course a trial, yet I have ever felt it a great mercy. One of the greatest of trials is, to have it cast upon one to make up one's mind,— on some grave question, with great consequences spreading into the future—and to be in doubt what one ought to do. You have not this trial—it is also a trial to wait and do nothing but how great a mercy is it not to have responsibility! Put your self then, my dear Child, into the hands of your loving Father and Redeemer, who knows and loves you better than you know or love yourself. He has appointed every action of your life. He created you, sustains you, and has marked down the very way and hour when He will take you to Himself. He knows all your thoughts, and feels for you in all your sadness more than any creature can feel, and accepts and makes note of your prayers even before you make them. He will never fail you— and He will give you what is best for you. And though He tries you, and seems to withdraw Himself from you, and afflicts you, still trust in Him, for at length you will see how good and gracious He is, and how well he will provide for you. Be courageous and generous, and give Him your heart, and you will never repent of the sacrifice.

Ever Yours affectionately in Xt John H Newman

110

To WILLIAM NEVILLE

A holiday abroad does no good

Hotel de Lucerne Luzerner hof Lucerne September 3 1866

My dear William,

Your note for £15 has come safely. It is not certain we shall want it—I trust not your kind additional £5 of it.

I fear I shall disappoint you much when I say that this trip has done me no good except what change of air *must* do. That I trust will show itself hereafter. As far as fidgetty symptoms go, I think I should have had them less at home, and have been able to meet them better. However, I have very little, thank God, to complain of here—though I certainly should have been better at home.

But what we both feel is want of good meals and want of sleep. I think neither Ambrose nor I have had more than two good nights' rest since we left England. It is all the same for that whether we are at Glion, Champéry, Interlaken, or here.

For myself, it arises, I think, from the food. I cannot digest such a nagging meal as a table d'hote dinner is. As to a restaurant's, I manage well enough. You order your two dishes and have as much as you can eat—but first a small piece of boiled, then a cold lobster salad, then a wing of pigeon, then some hard beef, then an impossible sweet bread, then some beans, and, to finish, some cruel ice, which simply destroys the working power of the stomach—and all these at vast intervals, and then the uncertainty, when it is put before you, whether you should be able to manage the particular dish or not, the suspicion with which you begin to eat and the impossibility of your getting your will to cooperate with your jaws, which is a great secret of food digesting well, the disgust at what you don't like, and the desire to get rid of it off your plate into your stomach as soon as you can, all this, in the event, not only does not answer the purpose of food, but murders sleep, when night comes. I have now (7 a.m.) my inside all disarranged by yesterday's dinner still—and as to sleep, I woke in discomfort at 12, and again at 2—and then, at half past 3 I woke for good—except a little dozing between 5 and 6. Then the beds, though new and good, are intolerable to me, and I cannot tell why. They make me restless. I wake with a crick in my neck—or a pain in my shoulders—or with my foot bare, from the blanket etc being pulled too much over my shoulders —and above all, they are so wonderfully hot. At this time my mattress lies against my wall, as I take it off my bed, before going to bed—the under mattress being harder. The upper mattress is springy, and I can't lie even—At Champéry I had to lie like a serpent in and out—and to sleep is impossible under such circumstances. The mattresses are new, filled with hair—there is no fault to be found with them, except that I cannot sleep on them. I have said nothing of the wine. It is all acid, Yvorne and all; and this I have been drinking now 5 weeks. I have tried to obey Dr Evan's order implicitly, but in vain. As to brandy, I have sometimes gone for it—but it is no support, and wishy washy. The only point in which we went out of Dr E's directions is in our coming down from our altitudes to Interlaken and Lucerne, but we have been brought down against our will by bad fare and bad weather. We were not high enough to get rid of fogs and rain—and if we had gone higher we should have got out of the Catholic region, except at Zermatt.¹ Also I am sure that a high place like that would be most dreary for any length of time. Then again in high places such as Champéry, there is no competition in hotels—and you are at the mercy of a stingy land lord.

Ambrose has been lamish—and Dr de Mussy who 'is here, assures him it is nothing more than a little sprain.

We were going to see Seelisberg today, the place which the poor F.R. Wards liked so much—but I am too tired.

You must not be surprised, if we come home a day or two earlier—for we are not doing much more than spend money. Our rooms had better be ready. I don't suppose we should start hence at once—but I doubt whether it will be prudent for you to write again. We have got all your letters from the Poste Restante.

Ever Yrs affly J H N

111

To R. W. CHURCH

England is being thrown into the background

The Oratory, Bm Septr. 21, 1866

What wonderful events have taken place lately! quite a new world is coming in; and if Louis Napoleon were to fall ill, the catastrophe would be still more wonderful. I don't quite like our being thrown so much into the background. Twenty-five years ago Rogers said one ought to go abroad to know how great England was—it is not so now—some foreign papers simply leave out the heading 'Angleterre' in their foreign news. And the fate of Austria, a state in some striking points like us, though in others different, is a sort of omen of what might happen to us in the future.¹ Then, I am quite ashamed at the past ignorance of the *Times* and other papers and at myself for having been so taken in by them. Think of the *Times* during the American civil war! And again on the breaking out, and in the course of the Danish War.² Really we are simply in the dark as to what is going on beyond our four seas—even if we

162

know what is going on within them. How dark, as even I could see, we are as to Ireland, from having been there. Some four years ago I met a man, he seemed some sort of country gentleman, at the inn of a country town—we got into conversation. I told him the hatred felt for England in all ranks in Ireland—how great friends of mine did not scruple to speak to me of the 'bloody English'—the common phrase—how cautious and quiet government people simply confessed they would gladly show their teeth if they were sure of biting; but he would not believe me—and that has been the state of the mass of our people. Even now they are slow to believe that Fenianism is as deeply rooted as it is. Every Irishman is but watching his opportunity—and if he is friendly to this country, it is because he despairs.

Don't think I am tempted to despair about *England*. I am in as little despair about England as about the Pope.[3] I think they have both enormous latent forces; and if, as they now talk, he goes to Malta, I shall think it is caused by some hidden sympathy of position. Misery does indeed name us acquainted with strange bedfellows. And, whatever the Pope will have to do, at least England must make some great changes, and give up many cherished ways of going on, if she is to keep her place in the world.

However, much all this is to an old man like me.

112

To BISHOP ULLATHORNE

Concerning Archbishop Manning

Rednall Jany. 8. 1867

My dear Lord,

Fr Bittleston tells me that you seemed to be disappointed that I am not in Birmingham, when the Archbishop is there. If you will kindly tell me what day or hour would be convenient to him, I will call upon him then at your house.

I will say to your Lordship, frankly, that I cannot trust the

Archbishop. It seems to me he never wishes to see a man except for his own ends. Last Spring he wrote to me flattering letters upon my Letter to Dr Pusey—and he followed them up by privately sending your Lordship for your approval an article intended for the Dublin Review in which I was severely handled for certain passages in it. I know other instances of such unsatisfactory conduct.

Just now he finds there is a general feeling afloat as to his treatment of me; accordingly he gives out that he has offered me this thing and that thing in vain—and is profoundly distressed at the distance of my behaviour towards him; and thus it is he compliments me now in the Dublin and it is his interest to see me in Birmingham, and, if I do not see him, to be able to say that he has tried in vain.

I cannot act towards him as if I trusted him—and I think that, as a matter of prudence, I never shall trust him till he has gone through purgatory and has no infirmities upon him. Certainly I have no wish to see him now; first because I don't like to be practised on; secondly, because I cannot in conversation use smooth words which conceal, not express thoughts; thirdly because I am not sorry he should know that I am dissatisfied with him. Of course his conduct to me is not special, but such as his conduct is to every one; but this is a further matter.

However, I propose to call on him, that he may not have the advantage of bringing against me that I have not done so.

Your Lordship's obt & affte Servt in Xt
John H Newman of the Oratory

113

To MARIANNE BOWDEN

Special prayers seemed to make a sick nun worse

The Oratory Bm May 29 1867

My dear Child,

It is no want of faith in you to put yourself simply into the hands of our dear Lord, that He may do with you what He will. He must not be supposed to turn a deaf ear to prayer, because He answers it in His own way. It is impossible that a blessing should not come to you in consequence of so many prayers made for you—and if He does not give the very favour asked for, it is because He has it in purpose to give you a greater. Any how, you are His—and prayer will make you more fully His.

I have to say the same about your Revd Mother's and Sister's charitable prayers for our Oxford undertaking. There is a very bad hitch—which it may take a long time to get over—and for myself I am really indifferent whether it is removed or not—but any how the ejaculations and prayers which have been offered for us, will not be in vain, but in some way or other will produce fruit.

Thank you for your congratulations on our Saint's Feast. Generally we have a very fine day—but we were unlucky this year—and had not many visitors—but St Philip is always St Philip, and, if he was with us, we can bear the absence of other guests.

I have placed your mortuary billet in our Sacristy

Pray for me & believe me Ever Yours
affectly in Xt John H Newman of the Oratory

P.S. And your Revd Mother must not forget me, tho' she has already done so much.

114

To WILLIAM MONSELL

Coming to terms with secular education

The Oratory Febry 9/68

My dear Monsell

I suppose we are as sure that Cardinal Cullen and the Irish Hierarchy, and that Archbishop Manning and the English, will fight tooth and nail against compulsory secular Education, as of any thing as yet future. There is an Article, I am told, in the Dublin lately on the subject, recommending a union with the

Anglicans and Wesleyans, to form a strong parliamentary opposition to it. And you must know better than I, what nevertheless I, rightly or not, take for granted, that with so strong an expression of opinion, few Irish Catholics will decline to follow their lead. If this be so, I don't see that you have a question before you, however you may regret it. Any how you have no question to ask of such as me, who am a priest like others, and like others have never been consulted by any bishop on the subject. I suppose the bishops consult with their respective chapters.

If, however, you want to know what I think, you must recollect I have a very contracted horizon. I can but judge from the few facts I know, and, were I in the world, as you are, I might at once change my judgement, however logically drawn from those few facts.

Now you know that I, as most or all of us, am, as a matter of principle, utterly opposed to education without religion, which I suppose is the scheme which you ask me about. And I have opposed projects tending that way for the greater part of my life. But now, if I was obliged to form a political judgement, I think I should concur in it, however grudgingly, and try to make the best of it and make terms with promoters of it.

It is forty years this very month, that the present Lord Malmesbury, whom I was presenting for his degree, told me that the repeal of the Test and Corporation Act was carried[1] (or resolved on by the Duke of W. [Wellington]) Ever since then the stream of opinion and legislation has been in one direction. It is cowardly to abandon a principle which you uphold as good and true, because you have suffered one or two defeats in maintaining it—but surely the time may come, after a long warfare steadily carried out in successive great reverses and uniform disappointments of your hopes, when it is as unwise and as headstrong to continue the war, as it would have been in Austria not to make peace after Sadowa. It may be very well for the Holy See, which is divinely intended to be the principle of immobility to continue its protests and to spurn the notion of concurrence or compromise; but that as little makes it its duty to forbid local hierarchies, according to their greater insight into local necessities, to act on their discretion, and as little justifies local hierarchies to refuse to political expedience what they cannot in principle originate or approve, what the Holy See cannot sanction, and must ignore, than it would have justified the Irish Hierarchy in 1829 and 1834 in refusing those concessions by which such great ecclesiastical and political advantages have accrued to Irish Catholics, the Holy See then, as it did, keeping silence.[2]

I cannot help saying I give up, after a long contest. Now here perhaps I am judging merely according to my contracted horizon, but, with this proviso, I say it seems to me as clear as day, that in a few years compulsory secular education will be the law. Some people say 'the Church of England, the Wesleyans, never will give in;' but I have been struck by the fact that the Guardian Newspaper (as it seems to me) is going round to the other side—and it says that numerous Anglicans are going round too—Moreover, it says that the orthodox dissenters have (if I understand it) gone round in a body.

Then we have the case of America—where secular education is (is it not?) the rule—and where, if you go by Fr Hecker and others, it answers so well for Catholics, that they would not alter it, if they could.[3] I know that circumstances are very different there; for we have to contend with a bigotry which does not exist there—but the question may be asked, whether these and the like great changes will not go a great way to destroy the bigotry under which we suffer.

Education is not exactly parallel to the case of Workhouses and Jails—nor is the case of London the same as that of provincial towns—but, as far as Birmingham is concerned, in spite of a bitter, active, anti-Catholic party, we have ever been treated well by the town—as in the work-house, which was in our hands for 14 years, so in the jail, which we have still;—and, speaking under correction, I do not know why we should not also be treated well in the case of secular schools. And, as far as I know, the liberal feeling in Manchester and Liverpool is quite as influential.

On the other hand, we might make terms—I mean, *you*, Catholic MP's might—there might be a provision, that some priest should be on each local board etc etc which you could not carry, if you set yourselves in opposition to a measure on which the country was set.

Moreover, to speak personally, how much we at the Oratory

should be at our ease, if we had not to keep poor schools! What a load of responsibility, anxiety, nay debt would be taken off us! Of course our great effort, and an anxious one, would be to bring our children round us on Sunday for religious instruction—a very serious task and duty—and it is done at Milan, Brescia, Turin, and I don't know why we should not do it too. And other religious bodies are in the same difficulty —and, as they are sure to meet it, so shall we be.

Every yrs affly John H Newman

115

To A STUDENT AT MAYNOOTH

On writing, particularly on writing Sermons

The Oratory, Birmingham March 2nd 1868

Dear Sir,

I would gladly serve you by answering the question which you ask had I anything to say which would be materially of use to you.

Also I know what able instructors you have at Maynooth, and I should shrink from interfering in a matter which requires an experience of young men which the Maynooth Professors have, and I have not. Besides, while I thank you heartily for the compliment you pay to my own mode of writing, and am truly glad if you and others have received pleasure from it, you must recollect that those who are expert in any work are often the least able to teach others; and for myself I must simply say that I have followed no course of English reading, and am quite at a loss to know what books to recommend to students such as yourselves.

As to the writing or delivery of sermons to which you refer, the great thing seems to be to have your subject distinctly before you; to think over it till you have got it perfectly in your head; to take care that it should be one subject, not several; to sacrifice every thought, however good and clever, which does not tend to bring out your one point, and to aim earnestly and supremely to bring home that one point to the minds of your hearers.

I have written some pages on the subject of preaching in a volume upon 'University Subjects' which I published when I was in Dublin. It is unfortunately out of print or I would have sent it to you. One great difficulty in recommending particular authors as models of English arises from the Literature of England being Protestant and sometimes worse—Thus Hume is a writer of good English, but he was an unbeliever. Swift and Dryden write English with great force, but you can never be sure you will not come upon coarse passages. South is a vigorous writer, but he was a Protestant clergyman and his writings are sermons. All this leads me to consider that everyone must form his style for himself, and under a few general rules, some of which I have mentioned already. First, a man should be in earnest, by which I mean, he should write, not for *the sake of writing*, but to bring out his *thoughts*. He should never aim at being eloquent. He should keep his idea in view, and write sentences over and over again till he has expressed his meaning accurately, forcibly and in a few words. He should aim at being understood by his hearers or readers. He should use words which are most likely to be understood—ornament and amplification will come to him spontaneously in due time, but he should never seek them. He must creep before he can fly, by which I mean that humility, which is a great Christian virtue, has a place in literary composition—He who is ambitious will never write well. But he who tries to say simply and exactly what he feels or thinks, what religion demands, what Faith teaches, what the Gospel promises, will be eloquent . without intending it, and will write better English than if he made a study of English literature. I wish I could write anything more to your purpose, and am, dear Sir,

Faithfully Yours in Christ, John H Newman of the Oratory,

116

To HENRY WILBERFORCE

A return to Littlemore

The Oratory Bm June 18/68

My dear Henry

Thank you for your affectionate letter and invitation—but I can't accept it. It is not much more than a week since I refused one from my sister. I have real duties here which make it difficult to get away; I am on a strict regime which I don't like to omit for a day—and I have an old man's reluctance to move. I have promised R W Church a visit for several years, and it must be my first.

I am gradually knocking off some purposes of the kind. When your letter came I was at Littlemore! I had always hoped to see it once before I died. Ambrose and I went by the 7 a.m. train to Abingdon, then across to Littlemore—then direct from *Littlemore* by rail to Birmingham where we arrived by 7—just 12 hours. The man of Ross has a name for planting—[1] at least I have begun something in that way at Littlemore, and Crawley has done as much again and much more tastefully. Littlemore is now *green*. Crawley's cottage and garden (upon my 10 acres which I sold him) are beautiful. The church too is now what they call a *gem*. And the parsonage is very pretty. I saw various of my people, now getting on in life. It was 40 years at the beginning of this year since I became vicar. Alas, their memory of me was in some cases stronger than my memory of them. They have a great affection for my Mother and Sisters —tho' it is 32 years since they went away. There is a large lunatic asylum—separated, however, from the village by the rail road—so it is no annoyance, rather it adds green to the place—nor is the rail road an annoyance, for it is in a cutting. It is 22 years since I was there. I left February 22 1846. I do not expect ever to see it again—nor do I wish it.

I am so glad to find you are so pleasantly placed. It would give me great pleasure to see your wife and daughters—some one said Harry [Wilberforce] is with you—is he not at Ushaw?

And say every thing most kind to your sister-in law, whom I should greatly like to see.

Ever Yrs affly JHN

117

To MISS M. R. GIBERNE

Newman has no wish to be in an official position in the First Vatican Council

The Oratory Bm Febry 10. 1869 Ash Wednesday

My dear Sister Pia,

I wonder whether you have as mild weather in France as we have here. I am sitting without a fire from choice, nor have I had one, except in the evening, for nearly a week past. One does not know what it means. There may be subterraneous fires, which are doing their best to find a vent.

Thank you for all your prayers. I said Mass for you on the 28th and 29th January and should have written to you, had I not been busy.

Don't be annoyed. I am more happy as I am, than in any other way. I can't bear the kind of trouble which I should have, if I were brought forward in any public way. Recollect, I *could* not be in the Council, unless I were a Bishop—and really and truly I am *not* a theologian. A theologian is one who has mastered theology—who can say how many opinions there are on every point, what authors have taken which, and which is the best—who can discriminate exactly between proposition and proposition, argument and argument, who can pronounce which are safe, which allowable, which dangerous—who can trace the history of doctrines in successive centuries, and apply the principles of former times to the conditions of the present. This is it to be a theologian—this and a hundred things besides. And this I am not, and never shall be. Like St Gregory Nazianzen I like going on my own way, and having my time my own, living without pomp or state, or pressing engagements. Put me into official garb, and I am worth nothing;

leave me to myself, and every now and then I shall do something. Dress me up and you will soon have to make my
shroud—leave me alone, and I shall live the appointed time.
Now do take this in, as a sensible nun, and believe me.

Ever Yours affly in Xt John H Newman

118

To JOHN HAYES

On his own method and aim in writing

The Oratory, Birmingham April 13, 1869

My dear Sir,

I saw the article you speak of in the 'Times', and felt flattered by the message which referred to myself.

The writer must have alluded in the sentence which leads to
your question, to my 'Lectures and Essays on University Subjects,' which is at present out of print. In that volume there are
several papers on English and Latin composition.

It is simply the fact that I have been obliged to take great
pains with everything I have written, and I often write chapters
over and over again, besides innumerable corrections and interlinear additions. I am not stating this as a merit, only that some
persons write their best first, and I very seldom do. Those who
are good speakers may be supposed to be able to write off
what they want to say. I, who am not a good speaker, have to
correct laboriously what I put on paper. I have heard that
Archbishop Howley, who was an elegant writer, betrayed the
labour by which he became so by his mode of speaking, which
was most painful to hear from his hesitations and alterations—
that is, he was correcting his composition as he went along.

However, I may truly say that I never have been in the practice since I was a boy of attempting to write well, or to form
an elegant style. I think I never have written for writing sake;
but my one and single desire and aim has been to do what is so
difficult—viz. to express clearly and exactly my meaning; this
has been the motive principle of all my corrections and re-

writings. When I have read over a passage which I had written a few days before, I have found it so obscure to myself that I have either put it altogether aside or fiercely corrected it; but I don't get any better for practice. I am as much obliged to correct and re-write as I was thirty years ago.

As to patterns for imitation, the only master of style I have ever had (which is strange considering the differences of the languages) is Cicero. I think I owe a great deal to him, and as far as I know to no one else. His great mastery of Latin is shown especially in his clearness.

Very faithfully yours, John H Newman

The Rev. John Hayes

P.S. Thank you for what you so kindly say of me in old times.

119

To LOUISA SIMEON

To a girl experiencing religious difficulties

The Oratory June 25. 1869

My dear Louisa Simeon

I have delayed writing to you, both as feeling the risk of my disappointing and disturbing instead of aiding you by what I might say—and also because I found you had been so good as to take up my suggestion as regards my Oxford Sermons. I thought they might for a while speak to you instead of a letter. I can never prophesy what will be useful to a given individual and what not. As to my Sermons, I was astonished and (as you may suppose) deeply gratified by a stranger, an Anglican Clergyman, writing to me a year or two ago to say that reading them had converted him from free thinking opinions, which he had taken up from German authors, or from living in Germany, I do not see how they could do so—but he said they did—and it was that, I think, which made me fancy it was worth while to recommend them to you.

You must begin all thought about religion by mastering

what is the fact, that any how the question has an inherent, irradicable [sic] difficulty in it. As in tuning a piano, you may throw the fault here or there, but no theory can any one take up without that difficulty remaining. It will come up in one shape or other. If we say 'Well, I will not believe any thing', there is a difficulty in believing nothing, an intellectual difficulty. There is a difficulty in doubting; a difficulty in determining there is no truth; in saying that there is a truth, but that no one can find it out; in saying that all religious opinions are true, or one as good as another; a difficulty in saying there is no God; that there is a God but that He has not revealed Himself except in the way of nature; and there is doubtless a difficulty in Christianity. The question is, whether on the whole our reason does not tell us that it is a duty to accept the arguments commonly urged for its truth as sufficient, and a duty in consequence to believe heartily in Scripture and the Church.

Another thought which I wish to put before you is, whether our nature does not tell us that there is something which has more intimate relations with the question of religion than intellectual exercises have, and that is our conscience. We have the idea of duty—duty suggests something or some one to which it is to be referred, to which we are responsible. That something that has dues upon us is to us God. I will not assume it is a personal God, or that it is more than a law (though of course I hold that it is the Living Seeing God) but still the idea of duty, and the terrible anguish of conscience, and the irrepressible distress and confusion of face which the transgression of what we believe to be our duty, cause us, all this is an intimation, a clear evidence, that there is something nearer to religion than intellect; and that, if there is a way of finding religious truth, it lies, not in exercises of the intellect, but close on the side of duty, of conscience, in the observance of the moral law. Now all this may seem a truism, and many an intellectualist will say that he grants it freely. But I think, that, when dwelt upon, it leads to conclusions which would both surprise and annoy him.

Now I think it best to stop here for the present. You must not suppose that I am denying the intellect its real place in the discovery of truth; but it must ever be borne in mind that its exercise mainly consists of reasoning—that is, in comparing things, classifying them, and inferring. It ever needs points to start from, first principles, and these it does not provide—but it can no more move one step without these starting points, than a stick, which supports a man, can move without the man's action. In physical matters, it is the senses which gives us the first start—and what the senses give is physical fact—and physical facts do not lie on the surface of things, but are gained with pains and by genius, through experiment. Thus Newton, or Davy, or Franklin ascertained those physical facts which have made their names famous. After these primary facts are gained, intellect can act; it acts too of course in gaining them; but they *must* be gained; it is the senses which *enable* the intellect to act, by giving it something to act upon. In like manner we have to ascertain the starting points for arriving at religious truth. The intellect will be useful in gaining them and after gaining them—but to attempt to *see* them by means of the intellect is like attempting by the intellect to see the physical facts which are the basis of physical exercises of the intellect, a method of proceeding which was the very mistake of the Aristotelians of the middle age, who, instead of what Bacon calls 'interrogating nature' for facts, reasoned out every thing by syllogisms. To gain religious starting points, we must in a parallel way, interrogate our hearts, and (since it is a personal, individual matter,) our own hearts,—interrogate our own consciences, interrogate, I will say, the God who dwells there.

I think you must ask the God of Conscience to enable you to do your duty in this matter, I think you should, with prayer to Him for help, meditate upon the Gospels, and on St Paul's second Epistle to the Corinthians, unless the translation of it disturbs you; and this with an earnest desire to know the truth and a sincere intention of following it.

When you are disposed, write again, and, if you wish, I will answer you

Yours affectly in Xt John H Newman

120

To AMBROSE ST JOHN

News from Birmingham, in rapid note form

August 19/69

My dear A

I have no news for you—Yours to William came yesterday. Fr Thomas has received John's. Poor Mr Moore, MP for Tipperary, who was so civil to me has died suddenly of inflammation of the lungs. Mrs Buckle has had an apoplectic stroke and Mr Buckle a second paralytic. I have settled with Creswell about the Tank with pipes, gutters etc it is to cost £42 and to be invisible; round, diameter 10 feet, depth 13. 5624 gallons of water—opening by a pipe on the lawn—to be finished in a month. Painting inside house begins in September and will last a month. Mule most amiable—has struck up a friendship with Austin's donkey. Cow out of favour in consequence. All that wretched Gip's puppies drown, I hear. Nero starving for want of bones—wont eat biscuit. Woodgate and Bramston dined with me at Rednall—they are my two oldest friends—I have known W since 1819 and B since 1822. Copeland is to Buxton. My £1300 has fallen down to £780. Sale of Sermons not so rapid. William Bellasis is leaving for some counting house. Edward Bellasis comes back for a while. Richard Bellasis comes here in a day or two to consult about going to Germany or not. Thomas Hoghton going for next term to Boulogne. Monsell spitting blood *Keep this to yourself*—Poor Morell asking if we want a mathematical tutor. Great chance of my book being dished, because I am an 'Hypothetical Realist'. Ignatius went for his holiday last Monday—Edward next Monday. We suspect that the Bishop as last year, does not mean to send a Celebret.[1] Wm sent down to him at once about it—but none has come. Wm thinks the old one ought to be endorsed by him. Perhaps the engraving is dear. Mrs Wootten went away on Monday for a holiday. Mrs Knight came on Monday. I called directly, but she was out. She called on me then—and I was out. I have done nothing yet to Library or Congregation

Room—I am so idle. Now I hope I have convinced you there is no news. Love to John. Please do not climb by yourself— and do not bathe in Tarns I rejoice to find the place suits you.

Ever Yrs affly JHN

121

To HENRY WILBERFORCE

'Plan after plan has crumbled under my hand'

The Oratory Aug. 20 1869

Confidential

My dear HW

Had I not been so very busy, I should have answered your former letter which made me very sad. It made me sad to hear you write as you did about your wife and about yourself, though I thanked you in my heart for your speaking out.

It is sad to hear any one speak as if his work was done, and he was but waiting to go—not sad, as if it were not *good to go*, but not good to be in the world still, with one's work done— for what does one live for except work? And then my thoughts glanced off from you and came down on myself with dismal effect—for what am I doing, what have I been doing for years, but nothing at all? I have wished earnestly to do some good work, and continually asked myself whether I am one of those who are 'fruges consumere nati'[1]—and have, to the best of my lights, taken what I thought God would have me do—but again and again, plan after plan, has crumbled under my hand and come to nought. As to the Oxford matter, my heart sank under the greatness of the task and I think it would have shortened my life, still it was work and service—and, when it was shut up, though I felt for the moment a great relief, yet it came upon me sorrowfully as a fresh balk and failure. Upon its settlement, I took up to write a book on some questions of the day, (you know the sort of questions, about faith etc) and now (in confidence) I think this will be stopped after my infinite pains about it. Our theological philosophers are like the old

177

nurses who wrap the unhappy infant in swaddling bands on boards—put a lot of blankets over him—and shut the windows that not a breath of fresh air may come to his skin—as if he were not healthy enough to bear wind and water in due measures. They move in a groove, and will not tolerate any one who does not move in the same. So it breaks upon me, that I shall be doing more harm than good in publishing. What influence should I have with Protestants and Infidels, if a pack of Catholic critics opened at my back fiercely, saying that this remark was illogical, that unheard of, a third realistic, a fourth, idealistic, a fifth sceptical, and a sixth temerarious, or shocking to pious ears? This is the prospect which I began to fear lies before me—and thus I am but fulfilling on trial what I said in my Apologia had hitherto kept me from trying, viz the risk of 'complicating matters further.' There was a caricature in Punch some years ago so good that I cut it out and kept it. An artist is showing to a friend his great picture just going to the exhibition—the friend says 'Very good, but could you not make the Duke sitting and the Duchess standing, whereas the Duchess sits and the Duke stands?' I cannot make a table stand on two or three legs—I cannot cut off one of the wings of my butterfly or moth (whatever its value) and keep it from buzzing round itself. One thing is not another thing, My one thing may be worth nothing, at the best—but at least it is not made worth something by being cut in half or turned inside out.

You must not for an instant suppose that I am alluding to the acts of any one whose *opinion* I have wished to have upon what I have written—but *through* a kind friend I come more to see than I did, what an irritabile genus Catholic philosophers are—they think they do the free Church of God service, by subjecting her to an etiquette as grievous as that which led to the King of Spain being burned to cinders . . . . .

Yrs ever affly John H Newman

To SISTER MARY GABRIEL DU BOULAY

The need for books that are truly educational

The Oratory Jan: 2. 1870

My dear Child,

A happy New Year to you and yours in the best sense of the word. I should have thanked you for your letter before now, had I not so many letters to write, and a book on hand, which now is nearly done, but which I cannot finish to my satisfaction. I generally write my books many times over—but never perhaps have I re-written one so often as this. I desire no better success than you say is attained by the Life of dear Mother Margaret.[1] Not that I doubt it will convert many—but there are two reasons for writing quite distinct from conversion, and, considering all things, I prefer them to any other reason— the one is to edify Catholics. Catholics are so often raw. Many do not know their religion—many do not know the reasons for it. And there is in a day like this, a vast deal of semi-doubting. There are those who only wish to convert, and then leave the poor converts to shift for themselves, as far as knowledge of their religion goes. The other end which is so important, is what I call levelling up. If we are to convert souls savingly they must have the due preparation of heart, and if England is to be converted, there must be a great move of the national mind to a better sort of religious sentiment. Wesleyans, Anglicans, Congregationalists, Unitarians,· must be raised to one and the same (what we used to call at Oxford) 'ethos'. That is the same moral and intellectual state of mind. To bring them to this, is 'levelling up' When you tell me that Mother Margaret's Life lays hold of hearts, moves other religionists without converting them, we must be thankful to do as much as that! If it manages to make 'men of good will' it is good three quarters of the way to bring 'peace on earth, and glory in the highest.' We cannot begin from the top, we must begin with the foundations. Pray for my book.

To BISHOP ULLATHORNE

Thoughts on the First Vatican Council, just beginning

The Oratory. Jany 28. 1870

My dear Lord

I thank your Lordshop very heartily for your most interesting and seasonable letter. Such letters, if they could be circu-
lated, would do much to re-assure the many minds which are
at present distressed when they look towards Rome. Rome
ought to be a name to lighten the heart at all times, and a
Council's proper office is, when some great heresy or other
evil impends, to inspire the faithful with hope and confidence;
but now we have the greatest meeting which ever has been,
and that at Rome, infusing into us by the accredited organs of
Rome and its partizans (such as the Civiltà, the Armonia, the
Univers, and the Tablet,) little else than fear and dismay.

When we are all at rest, and have no doubts, and at least
practically, not to say doctrinally, hold the Holy Father to be
infallible, suddenly there is thunder in the clear sky, and we are
told to prepare for something we know not what to try our
faith we know not how. No impending danger is to be
averted, but a great difficulty is to be created. Is this the proper
work for an Ecumenical Council? As to myself personally,
please God, I do not expect any trial at all; but I cannot help
suffering with the various souls which are suffering, and I look
with anxiety at the prospect of having to defend decisions,
which may be not difficult to my private judgement, but may
be most difficult to maintain logically in the face of historical
facts. What have we done to be treated, as the faithful never
were treated before? When has definition of doctrine de fide
been a luxury of devotion, and not a stern painful necessity?
Why should an aggressive insolent faction be allowed to 'make
the heart of the just to mourn, whom the Lord hath not made
sorrowful?' Why can't we be let alone, when we have pursued
peace, and thought no evil? I assure you, my dear Lord, some
of the truest minds are driven one way and another, and do not

know where to rest their feet; one day determining to give up all theology as a bad job, and recklessly to believe henceforth almost that the Pope is impeccable; at another tempted to believe all the worst which a book like Janus says,[1] others doubting about the capacity possessed by Bishops, drawn from all corners of the earth, to judge what is fitting for European society, and then again angry with the Holy See for listening to the flattery of a clique of Jesuits, Redemptorists, and converts.

Then again, think of the store of Pontifical scandals in the history of 18 centuries, which have partly been poured out, and partly are still to come. What Murphy inflicted upon us in one way, M. Veuillot indirectly is bringing on us in another.[2]

And then again, the blight which is falling upon the multitude of Anglican ritualists etc who themselves perhaps, at least their leaders, may never become Catholics, but who are leaving the various English denominations and parties (far beyond their own range) with principles and sentiments tending toward their ultimate absorption in the Catholic Church.

With these thoughts before me, I am continually asking myself whether I ought not to make my feelings public; but all I do is to pray those great early Doctors of the Church, whose intercession would decide the matter, Augustine and the rest, to avert so great a calamity. If it is God's will that the Pope's infallibility should be defined, then it is His blessed Will to throw back 'the times and the moments'[3] of that triumph which He has destined for His Kingdom; and I shall feel I have but to bow my head to His adorable, inscrutable Providence. You have not touched upon the subject yourself, but I think you will allow me to express to you feelings, which for the most part I keep to myself.

As to my book I have attempted it three or four times in the last 20 years, and could not get on. And I have in consequence felt that till it was actually *ended*, it really was not *begun*; I have had no confidence that I should be able to complete it. I have done so—but now that it is done, I think it will disappoint most people. It is not written against writers of the day, Mr Huxley or Professor Tindall, or Sir C. Lyell, or any one else. It is on a dry logical subject, or semi-logical, Assent. Of course, unless I thought the book had its use, I should not have made so many attempts to write it—but I am no judge of its worth.

Pray convey my best respects to the Bishop of Plymouth, and ask his blessing for us. I know well how much I owe to the kindness and sympathy of the American Bishops, and hope they are aware of the gratitude I feel towards them in consequence.

Thank you for what you say about St Girolamo and the Chiesa Nuova.[4]

Begging your Lordship's blessing, I am Yr obedient & affte Servt in Xt

John H Newman[5]

124

To REGINALD BUCKLER, O. P.

Further comment on the 'aggressive faction' in the Church

The Oratory Good Friday 15 April 1870

My dear Fr Buckler

Accept all the prayers and good wishes from me which are suggested by this most sacred time, and my congratulations in anticipation of Easter.

Thank you for your letter. You are quite right in supposing that my letter to Bp Ullathorne was most confidential, and that I had no hand whatever in its getting into circulation.

It was one of the most confidential letters that I ever wrote in my life. And I wrote it as an absolute duty.

I have no claim as a theologian—but I have a claim to speak as one who is now near 70 years old, and has experience of various kinds in ecclesiastical matters. My rule is to act according to my best light as if I was infallible before the Church decides; but to accept and submit to God's Infallibility, when the Church has spoken. The Church has not yet spoken, and till she has, not only is my freedom of thought in possession, and I may fairly consider myself right in what I think, and I have a very strong view of the present question. I think the movement party is going too fast. I recollect the text, Quisquis scandalizaverit *unum ex his pusillis* credentibus in me, bonum est ei magis si circumdaretur mola asinaria collo ejus, et in mare mitteretur.[1] I wish the Civiltà, the Univers, and other like publications would think of it. How differently things went in the case of the Immaculate Conception! Step after step was taken *towards* it. The Church patiently waited till all was ripe—No Council was necessary—the theological opinion grew into a dogma, as it were, spontaneously. But now it is as if certain parties wished to steal a march upon Catholics. Nothing is above board—nothing is told to the bishops generally before hand—the gravest innovation possible, (for it is a change in the hitherto recognized basis of the Church,) is to be carried by acclamation. —Deliberation is to have no part in the work. Open any theological book, and see what a different view is there presented to us. Turn to the first Council, in Acts xv, and there you find that before the settlement there was a 'magna conquisitio.' Slowness in decision, tenderness for weaker brethren, are first principles in the exercise of Ecclesiastical authority. Of course I should not have written so abrupt a letter to my Bishop except confidentially—but if you saw a railway train at full speed bowling over some unhappy workmen on the line, what could you do but cry out and gesticulate?

Very sincerely Yrs John H Newman

125

To AUBREY DE VERE

A reply to praise of the 'Grammar of Assent'

The Oratory Aug. 31 1870

My dear Aubrey de Vere,

It is a great pleasure to hear your commendations of two publications of mine—As to my Essay on Assent it is on a subject which has teazed me for this 20 or 30 years. I felt I had something to say upon it, yet, whenever I attempted, the sight I saw vanished, plunged into a thicket, curled itself up like a hedgehog, or changed colours like a chameleon. I have a succession of commencements, perhaps a dozen, each different from the other, and in a different year, which came to nothing. At last four years ago, when I was up at Glion over the Lake of Geneva, a thought came into my head as the clue, the 'Open Sesame', of the whole subject, and I at once wrote it down, and I pursued it about the Lake of Lucerne. Then when I came home, I began in earnest, and have slowly got through it.

Now you must not think, in consequence of my thus speaking, that I am sure myself that I have done any great thing—for I have felt very little confidence in it—though words like yours, and you are not the only person who have used such, are a very great encouragement to me—but I could not help feeling that I had something to give out, whatever its worth, and I felt haunted with a sort of responsibility, and almost a weight on my conscience, if I did not speak of it, and yet I could not. So that it is the greatest possible relief, at length to have got it off my mind—as if I heard the words 'he has done what he could' and, while I say this, I really am not taking for granted that your favourable criticism is the true one—and I recollect that what a man thinks his best work is often his worst, but then I think too that sometimes a man's failures do more good to the world or to his cause than his best successes—and thus I feel as if I could die happier, now that I have no Essay on Assent to write, and I think I shall never write another work, meaning by work a something which is an anxiety and a labour, 'Man goeth forth to his work and to his labours until the evening—' and my evening is surely come—though not my night.

Ever Yrs affly John H Newman

To MRS WILSON

To a lady who was troubled by the new definition of Papal infallibility

The Oratory, Oct 20. 1870

Private

My dear Mrs Wilson

It is a very difficult matter so to answer your sad letter as to be real use to you—and, unless I can so write, what is the use of writing at all?

I think there are some Bishops and Priests, who act as if they did not care at all whether souls were lost or not—and only wish to save souls on their own measure. If you directly asked your Confessor, whether you were obliged to receive the Pope's Infallibility, you acted imprudently—if he asked you, he was not only imprudent but cruel.

The rule in confession is, that when Priests differ in opinion, you may choose, which you will. If I were you, I should go to a Priest, who would not make it a point to bring up this question—though I fear there are few such in London.

Such unhappy times the Church has known before; nay far worse, for there have been two or three Popes at once, and the holiest men took opposite sides. It was so in the early Church too, when divisions lasted for 20 or 30 years. We are not in so bad a case.

For myself, I have at various times in print professed to hold the Pope's Infallibility; your difficulty is not mine—but still I deeply lament the violence which has been used in this matter.

However, there is a deeper question behind. When you became a Catholic, you ought to have understood that the voice of the Church is the voice of God. The Church defines nothing that was not given to the Apostles in the beginning, but that sacred deposit cannot be fully brought forward and dispensed except in the course of ages. It is not any argument against the Pope's Infallibility, that it was not defined as a truth till the 19th century.

Don't set yourself against the doctrine. Very little was passed, much less than its advocates wished—they are disappointed. Nothing is defined as to *what acts* ·are ex cathedra, nor to what things infallibility extends. Some people think the decree lessens the Pope's *actual* power.

Very truly Yrs John H Newman

127

To EMILY BOWLES

Should Catholics be educated at Oxford?

The Oratory April 30. 1871

My dear Child....

As to Catholic boys, the great evil is the want of a career—when they get to the top form, they fall back and are idle, as having nothing to look out for. They need a University. This is no fault of Catholicism—but, as far as I know of one man. Cardinal Wiseman was in favour of Oxford—till some one turned him round his finger,[1] and then he brought out a set of questions addressed to Catholic gentlemen, one of which was 'Do you wish your sons better educated than your priests?' as a *reason* against their going to Oxford. This was one chief reason, why it was decided that Catholic youths might not have a career. There are those who wish Catholic women, not nuns, to have no higher pursuit than that of dress, and Catholic youths to be shielded from no sin so carefully as from intellectual curiosity. All this is the consequence of Luther, and the separation off of the Teutonic races—and of the imperiousness of the Latin. But the Latin race will not .always have a monopoly of the magisterium of Catholicism. We must be patient in our time; but God will take care of His Church—and, when the hour strikes, the reform will begin—Perhaps it *has* struck, though we can't yet tell.

Ever Yours affectly John H Newman

To JAMES HOPE-SCOTT

On receiving a copy of an abridged version of the Life of Sir Walter Scott by J. G. Lockhart

The Oratory May 14. 1871

My dear Hope-Scott

Thank you for your book. In one sense I deserve it I have ever had such a devotion, I may call it, to Walter Scott. As a boy, in the early summer mornings, I read Waverley and Guy Mannering in bed, when they first came out, before it was time to get up; and long before that, when I was eight years old, I listened eagerly to the Lay of the Last Minstrel and to Marmion, which my Mother and Aunt were reading aloud. When he was dying, I was continually thinking of him, with Keble's words 'If ever floating from faint earthly lyre, etc' 6th after Trin.[1]

It has been a trouble to me that his works seemed to be so forgotten now. Our boys know very little about them. I think Fr Ambrose had to give a prize for getting up Kenilworth. Your letter to Gladstone sadly confirms it.[2] I wonder whether there will ever be a crisis and correction of the evil. It arises from the facilities of publication. Every season bears its own crop of books—and every fresh season ousts the foregoing. Books are all annuals; and to revive Scott, you must annihilate the existing generation of writers, which is legion. If it so fares with Scott, still more does it so fare with Johnson, Addison, Pope, and Shakespeare. Perhaps the competitive examinations may come to the aid. You should get Gladstone to bring about a list of classics, and force them upon candidates. I do not see any other way of mending matters. I wish I heard a better account of you.

Ever Yrs affly John H Newman

To MATTHEW ARNOLD

The Catholic Church and Democracy

The Oratory Decr. 3. 1871

My dear Mr Arnold,

Your letter, as those which you have written to me before now, is an extremely kind one. I am much pleased to have it—and I thank you sincerely for it—and with quite as intimate an interest have I read what you have lately written and also what you now send me.

The more so, as regards your letters as well as your writings, for the very reason that I am so sensitively alive to the great differences of opinion which separate us. I wish with all my heart I could make them less; but there they are, and I can only resign myself to them, as best I may.

It would have given me the greatest pleasure to have seen you, when you were here, had your time allowed of it. I had not heard of your coming.

Thank you for noticing the lines in the Spectator.

As to your questions, I agree with what you say about the Anglican and Catholic Churches relatively to democratic ideas. It was one of Hurrell Froude's main views that the church must alter her position in the political world—and, when he heard of la Mennais,[1] he took up his views with great eagerness. I have said the same in the beginning of the Church of the Fathers—'I shall offend many men when I say, we must look to the people' etc etc. I said this apropos of St Ambrose, and based my view upon the Fathers. Froude had seized upon it from the intuitive apprehension he had of what was coming, and what was fitting. We both hated the notion of rebellion—and thought that the Church must bide her time. This idea is expressed several times in the Lyra Apostolica. It often happens that those who will not bide their time, fail, not because they are not substantially right, but because they are thus impatient. I used to say that Montanus, Tertullian, Novatian, etc were instances in point, their ideas were eventually carried out—

Perhaps La Mennais will be a true prophet after all. It is curious to see the minute tokens which are showing themselves of the drawings of the Papal policy just now in the direction of the democracy. Of course the present Papacy is (humanly speaking) quite unequal to such a line of action—but it was the policy of Gregory vii—and, though we may have a season of depression, as there was a hideous degradation before Gregory, yet it may be in the counsels of Providence that the Catholic Church may at length come out unexpectedly as a popular power. Of course the existence of the Communists makes the state of things now vastly different from what it was in the middle ages.

My impression about Butler is with yours—but I cannot refer to any distinct passage.

Most truly Yours John H Newman

130

To LORD HOWARD OF GLOSSOP

Should there be a Catholic College at Oxford?

The Oratory April 27 1872

My dear Lord Howard,

. . . . .We are driven into a corner just now, and have to act, when no mode of action is even bearable. It is a choice of great difficulties. On the whole I do not know how to avoid the conclusion that mixed education in the higher schools is as much a necessity now in England, as it was in the East in the days of St Basil and St Chrysostom. Certainly, the more I think of it, the less am I satisfied with the proposal of establishing a Catholic College in our Universities; and I suppose the idea of a Catholic University, pure and simple, is altogether out of the question.

I think the Bishops ought to repeal their act of March 23, 1865, by which they virtually prohibited young Catholics from going to the existing Colleges. Some management of course would be required in relaxing the prohibition, so as not to seem to give a direct sanction to what can only be tolerated as the least of evils, but acts of management come easy to the Archbishop.

To meet the perils of this bold measure I would place a very strong Mission at Oxford. This is what our Bishop intended eight years ago, when he did me the great honour of entrusting the Mission to me. The Jesuits have now resumed it; could it be in better hands? They should have three or four of their best men there; they should have a handsome Church and imposing functions, good sermons, and unobtrusive gatherings and meetings in their Mission House. There should be nothing aggressive or polemical in their conduct; nothing loud; nothing like a Propaganda; but there should be a strong religious community, which would act as a support and rallying-point for young Catholics in their dangerous position, commanding their respect intellectually, and winning their confidence, and providing quiet opportunities for their being kept straight both in faith and in conduct.

As to a Catholic College, I think it would be a failure.

1. The names of the existing Colleges are historic, and carry with them a prestige. Who would not like to belong to Trinity or St John's? to Christ Church, Oriel, or Balliol? Youths like an old college, as they like an old University. You don't meet the existing difficulty by setting up a new College. If they at present go to Keble College, which is new, think what a name 'Keble' is to whole classes in the Anglican Church. Nor do I say that no youths will go to a new Catholic College, but that some will not. You will not have succeeded in clearing them all out from the Protestant Colleges; and your own College, after spending on it (say) £30,000, will be half-empty. The Holy See indeed might make entrance at a Protestant College a reserved case; but it would not make it a reserved case not to go to a Catholic College. You would not thus fill your rooms. There are parents who would not send their sons to Oxford at all, unless they could send them to an old College.

2. Would you forbid your youths to stand for a scholarship at Trinity, or a fellowship at Oriel? If not, how are you putting them on an equality with Protestant youths? if you do, what has become of your exclusive Catholic College?

3. Next a Catholic College is a new patch on an old garment.

The existing (Protestant) College discipline is in possession, and you are not answerable for it. It may be lax, but it works. There it is; but if you set up a new code of rules, such as a Catholic would prefer, will it work? You will come into collision with the custom of the place, and provoke comparison and rebellion.

4. Such stricter discipline, if it worked, would be a gain but I feel more and more that you would be obliged to take what you found in use. Your discipline would find the level of the discipline of the place. And besides, if it were ever so severe, it would not really counteract the temptations to unbelief and sin, against which it is directed. The true and only antagonist of the world, the flesh, and the devil is the direct power of religion, as acting in the Confessional, in confraternities, in social circles, in personal influence, in private intimacies etc etc. And all this would be secured by a strong mission worked zealously and prudently, and in no other way.

5. In a large University there are good sets and bad sets; and a youth has an opportunity of choosing between them. In a small, exclusive body there is no choice; and one bad member ruins for a time the whole community. Thus the open University, when complemented by a strong Mission, may be even safer than a close Catholic College.

6. If you set up a College, you make a great profession, whereas a Catholic Mission is a matter of course in a large town like Oxford, and already exists, and has been for many years. For a College you must make a great outlay; you create great expectations. Then, when things go badly, when your youths act amiss, or fail in the Schools, and you certainly would have these trials, where are you?

7. Then again a Catholic College with its Tutors etc professes intellectual Catholicity on the face of it, as a Mission does not. It is a direct challenge to Protestants. On the other hand it is at this very time prophesied at Oxford, that the principles of Catholics necessarily hinder them from following out the higher exercises of reason. Now we have lately had an ecumenical Council. Councils have generally acted as a lever, displacing and disordering portions of the existing theological system. Not seldom have they be[en] followed by bitter quarrels in the Catholic body. Time is necessary to put things to rights. When

Trent was the last Council, we enjoyed the stability and edification of three hundred years. A series of the ablest divines had examined, interpreted, adjusted, located, illustrated every sentence of the definitions. We were all of us on sure ground, and could speak with confidence, after Suarez, Lambertini, and a host of others. Now, as regards the force, limits, and consequents of the recent definitions, we have as yet nothing better to guide us, from the necessity of the case, than the Dublin Review and the Civiltà Cattolica. We have yet to learn what is precisely meant by 'inspiration', as applied to a book, and in what cases and under what conditions the Pope is infallible. Not to say that the Council is not yet finished. We could not have a more unfavourable time for getting into controversy.

These are some of the reasons which make me hesitate to recommend just now the establishment of a Catholic College in our Universities

JHN

131

To THE EDITOR OF *THE TIMES*

'No Pope can make evil good'

Sept. 9 1872

(For publication)

Sir

You have lately, in your article on the Massacre of St Bartholomew's day, thrown down a challenge to us on a most serious subject. I have no claim to speak for my brethren; but I speak in default of better men.

No Pope can make evil good. No Pope has any power over those eternal moral principles which God has imprinted on our hearts and consciences. If any Pope has, with his eyes open, approved of treachery or cruelty, let those defend that Pope, who can. If any Pope at any time has had his mind so occupied with the desirableness of the Church's triumph over her enemies, as to be dead to the treacherous and savage acts by which that triumph was achieved, let those who feel disposed say that in such conduct he acted up to his high office of maintaining justice and showing mercy. Craft and cruelty and whatever is base and wicked have a sure nemesis, and eventually strike the heads of those who are guilty of them.

Whether, in matter of fact, Pope Gregory xiii had a share in the guilt of the St Bartholomew massacre, must be proved to me, before I believe it. It is commonly said in his defence, that he had an untrue, one-sided account of the matter presented to him, and acted on misinformation. This involves a question of fact, which historians must decide. But, even if they decide against the Pope, his infallibility is in no respect compromised. Infallibility is not impeccability. Even Caiphas prophesied; and Gregory xiii was not quite Caiphas.

I am, Sir, Your obedient Servant, John H Newman

132

To R. W. CHURCH

It was reported that a 'threadbare looking individual' had been moved on in St Paul's Cathedral—and that it was Newman

December 22/72

My dear Dean,

On the contrary it was simply a bran new coat, which I never put on till I went on that visit to you—and which I did not wear twice even at Abbotsford—I thought it due to London. Indeed, all my visiting clothes are new, for I do not wear them here, and I am almost tempted, like a footman of my Father's when I was a boy, who had a legacy of clothes, to leave home, as he his place, in order to have the opportunity of wearing them. *They* (the clothes) must wish it, I am sure—for they wear out a weary time themselves in a dark closet except on such occasions, few and far between.

Don't fancy when I talked of a 'bore', that I had any other than that *general* feeling, which I ever had, that giving away one of my books is an impertinence, like talking of the shop. I used to say at Oxford that lawyers and doctors ever talked of the shop—but parsons never—now I find priests do—I suppose that, where there is *science*, there is the tendency to be wrapped up in the profession. An English clergyman is primarily a gentleman—a doctor, a lawyer, and so a priest is primarily a professional man. In like manner the military calling has been abroad a profession, accordingly they never go in mufti; but always in full military fig, talking as it were, *always* of the shop. Now I have a great dislike of this shopping personally. Richmond told someone that, when he took my portrait, I was the only person he could not draw out.

Now have I not really been talking of the shop enough for a whole twelve months, having talked of my dear self? But you see I have a motive—viz. lest you should dream you have trod on my toes, and so elicited from me the complaint that you have been 'bored' by me

Ever Yrs affly John H Newman

133

To R. W. CHURCH

A further comment on the episode in St Paul's

St Stephen's day 1872

My dear Dean, .

I hope to send you the book this evening. Perhaps I shall be obliged to delay.

Yes, I was morally turned out and I told you at the time, I did nothing but what you might have done at Chester or Carlisle, where you might not be known. I stood just inside the door listening to the chanting of the Psalms, of which I am so fond. First came Verger one, a respectful person, inquiring if I wanted a seat in the choir, half a mile off me. No I said—I was content where I was. Then came a second, not respectful, with a voice of menace—I still said No. Then came a third, I don't recollect much about him, except that he said he could provide me with a seat. Then came Number 2 again, in a compulsory mood, on which I vanished.

I am sure if I was a dissenter, or again one of Mr Bradlaugh's people, nothing would attract me more to the Church of England than to be allowed to stand at the door of a Cathedral—did not St Augustine while yet a Manichee, stand and watch St Ambrose? No verger turned him out.

Of course, knowing the nature of those men, I was amused, and told you and Blachford in the evening. You were annoyed, and said it was just what you did *not* wish, and that you would inquire about it.

I have not a dream how it got into the Papers—as mine is a Somersetshire one, I thought the paragraph had trickled out from Whatley.

Ever Yrs affly JHN

All Christmas blessings to you and yours.

134

To RICHARD HOLT HUTTON

An ecumenical letter at Christmas

The Oratory Decr 29. 1872

My dear Mr Hutton

I have nothing to write to you about, but I am led at this season to send you the religious greetings and good wishes which it suggests, to assure you that, though I seem to be careless about those who desire to have more light than they have in regard to religious truths, yet I do really sympathise with them very much, and ever have them in mind.

I know how honestly you try to approve yourself to God—and this is a claim on the reverence of any one who knows or reads you. There are many things as to which I most seriously differ from you but I believe you to be one of those to whom the angels on Christmas night sent greeting as 'hominibus bonae voluntatis' and it is a pleasure and a duty for all who could be their companions hereafter to follow their pattern of comprehensive charity here. I cannot feel so hopefully and tenderly to many of those whom you defend or patronize as I do to you—and what you write perplexes me often—but when a man is really and truly seeking the Pearl of great price, how can one help joining oneself in heart and spirit with him?

Most truly Yrs John H Newman

135

To MISS MUNRO

Submitting to God's will

The Oratory, Oct 21. 1873

My dear Miss Munro

It is very kind in you to write to me. I always hear about you with the greatest interest and anxiety. I know with what a true heart you desire to serve God—and that what you call your restlessness is only the consequence of that religious desire.

Be sure that many others besides you feel that sadness, that years pass away and no opening comes to them for serving God. Be sure that I can sympathise with you, for now for many years I have made attempts to break through the obstacles which have been in my way, but all in vain.

One must submit oneself to God's loving will—and be quieted by faith that what He wills for us is best. He has no need of us—He only asks for our good desires.

Ever yours affectionately, John H Newman

136

To CHARLES RUSSELL

On his correspondent's praise of 'A Letter to the Duke of Norfolk'

The Oratory Jany 19. 1875

My dear Dr Russell,

It is a great kindness in you to write to me, for you may easily suppose I am like a man who has gone up in a balloon, and has a chance of all sorts of adventures, from gas escapes, from currents of air, from intanglements in forests, from the wide sea, and does not feel himself safe till he gets back to his fireside. At present as I am descending, I am in the most critical point of my expedition. All I can say is that I have acted for the best, and have done my best, and must now leave the success of it to a higher power. Under these circumstances of course your letter is a great encouragement to me. Thanking you again, I am your affectionate friend.

John H Newman

137

To SIR WILLIAM HENRY COPE

The correspondent had sent Charles Kingsley's funeral sermon

The Oratory Febr. 13. 1875

My dear Sir William

I thank you very much for the gift of your sermon. The death of Mr Kingsley, so premature, shocked me. I never from the first have felt any anger towards him. As I said in the first pages of my Apologia, it is very difficult to be angry with a man one has never seen. A casual reader would think my language denoted anger—but it did not. I have ever felt from experience that no one would believe me in earnest if I spoke calmly, when again and again I denied the repeated report that I was on the point of coming back to the Church of England. I have uniformly found that, if I simply denied it, this only made newspapers repeat the report more confidently—but, if I said something sharp, they abused me for scurrility against the Church I had left, but they believed me. Rightly or wrongly, this was the reason why I felt it would not do to be tame, and not to show indignation at Mr Kingsley's charges—Within the last few years I have been obliged to adopt a similar course towards those who said I could not receive the Vatican Decrees. I sent a sharp letter to the Guardian and of course the Guardian called me names, but it believed me—and did not allow the offence of its correspondent to be repeated.

As to Mr Kingsley, much less could I feel any resentment against him when he was accidentally the instrument in the good Providence of God, by whom I had an opportunity given me, which otherwise I should not have had of vindicating my character and conduct in my Apologia. I heard too a few years back from a friend that she chanced to go into Chester Cathedral, and found Mr K. preaching about me kindly though of course with criticisms of me. And it has rejoiced me to observe lately that he was defending the Athanasian Creed, and, as it seemed to me, in his views generally nearing the Catholic view of things—I have always hoped that by good luck I might meet him, feeling sure there would be no embarrassment on my part, and I said Mass for his soul, as soon as I heard of his death.

Most truly Yours John H Newman

138

To MISS M. R. GIBERNE

On the death of Ambrose St John

The Oratory Jun. 4.1875

My dear Sister M. Pia

Great as our trial is, yours in some respects is greater. You indeed have not lost as we have a face and a voice always present—but then you have no partner nor confidant in your sorrow, and have no relief as having no outlet of it. This feeling of solitariness must be very oppressive—especially the very fact of *one* English friend being taken away, seems almost a commencement of the operation of that awful law which sooner or later must take us *all* away from this visible scene.

William is rather afraid you must be ill by your not writing—but I do not see that that is a sufficient reason for his thinking so. But any how write, if you have stamps.

This has come upon us as a great shock, but think how much worse it would have been, had he been subjected to a chronic derangement. As it was, his reason had returned enough, though he could not speak, for him to think, and he knew he was going, though we did not know it.

What a faithful friend he has been to me for 32 years! yet there are others as faithful. What a wonderful mercy it is to me that God has given me so many faithful friends! He has never left me without support at trying times. How much you did for me in the Achilli trial (and at other times), and I have never thanked you, as I ought to have done. This sometimes oppresses me, as if I was very ungrateful. You truly say that you have seen my beginning, middle, and end. Since his death, I have been reproaching myself for not expressing to *him* how much I felt *his* love—and I write this lest I should feel the same about you, should it be God's will that I shall outlive you. I have above mentioned the Achilli matter, but that is only one specimen of the devotion, which by word and deed and prayer, you have been continually showing towards me most unworthy. I hope I don't write too small for your eyes.

Ever Yrs affly John H Newman

139

To HELEN CHURCH

Dean Church's daughter had sent Newman 'The Hunting of the Snark'

The Oratory April 19. 1876

My dear Helen,

Let me thank you and your Sisters without delay, for the amusing specimen of imaginative nonsense which came to me from you and them this morning. Also, as being your gift, it shows that you have not forgotten me, though a considerable portion of your lives has past since you saw me. And, in thanking you, I send you also my warmest Easter greetings and good wishes.

The little book is not all of it nonsense; it has two pleasant prefixes of another sort. One of them is the 'Inscription to a dear child'; the style of which, in words and manner, is so entirely of the School of Keble, that it could not have been written had the Christian Year never made its appearance.

The other, 'the Easter greeting to every child etc' is likely to touch the hearts of old men more than of those for whom it is intended. I recollect well my own thoughts and feelings, such as the author describes, as I lay in my crib in the early spring, with outdoor scents, sounds and sights wakening me up, and especially the cheerful ring of the mower's scythe on the lawn, which Milton long before me had noted;—and how in coming down stairs slowly, for I brought down both feet on each step, I said to myself 'This is June!' though what my particular experience of June was, and how it was broad enough to be a matter of reflection, I really cannot tell.

Can't you, Mary, and Edith recollect something of the same kind? though you may not think so much of it as I do now?

May the day come for all of us, of which Easter is the promise, when that first spring, may return to us, and a sweetness which cannot die may gladden our garden

Ever Yrs affectionately John H Newman

140

To LORD BLACHFORD

Plans for a portrait to be painted by Ouless

The Oratory March 10, 1877

My dear Blachford

I want you and Church to answer me a question. I am pressed to sit for an oil painting. I dislike it extremely and wish to get off—but, being pressed, I have said I would go by the judgement of friends—of course I should not mention your names.

What makes me so averse to it is the very reason why I am pressed to it. On account of the vile thing put into the Exhibition several years ago.

The case was this. Mr Boyle, now of Kidderminster, brother to Patrick Boyle whom you may recollect at Oriel, pressed me years ago, in the name of Birmingham parties, to let me be taken. I resisted it for three years—till at last it seemed so ungracious in me, that, after various refusals, I consented. My alleged (and a true) reason for declining was that I had done nothing for Birmingham, and had no claim for such a distinction, my personal reason was that I had no wish at all to be put in a collection together with a set of liberal party men or town celebrities with whom I had nothing in common.

At last I consented and a painter was sent to me who came with a theory, intending it most kindly, which he gave in his defence, when my friends here cried out quite in grief, at his performance. He then said he meant to represent me as lamenting my Oxford position, circle etc etc.

Well, I suppose his employers did not like it either, for he could not get paid for it. A few weeks ago it was in a pawnbroker's shop—and lately has been bought as a speculation 'to be shown in the principal towns'.

I am now pressed by Mr Powell (of the firm of Hardman and Company) a Catholic, to let Mr W O[uless] A.R.A. paint me. He wants to do it for nothing and give us here, the picture which probably we shall neither like nor have room for. And here again I shall act ungraciously if I refuse—and I write to you, not necessarily to decide for me, but because I cannot refuse unless I am backed up, and must to my great disgust give in.

Yours affly John H Newman

141

To BISHOP ULLATHORNE

Trinity College makes Newman an Honorary Fellow

The Oratory Decr 18. 1877

My dear Lord,

I have just received a very great compliment, perhaps the greatest I ever received and I don't like not to tell you of it one of the first.

My old College, Trinity College, where I was an undergraduate from the age of 16 to 21, till I gained a Fellowship at Oriel, has made me an honorary Fellow of their Society. Of course it involves no duties, rights, nor conditions, not even that of belonging to the University, certainly not that of having a vote as Master of Arts, but it is a mark of extreme kindness to me from men I have never seen, and it is the only instance of their exercising their power once it was given to them.

Trinity College has been the one and only seat of my affections at Oxford, and to see once more, before I am taken away, what I never thought I should see again, the place where I began the battle of life, with my good angel by my side, is a prospect almost too much for me to bear.

I have been considering for these two days since the offer came, whether there would be any inconsistency in my accepting it, but it is so pure a compliment in its very title, that I do not see that I need fear its being interpreted as anything else.

Begging your Lordships blessing. I am,

Your obt and affectte servant in Xt
John H Newman

P.S. The Pope made me a D.D. but I don't call an act of the Pope's a '*compliment*'

142

To W. J. COPELAND

The Oratory Decr 20 1877

My dearest Copeland

All Christmas best wishes to you, and Pax hominibus bonae voluntatis.[1]

The grand Turkey has come safely.

The Trinity men have made me an 'Honorary Fellow' of their Society. *There's* news!

Of course you received my Proposed Scheme of Sermons some ten days ago. No hurry.

Ever Yours affly John H Newman

To MISS M. R. GIBERNE

She had asked Newman to describe his visit to Oxford

The Oratory In Fest. S. Joseph [19 March] 1878

My dear Sister M. Pia

Your letter just received made me both sigh and smile. I can only say with the 'Needy knife grinder',[1] 'Story, heaven bless you, I have none to tell you—' I assure you I made no record of my feelings when I went to Oxford, and recollect nothing. I know it was a trial to me and a pleasure—but I could not say more, if you put me on the rack. And, when you talk of my writing, you must recollect that it is trouble to me to write now, a trouble both to head and hand—and, there are so many letters which I am obliged to write, that, unless necessary, I shirk it.

Now I might sit for an hour till I had bitten the top of my penholder off, without being able to put down on paper my 'impressions, pains and joys, and reception'. If, 'like St John Chrysostom,' I was called to suffer, perhaps I might have something to say about my visit; but an Oriental is not a silent Englishmen, nor a Saint any earnest or token of what a hum-drum mortal is in the reign of Queen Victoria.

I can but tell you that the Trinity Fellows seem to be a pleas-ing set of men and very kind to me, but I suppose they are very far from the Church—that the Keble College people were very friendly and showed me over the magnificent buildings which they have erected, and that Pusey, whom I have not seen since 1865 looks much older. I had no time to go to Little-more—or indeed to do any thing beyond calling on Pusey, at Oriel, and at Keble College.

Ever Yrs affly JHN

I don't forget what I owe to your prayers

To ROBERT WHITTY, S.J.

Reports were in the newspapers that Newman was to be made a Cardinal

March 24. 1878

To Dr Whitty

Perhaps you have seen in the Papers a wild article about me in relation to the Holy Father. I have reason to believe it was not Roman news but composed in London; and that in consequence of the action of some very kind friends and well-wishers of mine, persons known or unknown to me. But I trust nothing will come of it, I am far from making light of dignities, but under the example and shadow of St Philip, I may be allowed to decline them. They are much to be prized, both when they open on a man opportunities and channels of serving God, and again when they are a means of sanctioning and rewarding his past attempts at service. Now I am too old to do any thing new, and wish only to have time to set my house in order before I go; so that honours would not be in my case any means of usefulness. And as their being a sanction of my past attempts, it would be a more simple, easy, and to me acceptable act on the part of superiors, if I was fortunate enough to deserve and obtain a few lines such as I believe have been vouchsafed to the Universe newspaper and the Dublin Review, to the effect that my writing had done service to the Catholic cause.

JHN

145

To BISHOP ULLATHORNE

How would Newman react to being offered a Cardinal's hat?

Birmingham, 2 February, Feast of the Purification
B.V.M. 1879

To the Right Reverend Lord, William Bernard,
Bishop of Birmingham.

My Right Reverend Father,

I trust that his Holiness and the most eminent Cardinal Nina will not think me a thoroughly discourteous and unfeeling man, who is not touched by the commendation of Superiors, or a sense of gratitude or the splendour of dignity, when I say to you, my Bishop, who know me so well, that I regard as altogether above me the great honour which the Holy Father proposes with wonderful kindness to confer on one so insignificant, an honour quite transcendent and unparalleled, than which his Holiness has none greater to bestow.

For I am, indeed, old and distrustful of myself; I have lived now thirty years 'in my little nest' in my much loved Oratory, sheltered and happy, and would therefore entreat his Holiness not to take me from St Philip, my Father and Patron.

By the love and reverence with which a long succession of Popes have regarded and trusted my St Philip, I pray and entreat his Holiness in compassion of my diffidence of mind, in consideration of my feeble health, my nearly eighty years, the retired course of my life from my youth, my ignorance of foreign languages, and my lack of experience in business, to let me die where I have so long lived. Since I know now and henceforth that his Holiness thinks kindly of me, what more can I desire?

Right Reverend Father, your most devoted
John H Newman[1]

146

To THE DUKE OF NORFOLK

The papers were saying that Newman had refused the Hat

The Oratory Febr. 20 1879

My dear Duke,

I have heard from various quarters of the affectionate interest you have taken in the application to Rome about me, and I write to thank you and to express my great pleasure in it.

As to the statement of my refusing a Cardinal's hat, which is in the papers, you must not believe it, for this reason.

Of course it implies that an offer has been made me, and I have sent my answer to it. Now I have ever understood that it is a point of priority and honour to consider such communications *sacred*. The statement therefore cannot come from me. Nor could it come from Rome, for it was made public before my answer got to Rome—It could only come then from some one who, not only read my letter, but instead of leaving the Pope to interpret it, took upon himself to put an interpretation upon it, and published that interpretation to the world. A private letter, addressed to Roman authorities, is *intercepted* on its way and *published* in the English Papers. How is it possible that any one can have done this?

And besides, I am quite sure that, if so high an honour was offered me, I should not answer it by a blunt refusal.

Yours affectly John H Newman

To R.W. CHURCH

News of 'official notice of my promotion'

The Oratory March 11. 1879

Private

My dear Church

I did not like to write to you till I had something like official notice of my promotion. This comes within this half hour. Yet not so much official as personal, being a most gracious message from the Pope to me.

He allows me to reside in this Oratory, the precedent for the indulgence being Cardinal de Berulle, Founder of the French Oratory in the 17th Century.

Haec mutatio dexterae Excelsi![1] all the stories which have gone about of my being a half Catholic, a liberal Catholic, under a cloud, not to be trusted, are now at an end. Poor Ward can no longer call me a heretic, and say (to H Wilberforce) he 'would rather a man should not be converted than be converted by me—' and another writer give it as a reason why I was not allowed to go to Oxford.

It was on this account that I dared not refuse the offer. A good Providence gave me an opportunity of clearing myself of former calumnies in my Apologia—and I dared not refuse it— And now He gave me a means, without any labour of mine, to set myself right as regards other calumnies which were directed against me—how could I neglect so great a loving kindness?

I have ever tried to leave my cause in the Hands of God and to be patient—and He has not forgotten me

Ever Yours affly John H Newman

To THE DUKE OF NORFOLK

The Duke had intervened in the matter of the Cardinalate

The Oratory March 12. 1879

My dear Duke

I have said all my life, and I repeat to myself now 'Never had a man such good friends'. Thanks for the letter.

Cardinal Manning has been to the Pope, and has got me a personal message for me from him quite as good as an official, and removes all my suspence [*sic*].

Also he has been so good as to explain all that took place at the time of his leaving England, and you will be glad to hear me say that I wish it all swept out of everyone's mind and my own—and shall be sorry if it is not so. I wish it known that I am quite satisfied, and am grateful to him for the trouble that he has taken in my matters.

Yours affly John H Newman

149

To HENRY BITTLESTON

Describing his reception by Pope Leo XIII

Via Sistina No 48 May 2 1879

My dear Henry,

Your letter came safe and thank you for it. I have been laid up with a bad cold ever since I have been here. Yesterday and today I have been in bed. It has seized my throat and continues hard. I have had advice, but it does nothing for me. The weather is so bad—I think it will not go till spring weather comes. It pulls me down sadly. Here great days are passing, and I a prisoner in the house. It answers to my general experience of Roman weather.

The Holy Father received me most affectionately—keeping my hand in his. He asked me 'Do you intend to continue head of the Birmingham House?' I answered, 'That depends on the Holy Father' He then said 'Well then I wish you to continue head;' and he went on to speak of this at length, saying there was a precedent for it in one of Gregory xvi's cardinals.

He asked me various questions—was our house a good one? was our Church? how many were we? of what age? when I said, we had lost some, he put his hand on my head and said 'Don't cry.' He asked 'had we any lay brothers'? 'how then did we do for a cook?' I said we had a widow woman, and the kitchen was cut off from the house. He said 'bene.' Where did I get my theology? at Propaganda? etc etc When I was leaving he accepted a copy of my four Latin Dissertations, in the Roman Edition. I certainly did not think his mouth large till he smiled, and then the ends turned up, but not unpleasantly—he has a clear white complexion his eyes somewhat bloodshot—but this might have been the accident of the day. He speaks very slowly and clearly and with an Italian manner.

William has had a letter to Austin on the stocks for some days. I hope it went a day or two ago.

Love to all

Ever Yours affly John H Newman

150

To LADY HERBERT OF LEA

Advice on dealing with a young son who had turned against religion

The Oratory Oct. 6 1879

Dearest Lady Herbert,

I have been thinking much about my best way, were I you, to affect your dear Son, and to secure his restoration, and I feel strongly, though it may seem cruel, that it is decidedly the best treatment is to leave him quite to himself [*sic*].

I take a great responsibility on me in saying this—for supposing this way did not succeed, I should be laying myself open to the charge of having by my do-nothing policy brought about that sad result.

But, you know, it frequently happens that medical men say of a patient—'Leave him alone—give him no physic—let nature act.'

Now I think that controversy is Lord P's *food*. He is supported, as on crutches, on asking and urging difficulties on the one hand and demolishing answers on the other. The best hope of his changing lies in his having no one to combat with him. Especially no one whom he loves or knows about. There is no *substance* in his scepticism, and this is most likely to come home upon him, if silence is offered to his restless activity of mind, and he has nothing brought before him to make him think that he is an object of anxiety to others. I doubt whether he would like to have his own way. Excuse this, but I feel it strongly—it gives him the best chance.

Most truly Yours J.H. Card. Newman

151

To ANNE MOZLEY

Written just after the death of his sister, Jemima

The Oratory Jan 6 1880

My dear Anne Mozley,

I am sorry to hear you have a cold. Thank you for telling me that Harry and Jane have the care of what dear Jemima left.

All I have to say is, what I dare say she told Jane, that about the date of 1850 I sent her (nothing of which I wish back) my sister Mary's copy of the Xtian Year (I think I gave it Mary, it was once mine, I know, it had the mark of her gloves on some of the pages, it was the first edition) my small Bible, which I had had from about the year 1807, miniatures back to back of my Father and my Mother's Father, and some other small things—one, a red morocco prayer book given me by my Mother in 1815. I only mention them, that Jane may know what to look for.

What I miss and shall miss Jemima in is this—she alone, with me, had a memory of dates—I knew quite well, as anniversaries of all kinds came round, she was recollecting them, as well as I—e.g. my getting into Oriel—now I am the only one in the world who knows a hundred things most interesting to me. E.g. yesterday was the anniversary of Mary's death—my mind turned at once to Jemima, but she was away.

Yours affectly John H Card. Newman

152

To JOHN RICKARDS MOZLEY

On death and eternity

The Oratory, Feb 26 1880

My very dear John,

Thank you for your affectionate letter, which I am glad to have, tho' how to answer it I scarcely know, more than if it were written in a language which I could not read. From so different a standpoint do we view things.

Looking beyond this life, my first prayer, aim, and hope is that I may see God. The thought of being blest with the sight of earthly friends pales before that thought. I believe that I shall never die; this awful prospect would crush me, were it not that I trusted and prayed that it would be an eternity in God's Presence. How is eternity a boon, unless He goes with it?

And for others dear to me, my one prayer is that they may see God.

It is the thought of God, His Presence, His strength which makes up, which repairs all bereavements.

'Give what Thou wilt, without Thee we are poor,
And with thee rich, take what Thou wilt away.'

I prayed that it might be so, when I lost so many friends 35 years ago; what else could I look to?

If then, as you rightly remind me, I said Mass for your dear Mother, it was to entreat the Lover of souls that, in His own way and in His own time, He would remove all distance which lay between the Sovereign Good and her, His creature. That is the first prayer, sine qua non, introductory to all prayers, and the most absorbing. What can I say more to you?

Yours affectly John H. Card. Newman

P.S. Cardinals don't wear mourning.

153

To GEORGE T. EDWARDS

A testament of faith

Febr. 24. 1887

My dear Mr Edwards,

My difficulty in writing breaks my thoughts and my feelings, and I not only can't say what I wish to say, but also my wishes themselves fare as if a dish of cold water was thrown over them.

I felt your letter, as all your letters, to be very kind to me and I feel very grateful to you. I don't know why you have been so kind, and you have been so more and more.

I will not close our correspondence without testifying my simple love and adhesion to the Catholic Roman Church, not that I think you doubt this; and did I wish to give a reason for this full and absolute devotion, what should, what can, I say, but that those great and burning truths, which I learned when a boy from evangelical teaching, I have found impressed upon my heart with fresh and ever increasing force by the Holy Roman Church? That Church has added to the simple evangelicism of my first teachers, but it has obscured, diluted, enfeebled, nothing of it—on the contrary, I have found a power, a resource, a comfort, a consolation in our Lord's divinity and atonement, in His Real Presence, in communion in His Divine and Human Person, which all good Catholics indeed have, but which Evangelical Christians have but faintly. But I have not strength to say more.

Thank you for the beautiful edition of the New Testament. I have a great dislike to heavy books

Very sincerely Yours John H. Card. Newman

154

To GERARD MANLEY HOPKINS

A view of the Irish situation and the Irish character

March 3. 1887

Dear Fr Hopkins,

Your letter is an appalling one—but not on that account un-trustworthy. There is one consideration however, which you omit. The Irish Patriots hold that they never have yielded themselves to the sway of England and therefore never have been under her laws, and never have been rebels.

This does not diminish the force of your picture—but it sug-gests that there is no help, no remedy. If I were an Irishman, I should be (in heart) a rebel. Moreover, to clench the difficulty the Irish character and tastes is very different from the English.

My fingers will not let me write more

Very truly Yrs J.H. Card. Newman

155

To MRS WILLIAM LANGFORD

Newman's last letter, arranging to see the niece he had not seen for forty seven years

The Oratory, Birmm Aug 2/90

My dear Grace,

Thank you for your wish to see me. I embrace it readily and I will see you whatever day next week suits you for that pur-pose.

Yours affectionately J.H.N.

P.S. I am sometimes engaged with the doctor.

Notes

Introduction

1. C.S. Dessain, *The Letters and Diaries of John Henry Newman* (1961) Vol. XI, p.xv.
2. The reference is to Sheridan's *The Critic*, Act III.
3. *Letters and Diaries* Vol. xi p. xvii.
4. Geoffrey Tillotson, *Newman: Prose and Poetry* (1955).
5. *Letters and Diaries* Vol. IV, p. 333.
6. Geoffrey Tillotson, op. cit., p. 19.
7. *Letters and Diaries* Vol. XI, p. 117.
8. Geoffrey Tillotson, op. cit., p. 25.
9. *Letters and Diaries* Vol. XX, p. 261.
10. *Letters and Diaries* Vol. XXIV, p. 53.

Letter 2

1. Newman added a later note: (This last rhyme 'cetera' I suspected is taken from Moore's Twopenny post bag). Thomas Moore published the *Twopenny Post Bag* in 1813, a collection of satires directed against the Prince Regent.

Letter 5

1. All men were speaking all good of me and were praising my luck. cf. Terence: *Andria*, I, i, 69–70.

Letter 7

1. 'Under-the-line-men' would be described today as those who had a third class degree. Newman was under the line.

Letter 9

1. Richard Whately, a senior Oriel man, a great influence on the young Newman.

Letter 10

1. Pusey had just been appointed Regius Professor of Hebrew and Canon of Christ Church.

Letter 11

1. Richard Hurrell Froude, Fellow of Oriel, had become Newman's great friend.

Letter 13

1. ethos, spirit.
2. passions.

Letter 14

1. either Caesar or no one at all.

Letter 16

1. Newman described the Lazaret, in an earlier letter as 'a quarantine house.'
2. I am a man and think nothing that is human is alien to me [second part of this quotation supplied] Terence: *Heautontimoroumenos*, I, i, 25.
3. well-wooded
4. end, work, activity.

Letter 17

1. scattered limbs.
2. nothing that is human is alien.

Letter 18

1. The Irish Church Temporalities Bill, suppressing ten Irish Bishoprics.

Letter 19

1. Edward Burton was Regius Professor of Divinity. William Sewell, of Exeter College, was a great pamphletter and a Tractarian until *Tract* 90.

Letter 21

1. The two Williams were her husband and her father-in-law.

Letter 30

1. Isaac Williams who was for a time curate at St Mary's and also at Littlemore.

Letter 31

1. Newman wrote over the top of this piece of news of Mrs Henry Wilberforce that she was better.

Letter 35

1. The Heads of Houses i.e. of the Colleges. The University opposed *Tract* 90 as well as the Bishops.

Letter 36

1. a kind of overcoat.

Letter 37

1. I am much more uncertain now than I was before. Terence: *Phormio*, 2, 4, 19.

Letter 41

1. Pusey's wife, who had died.
2. Pusey's young son.

Letter 45

1. W.G. Ward's book, *The Ideal of a Christian Church*, was an extremist Tractarian publication. Frederick Oakeley had the chapel in Margaret Street which was the centre of the London Tractarians and he was the nearest to Ward in his views.

Letter 49

1. *An Essay on the Development of Christian Doctrine.*

Letter 53

1. the novices or young men.
2. He was staying with his mother who thought perhaps he should not lodge in her house because he was a Catholic.
3. decide about building an Oratory house in London—Hansom was an architect.

Letter 55

1. See 'Town Churches' in the *Rambler*, V (Jan. 1850) illustrated with 'A Design for a Byzantine Church'. Pugin wrote a pamphlet attacking this.
2. Ambrose Lisle Phillips was a Catholic convert, an enthusiastic follower of Pugin.

Letter 60

1. O good Cross, long desired.

Letter 61

1. The coup d'état of Louis Napoleon was on 2 Dec.

Letter 62

1. The Little Oratory, a devotional confraternity for laymen.
2. necessity.

Letter 63

1. Miss Giberne had written, '... they like very much to go in "legno" [in a carriage] ... for the man I allow him two cigars a day, and for anything more he has no taste ...'
2. Lady Olivia Acheson, a convert lady who spent her time in good works in the Oratory parish.

Letter 65

1. The *Times* commented on the dubious justice of the verdict.

Letter 67

1. Lord and Lady Arundel—soon to be Duke and Duchess of Norfolk.

Letter 68

1. Newman added to this remark: (nor up to this date. March 7. 1876).
2. He also added later: (N.B. I had a great love for the place. When, at school, I dreamed of heaven, the scene was Ham. By chance years and years afterwards I found my Mother (who was very reserved in her feelings) had as great a love of it. She seemed so surprised. I love it to this day. William Neville and I passed the grounds in 1861).

Letter 69

1. A group of four Fathers, elected to help the Superior in the minor and practical business of the Oratory.

Letter 70

1. Ecclesiastes, 5:12.
2. Newman was the name of Wiseman's (and later Manning's) manservant.
3. St Philip sometimes mortified his disciples by getting them to look after his cat.

Letter 72

1. Mrs Partington lived in a house on the beach at Sidmouth and tried to keep out the Atlantic during a great storm in 1824.

Letter 76

1. Newman had written earlier, commenting on the strictness of the rules that Flanagan, the Novice Master, was imposing on the two novices. Flanagan replied, 'I see you are uneasy about the papers I sent you. You think them strict, and have a fear of my enforcing the rules with an iron hand. . . .'
2. Flanagan also wrote, 'Harry is in physic today—it appears he is subject to constipation—Ambrose has black dosed and pilled him . . .'

Letter 78

1. The Matron or 'Dame' for the Oratory School. Father Darnell was the first headmaster, under Newman.
2. This theologian in fact got into trouble with church authorities by writing a later republican book advocating the abolition of the Pope's temporal power.

Letter 80

1. the critical faculty.
2. Acts 5:4.

Letter 82

1. *Ecclesiastes* 11:1 and 4.
2. A red wine of southern Italy, Lachryma Christi.

Letter 83

1. The Roman Congregation of Cardinals which saw to the affairs of missionary countries. It still looked after England some years after the restoration of the English hierarchy.

Letter 85

1. 'Non ignara mali miseris succurrere disco.' Not a stranger to ill myself, I am learning to befriend those who are unhappy. Virgil: Aeneid, I, 630.

Letter 86

1. due honour and veneration, Council of Trent, Session XXV.
2. Richard Simpson, a clever convert, co-operated with Acton in bringing out the *Rambler*.

Letter 93

1. He puts down one and raises another. Psalm 74:8.
2. as needed.

Letter 95

1. Lord Edward Howard, M.P. for Arundel, was the only Catholic sitting in the House of Commons of a constituency in Great Britain.

Letter 96

1. This was Leopold I, first King of the Belgians and Queen Victoria's uncle. He married Princess Charlotte, the daughter of George IV and after her death in 1817 he remained in England at Claremont in Surrey. He was elected King of the Belgians in 1831.
2. Newman had had a fall and hurt his arm.
3. The pony at Rednal.

Letter 99

1. This was Jane Todd, a lady who had been a Tractarian and then became a Catholic, and who felt she owed her spiritual life and peace to Newman.

Letter 101

1. The Oratorians mentioned here are Austin Mills, William Neville, and Edward Caswall.
2. The story of the German flute is that it was carved from the bone of a murdered man and sang a song that discovered the murderer.

Letter 104

1. In April Napoleon III proposed to withdraw his troops from Rome and Pius IX was trying to settle his ecclesiastical differences with Victor Emmanuel.
2. In Scott's *Harold The Dauntless* Count Wittikin outwardly renounced heathenism in return for 'broad lands on the Wear and the Tyne.'

Letter 106

1. Macbeth, I, i, 1.

Letter 108

1. The *Letter to Pusey*.
2. *As You Like It*, II, vii.
3. *Aeneid* XII, 895: 'The gods affright me and Jupiter ranged against me.'
4. *Aeneid* I, 50–156.
5. St John 9:4.

Letter 111

1. The defeat of Austria at Sadowa in July ended the Austro-Prussian War and cut her off from Germany, leaving Prussia supreme there.
2. The *Times* backed the Southern States of America and then Denmark over the question of Schleswig–Holstein.
3. The question of the Pope's loss of temporal sovereignty was under discussion.

Letter 114

1. The repeal of the Test and Corporation Acts (1828) marked the end of the theory that Church and State were united in England.
2. Catholic Emancipation became law in 1829. A national system of education for Ireland began in 1834.
3. Hecker was a champion of the view that Catholicism in America should be American and therefore wished Catholics to accept the state school system.

Letter 116

1. John Kyrle was celebrated as a planter of trees in Alexander Pope's *Moral Essays*, Epistle III.

Letter 120

1. A Celebret vouched for a priest and enabled him to say Mass when he travelled.

Letter 121

1. born just to eat up the crops. Horace: *Epodes*, I, ii, 27.

Letter 122

1. Mother Margaret Hallahan, Newman's friend and foundress of the Dominican Congregation at Stone. She died in 1868.

Letter 123

1. Janus was the pseudonym of Döllinger and others in public letters attacking the Papacy and Ultramontanism, published eventually as a book.
2. Murphy was a violent Protestant who caused riots in Birmingham. M. Veuillot was the editor of the ultramontane newspaper *L'Univers*.
3. Acts 1:7.
4. Ullathorne had said he remembered Newman when passing St Philip's churches—San Girolamo and the Chiesa Nuova in Rome.
5. This letter, a most confidential one, became public.

Letter 124

1. Mark 9:41.

Letter 127

1. This person was H. E. Manning.

Letter 128

1. *The Christian Year*, Sixth Sunday after Trinity, penultimate stanza:— 'If ever floating from faint earthly lyre
   Was wafted to your soul one high desire,
   By all the trembling hope ye feel,
   Think on the minstrel as ye kneel.'
2. Hope-Scott's prefatory letter to Gladstone in this 1871 edition of Scott's *Life* spoke of a general decline in taste for Scott's novels.

Letter 129

1. La Mennais, or Lamennais, the Catholic priest and philosopher, was much concerned with democracy and it is presumably this facet of his thinking that was under discussion.

Letter 142

1. Peace to men of good will.

Letter 143

1. *The Friend of Humanity and the Knife-Grinder* by George Canning, 1797.

Letter 145

1. Bishop Ullathorne sent this to Rome (via Cardinal Manning), with a covering letter explaining that Newman would be glad of the honour but was fearful of living abroad. Manning despatched the letter without Ullathorne's explanation.

Letter 147

1. This change has been wrought by the right hand of the most high.

Index of Newman's Correspondents

ACTON, Sir John Dalberg (1834–1902), was educated partly in Germany as a pupil of Dollinger, becoming immensely learned and a liberal Catholic. In England he was in Parliament for a time and then engaged in journalism. He was actively against the definition of papal infallibility. He became Regius Professor of Modern History at Cambridge.

ALLIES, Eliza (1822–1902), married Thomas Allies in 1840 and became a Catholic in 1850. Her husband was an Oxford friend of Newman's; he became a Catholic too and was Lecturer in History at the Catholic University.

ARNOLD, Matthew (1822–88), the famous writer, was not a regular correspondent but the two letters extant from him to Newman express deep respect for Newman's writings and general influence. Matthew Arnold's brother Thomas was a Catholic convert and worked for Newman both at the Catholic University and at the Oratory School.

BADELEY, Edward Lowth (1803–68), educated at Brasenose College, Oxford. He met Newman c. 1837. He became a leading Tractarian lawyer and when a Catholic (1852), helped Newman during the Achilli affair.

BELAMY, A. A clergyman from Horsham who wrote to Newman. Nothing more is known about him.

BITTLESTON, Henry (1818–86), educated at St John's College, Oxford and in Anglican Orders. He was received into the Catholic Church by Newman in 1849, joined the Birmingham Oratory and is mentioned in the *Apologia*. He left the Oratory eventually and continued as a secular priest.

BLACHFORD, Lord—see Rogers

BLOXAM, John Rouse (1807–91), Tractarian liturgist and antiquary, Fellow of Magdalen College, Oxford and Newman's curate at Littlemore 1837–1840. In 1862 he was appointed Vicar of Upper Beeding in Sussex. He never became a Catholic though Newman had hopes that he would. He remained in friendly contact, however, and often visited the Birmingham Oratory.

BOWDEN, Charlotte or Chat or Chattie (1848–1933), youngest daughter of Henry Bowden, brother of J. W. Bowden.

BOWDEN, Elizabeth (1805–96), wife of J. W. Bowden. She became a Catholic in 1846.

BOWDEN, John William (1799–1844), Newman's close friend from undergraduate days and a Tractarian.

BOWDEN, Marianne or Mary Anne (1831–67), the delicate elder daughter of the above. She became a Visitation nun at Westbury.

BOWDEN, Marianne Frances (1839–1926), eldest daughter of Henry Bowden.

BOWLES, Emily (1818–1904), became a Catholic in 1843 and joined Cornelia Connelly's new religious congregation, the Society of the Holy Child Jesus. She quarrelled with the foundress, however, and left. She spent the rest of her life writing and translating religious books. Her brother joined Newman at Littlemore, became a Catholic with him and was a priest, belonging to the Birmingham Oratory for a time. Emily Bowles had Newman's confidence and he wrote to her freely.

BRAMSTON, John (1802–89), went up to Oriel in 1820 and met Newman two years later. He was in Anglican Orders and became Dean of Winchester.

BRETHERTON, Eleanor (born 1845), had Newman as her confessor from childhood. She married F. J. Watts. Newman kept in touch with her, visited her when she was ill and sent money for the children when times were hard.

BUCKLER, Reginald (1840–1927), became a Catholic in 1855 and a Dominican the following year. He was a spiritual writer.

CAPES, John Moore (1812–89), a Balliol man, originally opposed to the Tractarians, in Anglican Orders. He became a Catholic in 1845 and founded the *Rambler* in 1848. He rejoined the Church of England for a time but became a Catholic again.

CASWALL, Edward (1814–78), educated at Brasenose College, Oxford and a clergyman. He became a Catholic in 1847 and, after his wife's death in 1849, joined the Birmingham Oratory. He is known for the hymns he wrote and translated.

CHRISTIE, John Frederick (1808–60), an Oriel Fellow who became a friend of the leaders of the Oxford Movement. From 1847 he was Rector of Ufton-Nervet, Berks.

CHURCH, Richard William (1815–90), a Wadham man, later an Oriel Fellow, who met Newman in 1836. He was one of the Proctors who vetoed the proposal to censure Tract 90. After 1845 his friendship with Newman was suspended for twenty years but was marvellously renewed. He became Dean of St Paul's in 1871.

CHURCH, Helen, Mary, and Edith, daughters of the above. They sent Newman Lewis Carroll's books.

COPE, Sir William (1811–83), was a soldier and later in Anglican Orders. He was George Ryder's curate, then a minor canon and librarian of Westminster Abbey. He followed the Tractarians and collected all Newman's writings. Charles Kingsley's living was in his patronage.

COPELAND, William John (1804–85), Scholar and Fellow of Trinity, Oxford, a leading Tractarian and Newman's curate at Littlemore. He renewed his friendship with Newman in 1862 and brought other old friends back into touch.

DE VERE, Anthony (1814–1902), son of an Irish baronet who was educated at Trinity College, Dublin. He wrote poetry and was a friend of Tennyson and Browning. He became a Catholic in 1851 and in 1855 Newman appointed him Professor of Political and Social Science at the Catholic University.

DU BOULAY, Susan or Sister Mary Gabriel (1826–1906), received by Newman into the Catholic Church in 1850. She entered Mother Margaret Hallahan's Dominican community and was professed in the newly-opened convent at Stone. Newman had a great regard for this convent and its foundress.

EDWARDS, George T., an ecumenically-minded Anglican who in 1887 sent Newman a New Testament in large print, divided into four parts to be lighter to handle.

FABER, Frederick William (1814–63), Fellow of University College, took Orders in 1839. He became a Catholic in 1845 and founded a religious community which lived at St Wilfrid's, Cotton, near Alton Towers. He and his 'Wilfridians' joined the English Oratory in 1848. When the London Oratory was founded Newman put Faber in charge and when it became independent he was its Superior until his death.

FLANAGAN, John Stanislas (1821–1905), an Irishman who joined the Birmingham Oratory in 1848. He returned to Ireland in 1865 and became parish priest of Adare, remaining friendly to Newman and to the Oratorian community he had left.

FROUDE, William (1810–79), R.H. Froude's brother and a naval and railway engineer. His wife Catherine (née Holdsworth) had become friendly with Newman before her marriage. She became a Catholic but William never did, though always Newman's friend too.

GIBERNE, Maria Rosina (1802–85), friend of Newman's family and sister-in-law to Walter Mayers. She was an Evangelical, then a Tractarian, then a Catholic. She was an artist and an enthusiastic disciple of Newman, sometimes embarrassingly emotional but loyal. She became a Visitation nun at Autun, professed in 1863.

GORDON, John Joseph (1811–53), was in the Indian army before he took a Cambridge degree and became a clergyman of Evangelical views. He then felt the influence of the *Tracts* and of Newman's preaching. He became a Catholic in 1847 and joined the Birmingham Oratory. He died prematurely, much lamented by Newman.

HAYES, J., an Oxford man who had 'the cherished remembrance of having listened to your [i.e. Newman's] teaching from the Pulpit of St Mary's'. He was Vicar of Coalbrookdale, Salop, 1854–78.

HERBERT of Lea, Lady Mary (1822–1911), married Sidney Herbert. She was received into the Roman Catholic Church by Manning and became the friend and supporter of Herbert Vaughan.

HOLMES, Mary (1815?–78), accepted the doctrines of the *Tracts for the*

Times in 1839 and Newman was her director until her conversion to Rome in 1844. They corresponded to the end of her life. She was a governess, a well-read woman who was friendly with Thackeray and Trollope. At times she was embarrassing to Newman in her devotion to him, emotionally expressed.

HOPE-SCOTT, James Robert (1812–73), a Fellow of Merton College, adopted the views of the Tractarians and became their legal adviser. He became a Catholic in 1851. His first wife was the grand-daughter of Sir Walter Scott and he inherited Abbotsford through her, changing his name from Hope to Hope-Scott. His second wife was the eldest daughter of the fourteenth Duke of Norfolk. He was a rich and charitable man, having made a fortune as a parliamentary lawyer for the railway companies. He was Newman's good friend from 1837 and Newman often turned to him for advice.

HOPKINS, Gerard Manley (1844–89), the famous poet. A Balliol Exhibitioner, he followed Pusey at Oxford but became doubtful of the Anglo-Catholic position. He was received into the Roman Catholic Church in 1866 by Newman and became a Jesuit in 1868.

HOWARD, Lord Edward (1818–83), created first Baron Howard of Glossop in 1869, the second son of the thirteenth Duke of Norfolk. He sat in Parliament and interested himself in educational affairs. He was Chairman of the Catholic Poor Schools Committee.

HUTCHISON, William Antony (1822–63), a Cambridge graduate, a convert who joined Faber's community and then the Oratory. He went with Faber to start the London Oratory in 1849.

HUTTON, Richard Holt (1826–97), a Unitarian who was educated at University College, London. He intervened on Newman's side in the controversy with Kingsley and published a good short biography of Newman in 1891. He gradually came to accept the main tenets of the Church of England and indeed was increasingly sympathetic to Catholicism. His influence in literary circles was considerable.

KEBLE, John (1792–1866), Fellow and Tutor of Oriel, a leader of the Oxford Movement. He became Vicar of Hursley in 1836. As with Church, friendship was suspended for twenty years after Newman's conversion.

MACLAURIN, William, of Elgin, was educated in England and then at Glasgow University. He became an Episcopalian clergyman and Dean of Moray and Ross. When he became a Catholic, with his wife and child, in 1851, he suffered financially. There is a compassionate reference to him in a letter from Newman in 1867.

MANNING, Henry Edward (1808–92), undergraduate at Balliol and Fellow of Merton who became Archdeacon of Chichester. He became a Catholic in 1851 and was ordained priest after ten weeks. He founded the Oblates of St Charles in London, was Provost of the Westminster Chapter, Archbishop of Westminster in 1865 and a Cardinal in 1875. In later years he viewed Newman with hostility.

MAYERS, Walter (1790–1828), a clergyman of evangelical tenets who was Senior Classical Master at Ealing School. He influenced the schoolboy Newman and was for him 'the human means of the beginning of divine faith'.

MILLS, Henry Austin (1823–1903), educated Trinity College, Cambridge. He became a Catholic in 1846, joined Faber's community and with them became an Oratorian. He spent his life in Birmingham and is one of those mentioned at the end of the *Apologia*.

MONSELL, William (1812–94), educated Winchester and Oriel. He was M.P. for Limerick from 1847 until he was created Lord Emly in 1874 and held various offices in Liberal governments. He was received into the Catholic Church in 1850 and was Newman's friend and frequent correspondent.

MORRIS, John Brande (1812–80), Fellow of Exeter who assisted Pusey who was Hebrew Professor. He was an extreme and eccentric Tractarian, became a Catholic in 1846 and joined Newman's community at Maryvale. He left, was ordained and spent his life as chaplain to various patrons.

MOZLEY, Anne (1809–91), sister-in-law of Newman's sisters, lived in Derby, was in touch with the Oxford Movement and was engaged in literary work. Newman entrusted her with the editing of the letters of his Anglican period.

MOZLEY, John Rickards (1840–1931), the second son of Newman's sister, Jemima, was clever and had a successful academic career.

MUNRO, Miss G. (*c*. 1823–*c*. 1913), a convert, friend of Dr Whitty, who was received into the Catholic Church by Wiseman. Newman acted as her director.

NEVILLE, William Paine (1824–1905), educated at Winchester and Oxford, became a Catholic in 1851 and immediately joined the Birmingham Oratory. When Newman was old, Neville was his secretary and nurse. He was his chief literary executor.

NEWMAN, Charles Robert (1802–84), quarrelled with his family on his father's death and gave up Christianity. He was able but restless and relied on his brother J. H. Newman and the rest of the family for support.

NEWMAN, Elizabeth Good (1765–1852), Newman's aunt. He owed early religious instruction to her and was devoted to her. When Jemima Newman married, Aunt Elizabeth lived with her in Derby.

NEWMAN, Francis William (1805–97), undergraduate at Worcester College, Fellow of Balliol. He eventually held the chair of Latin at University College, London. Religiously, he began as an Evangelical, went on to become a Unitarian and espoused various eccentric causes. He published a rather bitter book about his famous brother after the latter's death.

NEWMAN, Harriett (1803–52), Newman's eldest sister. She married Thomas Mozley, an Anglican clergyman. She became out of sympathy with her brother's religious development and broke off relations two or three years before his conversion. Her only child, Grace (Mrs Langley) was Newman's last visitor.

NEWMAN, Jemima (1771–1836), née Fourdrinier, Newman's mother. A gentle Christian woman, who wrote letters of affectionate concern to her eldest son.

NEWMAN, Jemima (1808–79), Newman's second sister. She married John Mozley, printer and publisher in Derby. Although she was far from approving of Newman's conversion, she remained on more or less friendly terms and they corresponded regularly.

NEWMAN, John (1767–1824), banker, who married Jemima Fourdrinier in 1799, father of John Henry Newman.

NEWSHAM, Charles D.D. (1792–1863), became President of Ushaw College, Durham, in 1837. Newman admired him and sought his advice.

NORFOLK, Duchess of, Augusta (1820–86), wife of the fourteenth Duke, became a Catholic in 1850. Like her husband, she was a generous, charitable person.

NORFOLK, Henry Fitzalan Howard, fifteenth Duke of (1847–1917), succeeded his father in 1860 and was sent to the Oratory School the following year. He became a devout, active, public-spirited layman. To him Newman addressed his *A Letter to the Duke of Norfolk*, and he played an important part in securing Newman's cardinalate.

NORTHCOTE, James Spencer (1821–1907), an Oxford man who was greatly influenced by Pusey and Newman. He was curate at Ilfracombe. He, his wife and three of her sisters became Catholics 1845–6. He was editor of the *Rambler* 1852–4. After his wife's death, he studied for the priesthood under Newman and eventually became President of Oscott College and Provost of the Birmingham Chapter.

POPE, Simeon Lloyd (1802–55), educated at Trinity College, Oxford and took Anglican Orders.

PUSEY, Edward Bouverie (1800–82), educated Eton and Christ Church, Fellow of Oriel in 1823, Regius Professor of Hebrew and a Canon of Christ Church in 1828. He was an important Tractarian and their leader after 1845. Newman and Pusey corresponded frequently and intimately.

ROGERS, Frederic (1811–89), came to Oriel College in 1828 and was Newman's pupil. He was a Fellow of that college 1833–1845, an adherent of the Oxford Movement and Newman's close friend until religious differences caused them to part. Rogers became Permanent under Secretary of State for the Colonies. He was created Lord Blachford in 1871. From 1863 his old friendship with Newman was renewed.

RUSSELL, Charles William (1812–80), an Irish aristocrat, President of Maynooth. He was sympathetic to the Tractarians and a friend of Newman's.

RUSSELL, John Fuller (1814–84), a Cambridge man who was an antiquarian and writer on ecclesiastical affairs and sympathetic to the Oxford Movement.

RYDER, George Dudley (1810–80), one of Newman's students at Oriel. He took Orders and was influenced by the Oxford Movement. He, with his wife, children, sister, and her children were received into the Catholic Church in Rome in 1846. Newman acted as director to Ryder. His eldest son joined the Birmingham Oratory.

SIMEON, Louisa Edith (1843–95), eldest daughter of Sir John Simeon who was also a correspondent of Newman's. She married one of the Ward family.

ST JOHN, Ambrose (1815–75), undergraduate at Christ Church, held a studentship there and was curate to Henry Wilberforce 1841–3. Then he went to live at Littlemore just before becoming a Catholic. He was Newman's close companion until his death. See the tribute paid to him in the *Apologia*.

TALBOT, George (1816–86), an aristocrat, took Anglican Orders, became a Catholic and was ordained at Oscott in 1846. Newman refused his request to join the Oratory. He became a Canon of St Peter's and a Papal Chamberlain and was influential in church affairs in Rome. He was removed to an asylum in 1868.

ULLATHORNE, William Bernard (1806–89), after organizing the church in Australia, was put in charge of the Benedictine mission in Coventry and consecrated there in 1846 as Vicar Apostolic of the Western District. He was transferred to the Central District and became the first Roman Catholic Bishop of Birmingham in 1850.

WARD, William George (1812–82), the extremist Tractarian, a Fellow of Balliol, who became a Catholic in 1845, together with his wife, Frances. He taught philosophy and then theology at St Edmund's, Ware, and edited the *Dublin Review* 1863–78, making it an organ of extreme ultramontanism.

WESTMACOTT, Richard (1799–1872), sculptor. For much of his working life he was associated with the Royal Academy, becoming a member in 1838 and later professor of sculpture there. His well-known bust of Newman was done in 1841.

WHITTY, Robert (1817–95), born and trained for the priesthood in Ireland, ordained in England where he lived thereafter. He thought of becoming an Oratorian but became a Jesuit. He held important posts both as a secular priest and as a Jesuit, and was always attached to Newman.

WILBERFORCE, Henry William (1807–73), was Newman's pupil at Oriel, took Orders and had his first living at Bransgore. His wife became a Catholic in 1850 and he and the children followed. He turned to religious journalism.

WILBERFORCE, Mary (1811–78), née Sargent, wife of the above and sister-in-law of Manning and of George Ryder.

WILBERFORCE, Mary Frances (1800–80), née Owen, married William, the eldest son of the philanthropist in 1820. Newman dissuaded her from becoming a Catholic in 1834 and she did not take the step until 1852, followed by her husband in 1863.

WILBERFORCE, Robert Isaac (1802–57), brother to Henry and William and the second son of the philanthropist, was a Fellow of Oriel and a tutor there with Newman. He left Oxford in 1831 and became Archdeacon of the West Riding. He was the leading Tractarian theologian. He became a Catholic in 1854.

WILSON, Mrs Margaret, a convert who complained that she had been received too soon and who found great difficulty in accepting the definition of papal infallibility.

WILSON, Robert Francis (1809–88), was at Oriel College and Newman was his tutor. He took Orders and became Keble's curate at Hursley. For the last twenty-five years of his life he was Vicar of Rownhams, Hants.

WISEMAN, Nicholas (1802–65), Rector of the English College, Rome, 1828–40. Then he was Rector of Oscott and Coadjutor to Bishop Walsh in the Midland District. He was then in London, the last Vicar Apostolic of the London District, and in 1850 was made Archbishop of Westminster and a Cardinal. He was interested in the Tractarians and welcomed the Catholic converts.

WOOD, Samuel Francis (1810–1843), an Oriel man who became a barrister-at-law at the Inner Temple in 1835.